About the author:

Angela Dailey is a clinical social worker who has been treating all types of mental illness for 25 years. She also teaches psychology and sociology at the college level. She writes continuing education courses on topics related to attaining optimum mental health through healthy lifestyle choices and maintains a blog about nutrition and mental health at MentalHealthFood.net and its popular sister Facebook page at facebook.com/mentalhealthfood.

COOKING TO CURE

A nutritional approach to anxiety and depression

Angela Dailey, BA, MSW, LCSW

Cooking to Cure: a nutritional approach to anxiety and depression
Copyright: Angela Dailey
Published: February 12, 2015

The information and suggestions provided in this book are not intended as a substitute for advice from your physician. Consult with your physician before beginning any dietary regimen. Recommendations in this book are intended only as guidelines; needs of individuals will vary. The author shall not be liable for any injury or damage allegedly arising from any information or suggestions in this book.

Cover design by Angela Dailey and DeAnna Dailey
Illustration by Preston Baggette

For all of those suffering with anxiety and depression, and the people who love them, who are looking for more answers.

Gratitude

To my children, whose love and support for me, and each other, are the best things in my life.

Table of Contents

Preface

My interest in nutrition began around 1973 when someone gave me a copy of Adelle Davis's, book, "Let's Eat Right to Keep Fit". Adelle Davis was the forerunner of all the nutrition gurus we have today and probably 30 years ahead of her time. While she was the most popular and influential nutritionist during the 1960's and 1970's, some of her, at the time "radical", ideas were heavily criticized. She believed that in addition to many physical illnesses, mental and social ills like alcoholism and suicide could be prevented with proper nutrition. Now, close to 50 years after her original assertions, alcoholism and suicide have been linked to nutritional deficiencies and her ideas about processed and refined food, hydrogenated fats, and excessive sugar seem more relevant than ever. Her book gave me an appreciation for the connection between what we eat and how we feel, mentally as well as physically. I was about 17 years old then. I still own my original, now a bit yellowed, dog-eared, and battered, copy of that book as well as two of her other books I've had for nearly as long, "Let's Have Healthy Children" and "Let's Get Well". Although I confess to straying rather far off track at times over the years, those books influenced me profoundly throughout my adult life.

I had a friend at U.C. Davis at that time whose father worked as a television producer in the Bay Area of California. He suffered a rare stroke that carried a dismal prognosis. With the treatment they were able to offer, the doctors gave him a few months to live. Incredibly, a woman came into the same hospital on the same day with the same type of stroke. Her prognosis was, of course, the same. She received the available medical treatment. My friend's father contacted Adelle Davis. As I remember the story, because of the urgency of the situation, Adelle stayed up for 48 hours straight researching an individualized diet plan, involving both food and supplements, to help him. He followed her recommended protocol and fully recovered. The other stroke victim suffered the predicted outcome; she lived for a short time and died.

One of my first direct experiences with Adelle Davis's recommendations was with my 8-month old niece, Rebecca. Rebecca and her mother, Lorene, came from their home in Utah, to stay with us for a couple of months in our remote Montana cabin. Rebecca had what Lorene called "crying jags" where, for no apparent reason, she would scream and scream until she exhausted herself and fell asleep. We tried frantically to discover the source of her distress. Her diapers were dry, she was fed, held, rocked and cooed. Day after day, every waking minute was the same; Rebecca screamed. Nothing seemed to console or soothe her. Lorene said she behaved that way since she could remember. After two weeks, all of our nerves were frazzled. And we found no relief for poor Rebecca. We were 60 miles from the nearest doctor, where we would have taken her but Rebecca had already been to her doctor in Utah to no avail. It was then I thought of trying to find an answer in Adelle Davis's book, "Let's Have Healthy Children". Sure enough, Rebecca's symptoms were in the book. Adelle said Rebecca was suffering from a deficiency in calcium and magnesium and recommended it in the form of dolomite (a common mineral that occurs as crystals in large rock beds of limestone that is pulverized and made into tablets). She gave the recommended dosage and said the tablets should be crushed and added to her bottle. We saw an immediate improvement with the first bottle and after the second bottle,

Rebecca stopped the incessant screaming and never did it again! Rebecca began spending her waking hours smiling, playing, and enjoying the world around her. Lorene continued to add the dolomite to Rebecca's bottle until after she was eating a variety of solid foods and not taking a bottle anymore. Once her deficiency had been corrected she was, apparently, able to meet her need for calcium and magnesium with the addition of a variety of foods.

While the "truth" and power of nutrition as prevention and cure seemed obvious to me, apparently it was lost on mainstream Western society. Much like the electric car that was invented around the same time that Adelle Davis's books were popular, something that could have taken us into the 21st century healthier and cheaper in the long run, was swept aside as family farms were replaced by corporate agriculture and Western medicine steamrolled down a single track of looking at illness instead of health, prodded by ever-larger pharmaceutical companies that had much to gain from people being sick and nothing at all to gain from people being healthy. We became a fast-food, "quick-fix", culture. Why take the time to figure out the *cause* of a problem when we can just pop a pill to fix it *right now*? People stopped cooking and eating homemade meals at home as TV dinners made it easier for both parents to be wage earners outside the home without facing the time consuming chore of preparing foods and cooking. Pop Tarts replaced cooked breakfasts and canned Spaghetti-O's masqueraded as real lunches and dinners as processed foods of all kinds found their way to grocery stores on every corner across the country. Fewer people were growing their own food, buying fresh foods at their local markets, baking bread and cooking meals from wholesome, healthy ingredients. Who wanted to spend 2 hours making macaroni and cheese from "scratch" when you could buy it in a box and make it in 5 minutes? Not to mention, you could buy it *cheap.* We traded wholesomeness for convenience.

We were blind to the dangers of preservatives that were added to the food so it would keep longer on the grocery store shelves without spoiling. And to the effects of all the chemical ingredients that were in the packaged foods that we didn't recognize and couldn't pronounce. We trusted that they were not harmful. We had the FDA (Food and Drug Administration) looking out for us. No one would put anything in our food that would harm us, *right*? We didn't know that not only would many of those additives turn out to cause cancer and other serious diseases and disorders, but that even without the harmful additives, the processing of the food itself was stripping away much of our needed nutrients, without which our bodies were vulnerable from deficiencies and our immune systems weakened. Wheat and rice were stripped of their hulls and the center parts called "germ", which contained most of the fiber and necessary nutrients, to produce white flour and white rice, which were, in the process, stripped of their natural oils giving them a longer shelf life. We became accustomed to everything white and fluffy and refined, only vaguely resembling its natural state and depleted of its original nutrients. It never occurred to us that the cheese in that box of "macaroni and cheese" wasn't even real cheese. It was some kind of synthetic powder with artificial color and artificial flavor and a boatload of salt that was supposed to give the impression of melted cheese when it was reconstituted. Between that and the macaroni made from white flour and water, the only truly nutritious thing in the entire main course was the ¼ cup of milk that was added to it.

We became accustomed to prepackaged, canned, and boxed food. We were oblivious to their nutritional failings and to why that was important. And in between those nutritionally depleted meals we have the bagged chips, cookies, crackers and packaged cupcakes and fluffballs made of essentially nothing but white flour, white sugar, hydrogenated fat, and artificial color and flavor that also have very little, if any, nutritional value but instead pump us full of salt, sugar, trans-fat, and toxic preservatives and other chemicals. Add to that today's multi-billion dollar fast-food industry, and you have the current Western diet.

There is overwhelming evidence that the Western diet is responsible for myriad health problems including heart disease, hypertension, cancer, osteoporosis, obesity, celiac disease, diabetes, and some autoimmune disorders. The correlation is pretty clear – as our diet has included more processed and refined foods, the incidence of these health problems has increased. As we have increased harmful things in our diets, like refined salt, sugar, flour and hydrogenated oils, we have decreased the nutrients necessary for good health. While most of our attention has focused on the health consequences of the Western diet, those of us in the mental health field have seen a similar rise in many mental disorders including bipolar disorder, ADHD, schizophrenia, Alzheimer's disease and other types of dementia, as well as depression and anxiety disorders of all sorts. It doesn't seem too big a leap to suspect that the Western diet and its lack of nutrients necessary for physical health may also be responsible for the rising incidence of problems related to mental illness. There is a growing body of evidence that supports and confirms that suspicion.

Perhaps it was because of my early introduction to Adelle Davis's work, that when I began my education in psychology, I was shocked to discover there was nothing taught about the interface between nutrition and mental health. It seemed to me such a huge oversight. I took psychology classes and I took nutrition classes. But the nutrition classes were offered through the education department, not the psychology department. Rather than being a required part of the psychology program, they were not offered at all so I took them as electives in another department. And there was no information about the role nutrition played in *neuro*chemistry. In other words, how nutrients affect the brain. We knew some things about how nutrients were necessary for strong bones and teeth. But nothing was mentioned about how nutrients affect the serotonin levels in our brains. We knew that nutrients were necessary to "feel good" in our bodies. But not nearly enough emphasis, if any, was given to nutrients being necessary to feel good in our minds. Don't get me wrong; I feel I got an excellent education. I learned all about psychological disorders and how to treat them. But what I *really* wanted to know was what caused them in the first place. That was the part we knew a lot less about. But, even more frustrating than not having a lot of those answers, was a seeming lack of interest, in the field overall, in causation. Much like the medical model of looking at an illness as the problem and coming up with a remedy, mental illness has been approached in a similar way. We looked at a mental illness as the problem and came up with a treatment protocol, which likely included medication, some kind of talk therapy, or a combination of both. We routinely performed psychosocial assessments, which included a patient's social history, medical history, and current life situation. Sometimes we performed psychological tests that would give us information about the patient's personality traits or neurological functioning. We documented the patient's reported symptoms, any previous diagnoses, and recorded the most appropriate current diagnosis. Much like seeing a medical doctor for problems with depression, at no time has a nutritional analysis been part of a mainstream mental health diagnostic intake procedure. That huge piece of the puzzle has not been seriously considered as either the source of the problem, or as a remedy. Fortunately, that is beginning to change.

Researchers from around the world are looking at the relationships between nutrients and their effects on mental health. What they are finding is that deficiencies in certain nutrients are associated with disorders like depression and anxiety. And that correcting those deficiencies can reverse or improve symptoms in some people. As medical and mental health professionals are learning more about these relationships, so is the American public. The information about the links between nutrition and physical and mental health is making its way into nearly every home via daytime television talk shows, articles on the internet, and internet social media sites. More and more books are being published with information about preventing and treating various disorders with nutrition.

While there are a growing number of good books on this topic, none of them seemed to have exactly what I was looking for all in one place. And most of the information available emphasizes taking nutritional supplements rather than getting the nutrients from eating food. I am not completely against taking nutritional supplements. I take them myself sometimes. But, I think our bodies are designed to function best on proper food. Every food has many nutrients. Something like kale, for instance, is high in vitamin A. In addition to vitamin A, it also contains calcium, magnesium, phosphorus, potassium, vitamin K, zinc, copper, manganese, selenium, vitamin C, six different B vitamins, vitamin E, eighteen different amino acids (some of which we know play a big role in the creation of beneficial brain chemicals), fiber, beneficial fatty acids, and probably other things that we haven't even discovered yet. Many of these nutrients co-occur because they work together in performing their various beneficial tasks in our brains and other parts of our bodies. We are only just discovering the tip of the iceberg in regards to exactly how the different nutrients affect each other and how they work together. Taking supplements is somewhat of a gamble for several reasons. First, when we take a supplement in isolation, we may not be able to utilize that nutrient without its "helpers". For instance, calcium uses vitamin D to break down and become absorbable in the body. Calcium and magnesium also work together and taking too much of one can create a deficiency in the other. So, taking a calcium supplement alone, which many people do, without also taking vitamin D and magnesium at the same time can cause a deficiency in magnesium while the calcium is not fully absorbed. This can cause excess calcium in the body resulting in conditions like kidney stones. We also know that vitamin B6 is needed to convert the amino acid, tryptophan, to the neurotransmitter, serotonin and tyrosine and phenylalanine to dopamine. Basically, no single nutrient works alone. Every food contains multiple nutrients for that reason. It is impossible to replicate that complexity with supplements. Also, there is not always strict quality control with all supplements so the quality of the supplement can vary as well as the potential for contamination. In studies where nutrients were provided from food versus supplements, participants have consistently shown more positive results from the food. So, for the purposes of this book, we are going to trust that nature had this figured out a long time ago and for that reason, our emphasis for nutrition is going to be on whole, natural foods.

Another point I need to make is that when we are talking about improving depression and anxiety, there can be many contributing factors. Besides diet, some of the things to consider are exercise, stress management, fresh air, sunshine, adequate sleep, loving relationships, laughter, hobbies, volunteer work, music, prayer/meditation, yoga, sex, vacations, and recreation – all of which have been demonstrated to reduce symptoms of depression and anxiety. But, all of those things are topics for other books. Nutrition is only one piece of the puzzle and this book is intended to address that one, very important and too often overlooked, piece.

What I want for my clients, and everyone else who has an interest in a nutritional approach to treating depression and anxiety, is a book that explains the information in a way that anybody can understand it. A book that starts with the very basics like, "What is a nutrient?" I want a book that explains how nutrients affect the brain and our moods as well as how to get those nutrients from food. I want a book that has enough information to be helpful without so much information that it becomes mind numbing for the average reader. And, finally, I want a book with simple recipes showing us how to begin to use these foods in our everyday meals. And those recipes should have a complete nutritional breakdown so a person knows how much of which nutrients they are getting when they eat. Since that book wasn't out there, this is intended to be that book.

Angela Dailey, BA, MSW, LCSW

Chapter 1

Nutrients

This chapter is an overview of the different kinds of micronutrients and macronutrients, including a little bit about the way they work, what they are good for and where and how we get them. You will also learn about some of the symptoms of deficiencies and who is at highest risk of these deficiencies. Perhaps most importantly, you may be surprised to find the many ways that nutrients are effective in preventing and treating many well-known ailments such as cancer, dementia, heart disease, and brain disease, among others. This basic understanding of what nutrients are and why they are important will help you understand in later chapters why we need them for our brains to function properly by using nutrients to create neurotransmitters, which can decrease or even eliminate the need for prescription anti-depressants.

There are buzzwords that have become commonplace in food marketing, like "anitoxidants", "low-carb", and "natural" that seem to be misunderstood or not understood at all. For this reason, you will find in this chapter an explanation of what is an antioxidant, what is important to understand about carbohydrates and "low-carb" diets, as well as what the Glycemic Index is and a discussion of "natural" versus "organic" foods as well as raw versus cooked foods. You will also learn about "good fats" and "bad fats" because not all fat is bad! These are the highlights of what you will need to know when we start discussing the Western diet and its effects and what we should be eating for maximum physical and mental health.

What Is A Nutrient?

A nutrient is a chemical substance that provides nourishment essential for the growth and maintenance of life.

We get nutrients from the foods we eat. Different foods contain different amounts and types of nutrients. Nutrients include ***vitamins*** and ***minerals***, which are also called **"micronutrients"** because we need relatively small amounts of them. Nutrients also include **"macronutrients"** that we need in larger amounts, which include ***protein***, ***fat***, and ***carbohydrates***. Our bodies need varying amounts of all these things every day to function properly. Many physical and mental illnesses can result from a deficiency in any of these nutrients.

Nutrients can also be consumed in the form of supplements. While it is sometimes necessary to take vitamin and mineral supplements in pill or powder form, there are several reasons why getting nutrients from food is more beneficial. Nutrients that work together and depend on each other for optimum performance often co-occur in foods because that is their natural state. Because they need each other to work properly, they exist together in particular foods. When we take supplements independently of food, we run a greater risk of creating an imbalance. Some vitamins and minerals can be harmful in high doses. We are unlikely to consume them in dosages high enough to hurt us when we obtain them from their natural food source.

If you are not able to get all the nutrients you need from food, by all means, take supplements. Supplements are easily obtainable and relatively inexpensive. Because most experts would agree that getting nutrients from food is the best choice, the focus of this book is to provide you with the information you need to get all, or at least most, of your nutrients from the food you eat.

The following is an overview of vitamins and minerals (micronutrients) as well as protein, fats, and carbohydrates (macronutrients). Included is some brief information about how they are beneficial, some sources of the nutrients and symptoms of deficiency.

Micronutrients

Micronutrients include the 12 vitamins and 13 minerals that we need every day. Vitamins are either **water-soluble** or **fat-soluble** depending on whether they dissolve in water or in fat. Fat-soluble vitamins need to be consumed with some type of fat in order to be broken down and absorbed by the body. Water-soluble vitamins are easily accessible to the body because they are broken down in water. Excess water-soluble vitamins also leave the body easily through the urine. So, they typically need to be replenished more often then fat-soluble vitamins. Fat-soluble vitamins can be stored in the body in fat tissue. Water-soluble vitamins need to be consumed every day – sometimes several times a day – to keep them available to your body as the body will break them down quickly and excrete them out with urine. Provided you are consuming adequate amounts, fat-soluble vitamins don't have to be replenished every day and you don't have to consume them in your "daily requirement" amounts because your body will store them for use later. So, if your body needs 5,000 units of vitamin A per day and you consume 10,000 units, your body will store the excess and use it the next day. So, there is a little more leeway with the fat-soluble vitamins, provided you are consuming enough of them over a period of several days.

The water-soluble vitamins are vitamin C and the B-vitamins that make up the B-complex. These are the vitamins that are broken down and carried throughout the body in water. The fat-soluble vitamins are vitamins A, D, E, and K. These are the vitamins that require the consumption of fat in order to be used by the body. Following is a list of the water-soluble vitamins and the fat-soluble vitamins with an overview of how they are beneficial, symptoms of deficiencies, and food sources of the vitamins.

Water-soluble vitamins

Vitamin C

Vitamin C is good for combatting the common cold, preventing strokes, improving mood, preventing wrinkles, improving the immune system, and preventing and fighting some cancers. Vitamin C has also been successfully used to treat Bipolar Disorder.

Vitamin C deficiency causes scurvy, neurological (brain) damage, and can cause depression.

Sources of vitamin C:

- Citrus fruits like oranges, grapefruits, and tangerines
- Cantaloupe
- Kiwis
- Papayas

- Guavas
- Strawberries
- Dark leafy greens (kale, mustard greens, spinach, beet greens, turnip greens, Swiss chard, rainbow chard, collard greens, watercress, dandelion greens, purslane)
- Broccoli, cauliflower, brussels sprouts
- Bell peppers (yellow bell peppers provide the most vitamin C and green bell peppers provide the least)
- Red and green hot chili peppers
- Red cabbage
- Tomato juice

Keep in mind that vitamin C is destroyed by heat and air. So, for optimum vitamin C benefit, foods should be eaten raw, or minimally cooked, and as soon as possible after cutting or juicing. Orange juice, for instance, will lose more vitamin C the longer it is exposed to the air. Foods cooked quickly by steaming or sautéing will retain higher levels of vitamin C than those cooked at high temperatures for longer periods of time. Also, when cooked in water, as in boiling vegetables or cooking in soups or stews, the vitamin C will leach out into the cooking water and diminish with high heat and long cooking times.

There are 8 B-vitamins that make up the B-vitamin complex. They include thiamin, riboflavin, niacin, folate (also called folic acid or folacin), vitamin B6, vitamin B12, biotin, and pantothenic acid.

B vitamins work together to increase metabolism, reduce risk of heart disease, aid memory, aid in preventing cancer, reduce anxiety and depression, help maintain healthy digestion, reduce or eliminate symptoms of PMS, and are essential for healthy nerves and muscle function.

Thiamin (B1)

Thiamin is important for maintaining cellular function and a wide array of organ functions. Thiamin deficiency can lead to beriberi and/or Wernicke-Korsakoff syndrome. Symptoms include mental confusion, memory problems, fatigue, difficulty walking, pain, shortness of breath, delusions, hallucinations, and confabulation (making up stories to compensate for not remembering something).

Since alcohol interferes with the absorption of thiamin, as well as other B-vitamins, people who abuse alcohol are at highest risk of thiamin deficiency.

Sources of thiamin:

- Pork
- Liver
- Dark leafy greens
- Fortified (vitamins added) whole-grain cereals and breads
- Wheat germ
- Peas
- Lentils
- Almonds
- Pecans

Riboflavin (B2)

Riboflavin is required for the processing of dietary fats, carbohydrates, and proteins to convert these nutrients to energy. Riboflavin is also used for the continual process of renewal and regeneration of all cells and tissues in the body.

Riboflavin is destroyed by light. This is one reason that milk is sold in cartons rather than clear bottles.

Symptoms of riboflavin deficiency include swelling of the mouth, lips, and tongue, cracking at the corners of the mouth, rashes between the nose and mouth and on the genitals, itchy eyes that are sensitive to the light, numbness of the hands, and decreased sensitivity to touch, temperature, and vibration.

Sources of riboflavin:

- Dairy products such as milk, yoghurt, and cheese
- Liver
- Asparagus
- Spinach and other dark leafy greens (these must be cooked to absorb   riboflavin – it is not readily available in salads)
- Broccoli
- Beans
- Chicken
- Fish
- Eggs
- Fortified cereals and breads

Niacin (B3)

Like other B vitamins, niacin plays a role in processing carbohydrates, fats, and proteins into energy as well as keeping the nervous system functioning properly. Niacin is also responsible for making sex and stress-related hormones and also improves circulation and cholesterol levels.

Even a mild deficiency of niacin can cause indigestion, fatigue, canker sores, vomiting, and depression.

Severe deficiency causes a scaly rash on skin exposed to the sun, swollen mouth and tongue, vomiting and diarrhea, headache, apathy, fatigue, depression, disorientation, and memory loss. Severe deficiency is fatal if not treated.

The most common cause of niacin deficiency is alcohol abuse.

Sources of niacin:

- Chicken
- Turkey
- Liver
- Salmon
- Tuna
- Fortified cereals
- Beans
- Lentils
- Split peas
- Peanuts
- Whole wheat

Folate (B9)

Folate, or folic acid, helps the body break down proteins. It also helps form red blood cells and produce DNA, the building block of the human body, which carries genetic information. Folate is crucial in the development of a healthy fetus. It plays an important role in the development of the fetus' spinal cord and brain. Therefore, a deficiency can cause severe birth defects of the brain and spinal cord, known as neural tube defects.

Some types of cancers can be caused by folate deficiency including colorectal cancer.

Symptoms of deficiency include depression, fatigue, feeling lightheaded, headache, irritability, difficulty concentrating, forgetfulness, loss of appetite, weight loss, canker sores, swollen tongue, and poor growth.

Alcohol and many common medications block the absorption of folate.

Sources of folate:

- Dark leafy greens
- Asparagus
- Liver
- Beans
- Lentils
- Split peas
- Poultry
- Pork
- Shellfish
- Citrus fruits
- Sunflower seeds
- Peanuts

Vitamin B6

Vitamin B6 is necessary for the proper maintenance of red blood cell metabolism, the nervous system, and the immune system.

Vitamin B6 is required for the brain to produce serotonin, dopamine, and norepinephrine and for myelin formation.

Deficiencies can cause dermatitis (skin inflammation), depression, confusion, cognitive dysfunction, convulsions, and increased risk of heart attack.

Cooking and freezing destroy vitamin B6 so eating fruits and vegetables raw and other sources with the shortest cooking times required will help ensure maintenance of B6.

Mild deficiency of vitamin B6 is common in the U.S.

Sources of vitamin B6:

- Chicken
- Turkey
- Liver
- Cheese
- Eggs
- Seafood
- Bananas
- Carrots
- Peas
- Dark leafy greens
- Potatoes
- Avocado
- Watermelon
- Fortified cereals

Vitamin B12

Vitamin B12 deficiency causes neurological problems and is often misdiagnosed as Parkinson's Disease, Huntington's Disease, Multiple Sclerosis, Alzheimer's Disease, and autism. Low levels of Vitamin B12 can cause depression, severe mood swings, fatigue, nervousness, anxiety, clumsiness, loss of balance, confusion, memory loss, cognitive impairment, short attention span, tremors, delusions, paranoia, hallucinations, chest pains, digestive problems including colitis, sore mouth or tongue, irritability, vision problems, hearing problems, migraine headaches, and autoimmune disorders.

Many common medications block absorption of Vitamin B12 so can lead to deficiency. Vegan vegetarians are at risk of deficiency as well as babies that are breast-fed by mothers who are vegan vegetarians. People with Celiac Disease and the elderly are also at higher risk. Some estimates indicate that as many as 40% of Americans may be deficient in Vitamin B12.

Sources of vitamin B12:

Animal foods are the only natural sources of vitamin B12 but many foods including soy products and grain products are fortified with vitamin B12. Natural sources include:

- Liver
- Beef
- Poultry
- Fish
- Shellfish
- Egg yolks
- Milk
- Cheese

Biotin

As with other B-vitamins, biotin is involved in a number of things in the body including the production of energy from fats and carbohydrates (metabolic activities), enzyme functions and genetic processing.

A deficiency in biotin can cause depression, hair loss, scaly dry skin, sores on the nose and in the mouth, loss of appetite, nausea, numbness in the hands and feet, muscle pain and heart irregularities.

While a deficiency in biotin is not considered to be common, diabetics can be prone to biotin deficiency. Also, many prescription drugs block the absorption of biotin including antibiotics, sedatives, and anti-seizure medications.

Sources of biotin:

- Liver
- Egg yolks
- Salmon
- Beans
- Raspberries
- Pork
- Avocado
- Most fruits and vegetables contain at least some biotin and grain products will have some naturally and through fortification.

Pantothenic acid (B5)

Pantothenic acid is required by the body for cellular processes and maintenance of fat.

Symptoms of deficiency include irritability, fatigue, apathy, insomnia, numbness, and muscle cramps. A deficiency can also lead to hypoglycemia (low blood sugar). A deficiency in pantothenic acid increases risks of heart attacks and stroke. There is also a high correlation between pantothenic acid and rheumatoid arthritis. Patients with rheumatoid arthritis often have low levels of pantothenic acid and studies have shown that pantothenic acid can result in reduced levels of swelling and pain in people with rheumatoid arthritis.

Sources of pantothenic acid:

- Dairy products
- Liver
- Salmon
- Sunflower seeds
- Avocado
- Lentils
- Split peas
- Sweet potatoes
- Mushrooms
- Broccoli

Fat soluble vitamins

The fat-soluble vitamins are vitamins A, D, E, and K. Vitamins A and E must be consumed in the food we eat. The body can make vitamins D and K without them being consumed directly, but not in amounts adequate for long-term optimum functioning. Vitamin D can be converted by the body from exposure to sunlight. Vitamin K is created by bacteria in the intestines. Fat-soluble vitamins must be consumed with some type of fat or oil in order for the body to absorb the vitamins. So, while green leafy vegetables are an excellent source of these vitamins, they must be consumed together with meat, dairy products (not non-fat), oil, butter, or nuts for their fat content to utilize the fat-soluble vitamins. Sautéing kale in a small amount of olive oil or eating sweet potatoes with a small amount of butter will ensure good vitamin absorption.

Vitamin A

Vitamin A is commonly used topically and orally as

prescription treatments for acne and other skin conditions, including wrinkles. Oral vitamin A is also used as a treatment for measles and dry eye in people with low levels of vitamin A. Vitamin A is also used to treat a specific type of leukemia. Vitamin A from plant sources is made from **beta-carotene**, which is converted directly to vitamin A in the body. Vitamin A from plant sources has antioxidant properties and plays a key role in keeping the immune system strong. Vitamin A derived from animal sources like meat and milk, has already been converted to vitamin A and while it still delivers many of its benefits, it is thought to have less powerful antioxidant properties than beta-carotene. Vitamin A helps maintain healthy eyesight, particularly the ability to see in dim light, and healthy skin, teeth, and bones.

Sources of vitamin A:

- Any type of animal liver is high in vitamin A
- Cream
- Whole or 2% milk and yoghurt (Vitamin A is in fat so will not be present in skim milk or fat-free yoghurt unless it is added. Since it is fat soluble, you cannot absorb the vitamin A from skim milk)
- Herbs and seasonings including:
- Parsley
- Basil
- Marjoram
- Dill
- Oregano
- Paprika
- Red pepper
- Cayenne
- Chili powder
- Orange, red, and dark green fruits and vegetables including:

- Carrots
- Winter squash (butternut, acorn, banana squash)
- Apricots
- Cantaloupe
- Red and dark green leaf type lettuces
- Dark leafy greens
- Sweet potatoes

　　　* A note about sweet potatoes vs. yams…. what are labeled "yams" in our grocery stores in the U.S. are actually sweet potatoes. There are varieties of sweet potatoes that are lighter colored and yellow on the inside (these are called "sweet potatoes" in the grocery store) and varieties that are darker colored and orange on the inside (these are called "yams"). The darker colored ones (yams) have much higher vitamin A content and, in general, are more nutritious than the lighter colored ones. When I refer to "sweet potatoes", I mean the darker colored variety labeled as "yams". I don't refer to them as yams because a yam is actually an African food that is quite different, both in appearance and nutritional content, than the sweet potatoes we call yams in the U.S.

Vitamin D

Your body naturally makes Vitamin D when you expose your skin to the sun. In addition, Vitamin D is added to some foods such as milk and other dairy products, soymilk, tofu, and fortified cereals.

Vitamin D promotes absorption of calcium for bone health, boosts immune function, reduces inflammation, promotes healthy neuromuscular function, reduces risk of infection, and protects against some forms of cancer. It may reduce the risk of developing multiple sclerosis, as well as playing a key role in keeping the brain working well later in life. It is linked to maintaining a healthy body weight and reducing the severity and frequency of asthma symptoms. Vitamin D also helps regulate blood pressure, reduces stress and tension, relieves body aches and pains by reducing muscles spasms, improves cardiovascular health, helps fight depression and reduces wrinkles.

Sources of vitamin D:

- "Fatty" fish like herring, salmon, mackerel, sardines, and tuna
- Raw fish will usually have a higher vitamin D content than cooked fish. Sushi with raw fish is a good source of vitamin D.
- Eggs
- Mushrooms

Vitamin E

Vitamin E acts as a metabolism booster, anti-inflammatory, reduces risk of Alzheimer's; helps prevent cancer, heart disease, stroke, cataracts, and signs of aging. Topically reduces scars and age spots and promotes wound healing. Women find relief from the discomfort of fibrocystic breast disease. It is used for treating cancer, diabetes, diseases of the brain and nervous system including Alzheimer's disease and other dementias, Parkinson's disease, night cramps, restless leg syndrome, and for epilepsy, along with other medications. Vitamin E is also used for Huntington's chorea, and other disorders involving nerves and muscles. Vitamin E is also used for cataracts, asthma, respiratory infections, skin disorders, aging skin, sunburns, cystic fibrosis, infertility, impotence, chronic fatigue syndrome (CFS), peptic ulcers, for certain inherited diseases and to prevent allergies. It is also used for improving physical endurance, increasing energy, reducing muscle damage after exercise, and improving muscle strength.

Sources of vitamin E:

- Sunflower seeds
- Almonds
- Peanuts
- Pine nuts
- Hazelnuts
- Olives
- Dark leafy greens
- Apricots
- Papaya
- Broccoli
- Avocado
- Basil
- Parsley
- Oregano
- Paprika
- Red chili powder
- Wheat germ
- Plant oils such as wheat germ oil, avocado oil, and olive oil

Vitamin K

Vitamin K is important for strong bones and reduces the risk of bone fractures. It also reduces the risk of heart disease, strokes, and varicose veins by preventing arterial calcification. Vitamin K prevents against prostate cancer, dementia and other brain disease.

Sources of vitamin K:

- Dark leafy greens
- Prunes

- Cucumbers
- Cabbage
- Broccoli
- Asparagus
- Brussels sprouts
- Green onions (scallions)
- Chili powder
- Curry
- Paprika
- Cayenne
- Basil
- Sage
- Thyme
- Parsley
- Coriander
- Marjoram
- Oregano

Minerals

Major minerals include calcium, chloride, magnesium, phosphorus, potassium and sodium. Sulphur has also been garnering a lot of attention recently. **Trace minerals** are minerals that are needed in smaller amounts and they include chromium, copper, fluoride, iodine, iron, selenium, and zinc.

Phytonutrients are another category of nutrients that are found only in plants. Many of these important chemicals are found in colorful fruits and vegetables. Some of the better-known phytonutrients are the carotenoids, like beta-carotene, lutein, lycopene and zeaxanthin, as well as flavonoids.

Major Minerals

Calcium

The body needs Vitamin D to absorb calcium. Many foods that are fortified with calcium, like milk, are also fortified with vitamin D. Calcium will be best utilized if you have adequate levels of vitamin D. Calcium is also best absorbed in the presence of fat, like the fat-soluble vitamins. Remember some of the fatty fish that are high in vitamin D? They are also high in calcium, a good example of nature "pairing" or combining nutrients in food for optimum utilization.

Your body needs calcium to build and maintain strong bones. Your heart, muscles and nerves also need calcium to function properly. Calcium plays an essential role in blood clotting, muscle contraction, nerve impulse transmission, preventing osteoporosis, relieving symptoms of PMS, and bone and tooth formation.

Sources of calcium:

- Dairy products like milk, yoghurt, and cheese
- Dark leafy greens
- Flax seeds
- Almonds
- Soy products like soybeans, soy milk, and tofu
- Sesame seeds
- Brazil nuts
- Many common cooking herbs, especially savory

Chloride

Chloride is an ingredient in salt. We generally meet, and sometimes exceed, our chloride needs through the use of table salt.

Chloride moves in and out of your cells when necessary to maintain the proper balance of fluid and electrolytes. When the pH of your blood changes, chloride acts as a buffer, which is a substance that neutralizes your blood. If your blood becomes too acidic or too alkaline, chloride will bring the pH of your blood back to neutral. It also helps maintain proper blood volume and blood pressure.

Sources of chloride:

- Our main source of chloride is via sodium chloride, or salt
- Tomatoes
- Lettuce
- Celery
- Olives
- Seaweed
- Rye
- Wheat
- Barley
- Dark leafy greens
- Watermelon
- Pineapple

Magnesium

Magnesium can lower blood pressure, and is used for treating heart disease and osteoporosis. Type 2 diabetes is associated with low magnesium. In addition to heart health and development and maintenance of strong bones and teeth, magnesium plays a crucial role in the transmission of nerve impulses, body temperature regulation, detoxification, and energy production. Magnesium also relieves symptoms of PMS and menopause and minimizes the risk of premature labor. Magnesium is also beneficial in treating insomnia, constipation, depression, anxiety, and panic attacks. Magnesium is a laxative (Milk of Magnesia is magnesium) and a muscle relaxer. Soaking in hot water with Epsom Salt (magnesium) will relieve sore, strained muscles.

Sources of magnesium:

- Rice
- Halibut
- Wheat and oat brans
- Barley
- Artichokes
- Buckwheat flour
- Pumpkin seeds
- Dark chocolate
- Flax seeds
- Sesame seeds
- Brazil nuts
- Sunflower seeds
- Almonds
- Cashews
- Molasses
- Soybeans
- Dark leafy greens

Phosphorus

Some amount of phosphorous is present in nearly every food.

Phosphorus works together with calcium in the building and maintenance of strong teeth and bones. It also aids in digestion, boosts energy and alertness, and regulates reproductive hormones. Phosphorus is essential for proper cell reproduction, memory, concentration and other mental activities.

Sources of phosphorus:

- Rice and oat bran
- Wheat germ
- Pumpkin seeds
- Cheese (especially parmesan)
- Sesame seeds
- Brazil nuts
- Pine nuts
- Flax seeds
- Soybeans

Potassium

Potassium is a critical electrolyte that is abundantly present in seawater (and sea salt) and soil.

Potassium contains a positive electrical charge and works closely with chloride in regulating blood pressure and PH balance. Potassium is necessary for the heart, kidneys, and other organs to work normally. Potassium allows our muscles to move, our nerves to fire, and our kidneys to filter blood. The right balance of potassium literally allows the heart to beat.

Sources of potassium:

- Beans
- Dark leafy greens

- Sweet potatoes
- Apricots
- Winter squash (acorn, butternut)
- Yoghurt
- Salmon
- Avocados
- Mushrooms
- Bananas
- Nuts, like almonds and peanuts
- Citrus fruits
- Milk
- Potatoes
- Raisins
- Dates
- Prunes
- Carrots

Keep in mind that potassium is lost in liquid when boiling fruits and vegetables containing potassium. The potassium leaches out into the water so is not a problem for soups and stews when the liquid is consumed. But, when boiling potatoes, or other vegetables or fruits, draining off the liquid pours most of the potassium down the drain. A better way to maintain the potassium level in potatoes is to eat them baked with the skins. Sautéing and cooking with the minimum amount of water is recommended for retaining potassium.

Sodium

As with chloride, our main source of sodium is sodium chloride, or salt. Many fruits and vegetables contain sodium naturally. Sodium is lost through sweating, so people who live in hot climates or who sweat a lot as a result of exercise or physical labor need to consume more salt than people who live in colder climates or have a more sedentary lifestyle. Typically, we get plenty of sodium from using salt in cooking and added at the table. If we eat much processed food (boxed or commercially canned food) we probably have more sodium than we need.

Sodium is important for regulating the contraction of the heart and other muscles. Sodium also regulates fluids in the body, reduces risk of heat stroke, removes excess carbon dioxide from the body, and is an important element in the development of the brain. Sodium aids in the keeping the mind sharp.

Sources of sodium:

- Sea salt
- Celery
- Olives
- Kelp
- Dark leafy greens

Trace Minerals

Trace minerals are minerals that we just need a "trace" of. But just because we only need a small amount of them doesn't mean they aren't very important. Iodine, for instance, is a trace element needed in small amounts but iodine deficiency is the single most common cause of mental retardation and brain damage in the world. It is rare to see a deficiency in the U.S. because iodine is added to most table salt to ensure that people get enough of it. It is naturally present in sea salt and food that comes from the sea like saltwater shellfish, sea fish like cod, haddock and perch, and kelp. Iodine deficiencies also cause underactive thyroids, and goiters (enlarged masses growing on the thyroid glands at the front of the neck). Iron is another trace mineral and lack of adequate iron is one of the most common nutritional deficiencies. Iron deficiency can cause anemia, which can result in a lack of energy and reduced ability to fight infection, among other things. One of the best sources of iron is red meat.

Chromium

Chromium helps maintain normal blood sugar and insulin levels. Chromium boosts metabolism, prevents hypertension, and helps regulate fat and cholesterol. Chromium is used to treat memory problems and Alzheimer's disease.

Sources of chromium:

- Eggs (yolks have a much higher chromium content than whites)
- Brewer's yeast
- Beer
- Molasses
- Sweet potatoes
- Corn
- Whole grains
- Red meat
- Poultry
- Seafood
- Tomatoes
- Broccoli
- Onion
- Garlic
- Chili peppers
- Green peppers
- Beets
- Mushrooms

- Grape juice
- Bananas

Copper

Copper is important for bone and connective tissue production. It also helps the body eliminate free radicals (free radicals can damage cells and are believed to accelerate the progression of cancer) and contributes to producing melanin (the dark pigment found in the hair, skin and eyes). Copper is also important in the absorption of iron. So, even if you consume adequate amounts of iron, if you don't have enough copper, you won't be able to absorb the iron and can still become anemic.

Sources of copper:

- Liver
- Oysters
- Sesame seeds
- Cocoa powder
- All kinds of nuts with cashews having the highest content
- Calamari
- Lobster
- Sunflower seeds
- Sun dried tomatoes
- Pumpkin seeds
- Basil
- Marjoram
- Oregano
- Thyme
- Savory
- Parsley

Fluoride

Fluorite is a common mineral and the chief source of fluoride. Fluoride is added to drinking water in many places, and in toothpaste and other products, to prevent tooth decay. The addition of fluoride to drinking water has been controversial since the practice began in the 1940's. Prior to this, no commercial products contained fluoride. Since then, drinking water, toothpaste, mouthwash, as well as many prescription medications contain fluoride. In addition, many pesticides contain fluoride so many foods absorb the fluoride from the soil. Also, commercially made beverages including juice, bottled teas, and domestic beers contain fluoride from the water used in the drinks. Most processed foods contain fluoride. Black tea and grapes often contain significant amounts of fluoride absorbed from the soil. Nowadays, getting enough fluoride is seldom a problem. The controversy involves getting too much fluoride because of the possibility of overexposure. Even Teflon contains fluoride and eating from Teflon pans is therefore a source of fluoride. Toxic levels of fluoride, which vary from person to person, may cause the tooth defect dental fluorosis, and skeletal fluorosis, a painful bone disease. Some fluoride is naturally present in small amounts in water and fresh fruits, vegetables, and fish. The best way to get enough fluoride without getting too much fluoride is to eat fresh non-processed foods and drink spring water.

Iodine

Iodine is important in the function of the thyroid gland, metabolism, and reproduction, growth, and development. Iodine deficiency can cause retarded brain development called "cretinism", infertility in women, fatigue, depression, high cholesterol, weight gain, and goiters.

Sources of iodine:

- Sea salt contains iodine naturally and commercial table salt often has iodine added. The label on the salt container will say, "iodized".
- Seafood and sea fish
- Kelp
- Seaweed (such as the kind used in making sushi)
- Watercress
- Dairy products
- Potatoes (skins have the highest content)
- Beans
- Corn
- Peas
- Turkey
- Rice
- Eggs

Iron

The body needs iron to produce red blood cells. Iron prevents anemia, which causes fatigue, lethargy and weakness. Iron is important for concentration and other important brain functions. Iron is used to treat insomnia. Iron is a vital element for muscle contraction and is used to treat Restless Leg Syndrome. Iron plays a key role in maintaining a strong immune system. Cooking with cast iron cookware will add iron to the food. An old remedy for lack of energy was to stick a rusty nail in an apple overnight then, after removing the nail, the apple was eaten the next day. The iron from the rust would leach into the apple and give the person a "boost".

The most bioavailable iron comes from red meat. In other words, our bodies can utilize some iron from plants but we can break down and use the iron from meat better.

Sources of iron:

- Beans
- Soybeans
- Molasses
- Spinach
- Red meat (especially liver)
- Chocolate
- Clams, oysters, mussels
- Pumpkin seeds
- Sesame seeds
- Sun-dried tomatoes
- Sunflower seeds
- Dried apricots
- Raisins

Selenium

Selenium content in food can vary widely depending on how selenium rich or poor the soil was where the plants were grown or animals were raised. Some areas of the United States generally have higher selenium content in the soil, particularly the high plains areas including Nebraska and the Dakotas. People who live in those areas typically have diets higher in selenium than in other parts of the U.S. or world where the soil contains less selenium and most foods are obtained locally. Selenium content analyses will vary widely for this reason. Brazil nuts are much higher in selenium than other foods and should only be eaten occasionally because of this.

Selenium improves the immune system against bacterial and viral infections, against cancer cells and herpes virus, cold sores, and shingles. It also regulates cholesterol and benefits the skin during healing from burn injuries. Selenium contributes to healthy skin and shampoo containing selenium can alleviate dandruff problems.

Sources of selenium:

- Brazil nuts
- Tuna
- Cod
- Turkey
- Chicken
- Beef
- Sunflower seeds
- Eggs
- Cottage cheese
- Brown rice

Zinc

Zinc is important for proper functioning of the immune system and the healing of wounds. It supports normal growth and development during pregnancy, childhood, and adolescence and is required for proper sense of taste and smell. While zinc is present in plant foods, it is more "available" to the body from animal foods. Oysters are higher in zinc by far than any other food.

Sources of zinc:

- Oysters
- Beef
- Crab
- Lobster
- Pork
- Beans
- Chicken

- Yoghurt
- Cashews
- Chickpeas
- Oats
- Milk
- Cheese

Macronutrients

Macronutrients include ***protein***, ***fats***, and ***carbohydrates***. These three things are what provide our calories. Micronutrients do not provide calories. We need calories for energy. The only other substance that provides calories is alcohol. Alcohol is not considered a macronutrient because, unlike protein, fat, and carbohydrates, we do not need alcohol to survive.

Protein

Protein is made up of building blocks called **amino acids**. There are many amino acids but 20 of them are called "standard amino acids" and together make a complete protein. Eleven of the 20 are called "non-essential", which is a little misleading because it implies that they are not important. They are important. "Non-essential" means that the body can manufacture them on its own. The other nine amino acids are called "essential" because they cannot be manufactured by the body. These must be consumed by eating proteins that contain those amino acids.

The 11 "non-essential" (manufactured by the body) amino acids are:

- Alanine

- Arginine
- Asparagine
- Aspartic Acid
- Cysteine
- Glutamic Acid
- Glutamine
- Clycine
- Proline
- Serine
- Tyrosine

The 9 "essential" (not manufactured by the body) amino acids are:

- Histidine
- Isoleucine
- Leucine
- Lysine
- Methionine
- Phenylalanine
- Threonine
- Tryptophan
- Valine

Protein from animal sources such as meat, dairy products, and eggs are called "complete proteins" because they contain all 9 of the "essential" amino acids in the proper ratio to each other to be utilized by our bodies as protein. Plant proteins, like what is contained in vegetables, fruits, grains, and legumes (beans, lentils, split peas) are usually "incomplete" because plant proteins have some of the essential amino acids, but not necessarily all 9 of them. Or, even if all 9 of them are present, they will not be in a ratio that will allow much of the protein to be useable. However, plants can be combined to include all 9 of them in useable ratios. It is necessary to have all 9 of them for the body to properly utilize the protein. The protein in soy is considered to be the most compete form of plant protein with a quality (amount and ratio) comparable to animal protein.

Later, we will be referring specifically to four of these amino acids because of their particular role in the production of hormones and neurotransmitters that affect anxiety and depression. Those are *tryptophan*, *phenylalanine* (essential amino acids), *tyrosine,* and *glutamine* (non-essential amino acids).

Fat

Fat is something the body needs in order to absorb fat-soluble vitamins and minerals. Without fat, you would be deficient in these nutrients. Fat also provides energy. We need fat for healthy skin, healthy cells, and regulating the production of sex hormones. Fat is also important for brain development and function.

Good Fat and Bad Fat

There are three types of fat: *saturated, unsaturated,* and *trans fat.* Trans fat is considered "bad" fat. Bad fat contributes to heart disease, obesity, and high blood pressure. Unsaturated fat is considered "good" fat. Good fat can lower cholesterol, lowering your risk of heart disease. So, "good" fat gives you all the benefits of the fat we need without the undesirable effects of "bad" fat. Saturated fat used to be considered "bad fat" but more recently is thought to be beneficial in moderation.

Unsaturated fat is oil that comes from plants like olive oil and flax oil and fatty fish like salmon and tuna. **Saturated fat** is fat that comes mostly from animals, like the fat that is in meat and the fat that is in milk, which of course is cream, from which butter is made. Foods from plants that contain saturated fat include coconut, coconut oil, palm oil and palm kernel oil (often called tropical oils) and cocoa butter. **Trans fat** is a man-made type of fat. It is made by taking an unsaturated fat like soybean oil or cottonseed oil that is liquid in its natural state and adding hydrogen atoms to it to make it solid. It is then called "hydrogenated oil" or "partially hydrogenated" oil. It is what solidifies oil into margarine. The original purpose for this was to give unsaturated fats a longer shelf life. Oil will oxidize, or become "rancid", much more quickly than its hydrogenated manufactured cousin. So, when added to cookies, cakes, breads, and other kinds of processed foods bound for grocery store shelves, hydrogenated oil would allow these products to keep longer without spoiling. Unsaturated fats are better for you, in part, because trans fats basically turn to sludge in your arteries, while vegetable oil does not. Also, many types of unsaturated oils contain beneficial things including omega-3 fatty acids, which have been implicated in lowering risk of heart disease and stroke as well as aiding in decreasing symptoms of depression and anxiety.

Hydrogenated oil was considered a technological marvel and touted as better for us than saturated fat because it contains "no cholesterol". So, we were told to eat margarine rather than butter because saturated fats, like butter, were full of cholesterol and among the biggest contributors to heart disease. As it turns out, that isn't entirely true. Our bodies were designed to utilize certain amounts of saturated fat. Not so of its artificial cousin, trans fat. Most experts now agree that trans fat is much worse for us than saturated fat and should, ideally, be avoided altogether while saturated fat in moderate amounts is not harmful and even has some benefits. This is very good news for those of us who enjoy cream in our coffee and find that a baked sweet potato is just not the same without a little butter.

Another way to compare the three is by understanding that unsaturated fat raises your HDL (good) cholesterol and lowers LDL (bad) cholesterol. Saturated fat and trans fat both raise LDL (bad) cholesterol. However, trans fat not only raises the LDL (bad) cholesterol, it also lowers the HDL (good) cholesterol. So, the best source of fat is unsaturated fat while saturated fat is beneficial in moderation and as a part of a balanced, healthy lifestyle that includes unsaturated fats primarily. Trans fat has no benefits and is just bad for you.

Since unsaturated fat is the "good for you" fat and since it is shown to be helpful in alleviating symptoms of depression and anxiety, for the purposes of this book it is recommended that unsaturated fat be your primary source of fat. Although coconut oil contains saturated fat, recent findings suggest that it may have beneficial health benefits, including some promising implications in alleviating symptoms of Alzeimer's disease. More research to determine the possible benefits of coconut oil is ongoing.

Sources of Bad Fats (Trans Fats) include:

- Fast food
- Junk food
- Processed fried foods and snacks such as doughnuts, potato chips, fried cheese sticks

Sources of Saturated Fats include:

- Cream
- Butter
- Fatty meats

- Coconut oil

Sources of Good Fats (Unsaturated Fats) include:

- Olive oil
- Flax oil
- Nuts and seeds like sunflower and pumpkin seeds
- Avocado
- Tuna
- Salmon

Omega-what's?

We can't talk about fat without talking about **omega-3 fats** and **omega-6 fats**. This is because *if there were only one thing we were going to change about our diets, this should probably be that thing*. Omega-3's and omega-6's are fatty acids that control inflammation in the body. Omega-3's are basically anti-inflammatories, suppressing the flammatory response. Omega-6's excite the flammatory response. So, between the two, they regulate inflammation in the body. The body needs some inflammation to protect itself and heal from various kinds of damage. Inflammation also triggers the immune system to fight diseases. But, chronic inflammation may be at the root of all major illnesses. It's important to have both kinds in our diet but it's important to have them in the proper balance. Ideally, we would consume them in equal amounts. In other words, in a ratio of 1:1. The problem with the modern Western diet is that we have created a huge imbalance of these two important fatty acids where we now consume around 20-25 times as much omega-6's as omega-3's, or in a ratio of 20-25:1. This is because omega-6's are found in seed oils like soybean oil, safflower oil, and corn oil that is used in fast foods and in processed foods like cookies, chips, crackers, and other snack foods. These high proportions of omega-6 fatty acids *increase* inflammation. The imbalance between omega-3 and omega-6 fatty acids may also contribute to obesity, depression, dyslexia, hyperactivity and even a tendency toward violence.

Omega-3's are found in flax seed oil, fatty fish like salmon, cod, and sardines, and walnuts. Walnuts are also a good source of omega-6 fatty acids. Other "good" sources of omega-6's are other kinds of nuts like almonds and peanuts, and seeds like sunflower seeds, pumpkin seeds, and sesame seeds. While some of the "good" foods, like almonds and avocados, have a high omega-6 to omega-3 ratio, they also have many redeeming qualities. These whole, natural foods are also good sources of many other important nutrients and fiber.

So, the omega-3's and omega-6's are both good for us, *as long as we eat them in close to equal proportions.* Luckily, as with so many foods that contain important nutrients, omega-3's and omega-6's co-occur in many foods. And, like so many other things, if we obtain them by eating them in their natural state, the balance will pretty much take care of itself. It would be difficult to consume 20-25 times more omega-6 than omega-3 if we were just eating whole, natural food. The only reason this has become a problem is because our Western diet is grossly overloaded with omega-6 fatty acids in processed food. It is one very good reason to avoid processed food. Processed food, in general, has way too little of the good things we need, and a whole lot of the bad things that we not only don't need, but that are making us very sick, both physically and mentally.

Low levels of omega-3 fatty acids are associated with depression. High levels of omega-6 fatty acids are associated with depression. An imbalanced ratio of omega-6's to omega-3's is associated with depression. Lowering levels of omega-6's and raising levels of omega-3's improves depression and lowers the risk of becoming depressed. Currently the Japanese government recommends omega fats in a 4:1 ratio. The incidence of heart disease, stroke, depression, and anxiety all have historically been much lower in Japan than in the US. The Japanese also typically eat a lot of fatty fish, which are high in omega-3's. The US government recommends a ratio of 10:1. While even that would be a tremendous improvement over the current Western diet, most of the recent available research in depression and anxiety would agree that ratio is too high.

There are 3 kinds of omega-3 fatty acids: alpha-linoleic acid (ALA), eicosapentaenoic acid (EPA), and docosahexaenoic acid (DHA). EPA and DHA are the kinds that are most beneficial in treating depression and anxiety.

ALA is found in plants and of the 3 kinds is the one we generally get the most of from our food. Some ALA will convert to EPA and DHA in most people. How much is converted depends on several factors. Saturated and trans-fats, some prescription medications, deficiencies in vitamins B6, B3, and C or in the minerals zinc and magnesium, excessive alcohol consumption and some health conditions like diabetes can interfere with conversion. Also people with certain ethnic heritages including Native American, Inuit, Norwegian, and Welsh-Irish may not effectively convert ALA to EPA or DHA in the body. Meeting your needs for other nutrients by eating a variety of healthy, whole food is crucial for proper conversion of ALA to EPA and DHA. If you share one of the aforementioned ethnic heritages, how much ALA you are able to convert is difficult to say. You will be able to convert some, but may need to consume much more ALA, perhaps as much as 5 times more, in order to convert enough to EPA and DHA. ALA is found in many types of nuts and seeds as well as plants. The best source of readily available ALA is in flax seed and flax seed oil.

Smaller amounts can be found in:

- Kale
- Spinach
- Mustard greens
- Algae
- Brussels sprouts
- Watercress
- Parsley

EPA and DHA seem to have the most health benefits overall and specifically in regards to mental health. EPA and DHA are especially low in the Western diet. EPA and DHA are found in:

- Fatty fish such as salmon (wild caught will have higher levels of omega-3's than farmed because of what they eat), sardines, herring, mackerel, trout (Lake Trout is highest), and tuna.
- Cod liver oil
- Grass fed meat (meat that comes from feedlots is typically high in omega-6 and low in omega-3 because of what they are fed)
- Wild game

The surest way to meet your needs for EPA and DHA is to eat fatty fish several times a week. Some people will be able to convert a substantial amount of ALA to EPA and DHA. Those who cannot convert it as efficiently should consume more from sources that are high in ALA, like flaxseed oil, which has about 5 times more omega-3 in the form of ALA than omega-6, or a ratio of about 1:5. Being conscientious about eating vegetables that have a higher ratio of ALA to omega-6 like dark green leafy vegetables, will also help ensure a good balance.

Use the Nutrition Content Table beginning on page 126 to find foods that have a positive ratio (1:1 or better) of omega-6 to omega-3. Some examples are Coho Salmon (1:7), raw pink salmon (1:22), cherries (1:1), cantaloupe (1:1.25), mangos (1:2.5), arugula (1:1.25), green beans (1:1.5), broccoli (1:1.25), cabbage (1:1.5), cauliflower (1:3), kale (1:1.5), leaf lettuce (1:1.25), romaine lettuce (1:1.3), mustard greens (1:1), turnips and turnip greens (1:4), squash (1:2), spinach (1:5), rutabagas (1:1.75), and kidney beans, navy beans and pinto beans which all have a ratio of about 1:1.5.

Carbohydrates

Carbohydrates provide energy to cells in your brain, red blood cells, and muscles. There are three types of carbohydrates: **Starch, Sugar,** and **Fiber.**

Starch

Starchy foods include:

- Potatoes
- Wheat
- Corn
- Rice
- Pasta
- Cereals
- Bread
- Crackers

Fiber

Fiber is found naturally in the plants, nuts and seeds that we eat. Meat and dairy products do not contain fiber. Fiber comes in two types: *soluble* and *insoluble.* Both types are very important for digestion, and prevention of heart disease, diabetes, obesity and constipation. Some foods only contain one type and some foods, like fruit, usually contain both.

Soluble fibers attract water and form a gel, which slows down digestion. Soluble fiber delays the emptying of your stomach and makes you feel full, which helps control weight. Slower stomach emptying may also affect blood sugar levels and have a beneficial effect on insulin sensitivity, which may help control diabetes. Soluble fibers can also help lower LDL ("bad") blood cholesterol by interfering with the absorption of dietary cholesterol.

Sources of soluble fiber include:

- Oatmeal
- Lentils
- Apples
- Oranges
- Pears
- Oat bran
- Strawberries
- Nuts
- Flaxseeds
- Beans
- Split peas
- Blueberries
- Psyllium
- Cucumbers
- Celery
- Carrots

Insoluble Fiber is considered gut-healthy fiber because it has a laxative effect and adds bulk to the diet, helping prevent constipation. These fibers do not dissolve in water, so they pass through the gastrointestinal tract relatively intact, and speed up the passage of food and waste through your gut. Insoluble fibers are mainly found in whole grains and vegetables.

Sources of insoluble fiber include:

- Whole wheat
- Whole grains
- Wheat bran
- Corn bran
- Seeds
- Nuts
- Barley
- Couscous
- Brown rice
- Bulgur
- Zucchini
- Celery
- Broccoli
- Cabbage
- Onions
- Tomatoes
- Carrots
- Cucumbers
- Green beans
- Dark leafy green vegetables
- Raisins
- Grapes
- Fruit
- Root vegetable skins (such as beets, turnips, potatoes)

Sugar

Sugar is the third form of carbohydrate and includes several different types. The more common types are *sucrose, glucose* (also called *dextrose*), *fructose, maltose,* **and** *lactose.* All forms of sugar occur naturally in foods. In its natural state, sugar is considered **unrefined.** When sugar is processed from food, it is available to us in more concentrated forms and is called **refined** sugar.

Sucrose is the most common refined sugar and is what we typically use as granulated sugar for sweetening food, such as cereals, drinks, and for use in baking. Granulated sugar is extracted from both sugarcane and sugar beets. Sugarcane is a tall fibrous grass with sweet juicy stalks. It is grown in tropical and subtropical climates. Sugar beets are large tuberous roots grown in temperate climates in the U.S. as well as other parts of the world. Sugar beets are not the same as the red beets we normally eat. Sugar beets, while they have high sugar content, are unpalatable in their natural state. Sucrose also occurs alongside glucose and fructose in some fruits and vegetables. Molasses is a byproduct of granulated sugar. It is present in sugarcane and is separated in the process of making "white" sugar. Brown sugar is refined sugar that still retains some of the molasses, which is what gives it its brown color. Dark brown sugar has more molasses than light brown sugar. Molasses is the only sweetener that has any appreciable nutritional value but its use is limited due to its strong flavor.

Glucose is produced in fruits and vegetables through the process of photosynthesis. Most ingested carbohydrates are converted to glucose during digestion.

Fructose is the type of sugar in fruit, some root vegetables, and honey. It is the sweetest of the sugars.

Maltose is formed during the fermentation of grains like barley and is converted to malt, which is used as flavoring in drinks and some processed foods. It is less sweet than sucrose, glucose, or fructose. Like glucose, it is formed in the body during digestion of starch.

Lactose is the sugar that is found naturally in milk. It is broken down during digestion by the enzyme lactase, which is present in children but some adults stop producing the enzyme, which results in lactose intolerance, or the inability to digest lactose.

What is an antioxidant?

Antioxidants are substances that protect cells from the effects of oxidation, a process that can destroy the body's cells and DNA by producing or activating "free radicals". Free radicals are cells that are less stable and more volatile and seek to damage other cells. Over time, this damage can be irreversible and can lead to disease, particularly cancer. Exposure to radiation, tobacco smoke, and other environmental toxins and even fried foods can produce free radicals. Antioxidants neutralize free radicals, preventing them from damaging other cells. Antioxidants can also repair some damaged cells. Antioxidants may play a role in preventing cancer and some neurological disorders as well as strengthening the immune system. While there are too many to list, some of the known antioxidants include:

- Vitamin A (best from beta-carotene)
- Vitamin C
- Vitamin E
- Selenium
- Zinc
- Bioflavonoids

*Bioflavonoids are pigments that give fruits, vegetables, and flowers their color. Bioflavonoids are antioxidants, antihistamines, and anti-inflammatories. Some of them also act as antidepressants. Curcumin, for instance, the yellow pigment of curry, has been shown to possess antidepressant activity in various animals.

There are many substances contained in food, especially fruits and vegetables, that act as antioxidants. Many of these substances are known but many remain undiscovered. The complexity of the chemical composition of food is the subject of a large body of research. New discoveries are happening every day that add to our understanding of the role these substances play. Clinical trials demonstrating the effectiveness of antioxidants have mixed results. This could in part be due to the isolating of the substances in the experiments. When we look at the effects of one substance or nutrient alone, we are not seeing it in its natural context where it is likely working together with other substances, including other antioxidants. The best antioxidant protection is going to come from consuming them via the food in which they naturally occur. A diet rich in a variety of fruits and vegetables is the best way to insure continuous renewal of various antioxidants. Eating fruits and vegetables that are free of toxins like pesticides will help insure the optimum benefit from antioxidants. Theoretically, the more toxins we introduce to our bodies, the more antioxidants we need to help counter the harmful effects. So, the best formula is low toxin consumption and high antioxidant consumption.

The Low-Down on Low-Carb

Because "Low-Carb" is one of the buzzwords for diets currently, it is important to understand a few things about how carbohydrates work.

Counting grams of carbohydrate alone is misleading because carbohydrates include fiber. Fiber is not digested and does not break down in the body into glucose like the two other types of carbohydrate, starch and sugar. Both starch and sugar break down into sugar in the body. So, when we eat starchy foods like pasta and potatoes, the starch is converted to sugar in basically the same way as if we ate sugar right off of a spoon. The difference is that the starchy foods have some nutritional value and, oftentimes, some fiber as well. Fiber will slow the process of starch breaking down into sugar, which is good because our blood sugar doesn't spike. Whereas refined table sugar, has little to no nutritional value and contains no fiber. So starch is converted to sugar but has some redeeming value. Those are considered "good carbs". The "good carbs" are the fiber carbohydrates and starch carbohydrates because they serve important functions and are contained in food along with other beneficial nutrients. That's one of the reasons whole grains are a better choice than refined grains, like white flour or white rice. With white flour and white rice, the hulls and bran have been removed from the grains of wheat and brown rice, removing most of the nutrients and the fiber. Most of what you have left is starch. Refined sugar and starchy low-fiber, low-nutrient foods are "bad carbs".

Sometimes you will come across the terms, "net carbs" or "active carbs". That means the total carbohydrates minus the number of carbohydrates that are fiber. In a protein snack bar for instance; the nutritional analysis on the label will have a breakdown that includes Carbohydrate 25g., Fiber 3g., Sugars 12g. That means there are a total of 25 grams of carbohydrate; 3 of them are from fiber and 12 of them are from sugar. That means 10 grams are from some kind of starch. Your body will convert the starch to sugar. But it will not convert the fiber to sugar. You can deduct the grams of fiber from the total carbohydrates and that will give you your "net carbs" or "active carbs". In this case it would be 25 total grams minus 3 grams of fiber for a total of 22 "net carbs". Those are the carbs that your body is going to use as sugar. So, those are the carbs that you "count" when you are counting carbs.

Whole wheat flour has about 87 grams of carbohydrates per cup. White flour has about 92 grams of carbohydrate per cup. But that cup of whole wheat flour has 15 grams of fiber making the "net carbs" equal 72 grams. The white flour has only 3 grams of fiber leaving it with 89 grams of net carbs! Not to mention that most of the nutrients have been removed from the wheat in the process of making white flour. This means that the net carbs are much higher and the nutritional value is much lower than whole wheat flour.

Brown rice has about 45 grams of carbohydrates per cup, cooked. It has 3.5 grams of fiber for a total of 41.5 net carbs. White rice has about 45 grams of carbohydrate but only about .5 grams of fiber leaving a net carb count of 44.5. And, as with the white flour, most of the nutrients have been removed in white rice.

The Glycemic Index

The glycemic index is a way of measuring how fast the carbohydrates in different foods break down into sugar in the body. The foods that score high on the GI break down the fastest. The idea of using the GI is to consume carbohydrates on the lower end of the scale – those that have a lower carbohydrate content or convert to sugar more slowly to avoid spiking our blood sugar. Foods on the low end of the GI have a lower carbohydrate content or have a higher fiber and nutrient content, slowing the digestive process. This allows the body to convert carbohydrates to sugar more slowly as it is busy processing other things at the same time. In the absence of fiber and nutrients, sugar and starch are converted very quickly, flooding the blood with sugar. This causes the pancreas to produce high amounts of insulin in response to the sugar. The resulting spikes of insulin then cause the blood sugar levels to drop making us feel hungry, tired, and lacking concentration. This often drives us to eat more carbohydrate-laden foods to bring our blood sugar back up, producing more insulin again and the vicious cycle continues. We avoid this cycle if we avoid foods that are high on the Glycemic Index. Eating foods that contain low or moderate amounts of sugar and starch and high amounts of fiber and other nutrients allows the pancreas to operate at a reasonable level without being overworked. It allows the body to use appropriate amounts of sugar as energy without excess being stored as fat.

The glycemic index separates carb-containing foods into three general categories: (1) High Glycemic Index Foods (GI 70+), that cause a rapid rise in blood-glucose levels. (2) Intermediate Glycemic Index Foods (GI 55-69) causing a medium rise in blood-glucose. (3) Low Glycemic Index Foods (GI 54 or less), causing a slower rise in blood sugar.

"Natural" vs. "Organic"

Many people are confused about the difference between products labeled, "All Natural" and "Organic". When a product is labeled, "Natural", it simply means that there are no artificial ingredients added during the processing or packaging of the product. These include things like artificial sweeteners, artificial flavorings, artificial colors, preservatives, etc. It does not, however, tell you anything about what that product was exposed to prior to packaging or processing. In other words, hamburger can be labeled "all natural" as long as when it is processed or packaged, nothing artificial was added. It has nothing to do with what the animal that hamburger came from was fed or exposed to. The animal could have been given antibiotics, growth hormones, fed genetically modified feed and grain, or grazed on pasture that was treated with pesticides and herbicides. All of these will be present to some extent in that meat. Milk is another good example. Milk can be labeled "all natural" as long as no artificial coloring, flavorings, preservatives, etc., were added to the carton. But whatever medicines the cow that milk came from was treated with, and whatever chemicals the cow ingested, are likely to be present in the milk. Likewise, green beans, or any other vegetables, fruits, nuts, grains – basically any kind of food that occurs naturally – can be labeled "all natural" as long as no artificial ingredients were added to it after it was harvested. But while it was growing, it could have been saturated with chemical pesticides and herbicides and grown in soil with synthetic chemical fertilizers that can be absorbed by the plant. Some of the chemical spray can be washed off, but not necessarily all of it.

On the other hand, if something is labeled, "organic", it generally means that it was grown free of synthetic chemicals, irradiation, sewage sludge, or genetically modified organisms. Certification for organic meat forbids use of growth hormones, antibiotics, genetically modified feed, or animal by-products in the feed at any time throughout the animal's life. It also means that they did not graze on chemically treated pasture or eat other types of chemically treated feed.

There are many reasons to eat organic food. Organic food is generally more nutritious than non-organic food. The soil that organic foods are grown in is usually more nutrient-rich than soil that has been stripped of its nutrients and replaced with chemical fertilizers that are designed more for rapid growth and higher yields than nourishing the plants. A tomato grown in soil that has been leached of its nutrients relying on chemical fertilizers will not have as much nutritional value as a tomato grown in soil that is rich in the nutrients that make it grow strong enough to resist diseases and insects without chemical additives. Those nutrients are absorbed by the plant and, generally speaking, a side-by-side comparative analysis of any two foods, one grown organically and one grown with synthetic fertilizer, pesticides, and herbicides, will show the organic food to have more nutritional value. Also, many of the chemicals used in the growing and production of non-organic foods are linked to serious diseases including various types of cancer. Those chemicals also soak into the ground, eventually making their way into wells and aquifers that supply communities with drinking water.

If we are strictly concerned with our immediate personal health, fruits and vegetables that have peels or rinds that will be removed before eating are less of a threat as, for the most part, the harmful chemicals will not penetrate to the inside. Examples would be bananas, avocados, and oranges (provided you don't use the orange peel as flavoring in something else). But I remember standing on the Caribbean side of Costa Rica with a large banana plantation on my left and the crystal clear ocean on my right. The bananas, even though the bunches are wrapped in what looks like some kind of burlap for protection, are heavily sprayed with pesticides. The rain washes all of those pesticides into the ocean and from where I was standing, the once thriving coral reefs were bleached white and completely dead for as far as I could see and well beyond. It was at that moment I realized that it's about more than just about the banana.

While the impact of commercial agriculture on our health, and the planet, is significant and there is plenty to be said about it, it is a topic for another book. For the purposes of this book, we want to be aware of getting as much nutrition as possible from the food we eat. Also, because we know that many of the harmful chemicals used in commercial agriculture are linked to many physical diseases and disorders, it stands to reason that they may also be involved in some of the mood disorders, like depression and anxiety, that are rampant in today's Western world. Chemicals that we ingest, whether they are in the form of nutrients or toxins, affect our bodies, and brains in particular, in myriad ways that we do not yet fully understand. When we are trying to correct "chemical imbalances" in our brains, it makes sense to feed our brains with good chemicals (nutrients) and avoid feeding it toxic chemicals that may have adverse effects.

I eat organic food whenever it is reasonably possible. I live in a remote rural part of Montana where organic food is not as readily available as it is in many other places and what is available is expensive. I have gardens and a greenhouse where I grow a substantial amount of my own food and freeze much of it for the winter months. I have a dear friend who supplies me with organic, free-range eggs. I hunt big game, like elk and antelope (thank you, Jim Karas, for never failing to correct me by pointing out that they are, technically, "pronghorn" and not antelope) as well as game birds like pheasant and Hungarian Partridge because wild meat is leaner and free of the chemical additives that are common in commercially raised meat. When I buy meat, I try to buy organic meat. While I try to be conscientious about what I buy and eat, I would not consider myself to be a fanatic, with one exception: liver. I will not eat liver from any commercially raised animal unless it is organic. The liver is the body's primary filter. While some amount of antibiotics, hormones, pesticides, herbicides, preservatives and other harmful additives are stored in the fat and other body tissue, most of it makes its way to the liver. The liver attempts to detoxify the body by eliminating the body of the harmful substances. What the liver is not able to break down and eliminate remains stored in the liver. So, while liver is one of the most nutritious foods we can eat, the liver is the most toxic part of the animal if it has been raised commercially and not organically. I would rather have the nutrition without the toxins.

Raw vs. Cooked Food

There is considerable debate about the pros and cons of various popular diets including diets that lean heavily towards meat consumption, like the Paleo Diet, versus vegetarian plant-based diets. Some vegetarians will eat eggs and dairy products with the rationale that animals are not killed in the harvesting of eggs and milk. "Vegan" vegetarians do not eat any animal products, including eggs and milk or other dairy products. There is yet another subset of, usually vegetarian although a very small number of meat eaters fall into this category, people who believe that humans are designed to eat only raw food. All sides have plausible arguments, although we really don't know exactly what all of our ancestors ate. We know that some of them ate meat. We also know that gorillas, with whom we share common ancestors and 98% of our DNA, are primarily vegan with the exception of some insects.

One of the problems with eating nothing but raw fruits and vegetables, or even primarily raw fruits and vegetables, is that it would require over 50% of our waking life to chew what we would need to survive and be healthy. We basically would never be able to do anything else but gather, prepare, and eat food. People who eat primarily raw food are heavily dependent on electric blenders to "pre-chew" the food so it can be broken down and digested faster, as well as consumed faster. A "smoothie" made of 2 quarts of raw vegetables that would take an hour or more to chew will blend down to a couple of cups of pulpy liquid that you can drink in minutes. The blender probably does a better job of "chewing" than we do, which is also going to cut down on digestion time.

Cooked food is already partially broken down and is easier to digest than raw food. Cooking usually reduces the volume of food, making it easier to consume more food in much less time. Cooked food also makes many more nutrients available to us. However, the flip side of this is heat, especially high heat and prolonged heat, destroys some nutrients, especially the water-soluble nutrients like vitamin C and the B vitamins. Some minerals, like potassium, leach out of vegetables into cooking liquid. So vegetables that contain significant amounts of potassium, like carrots and potatoes among others, should not be boiled in water with the water thrown away. It is best to steam, bake, grill, broil, sauté, or roast vegetables to maintain more of the nutrients. If vegetables are cooked in water, the water should be consumed rather than discarded, as you would do with soup or stew for instance. You can also save cooking water as stock to use later.

While cooking food makes more nutrients available to our bodies, makes it possible to consume more food in less time, and makes digestion easier because the food is already partially broken down, raw vegetables have enzymes and microbes that aid in digestion. These enzymes and beneficial bacteria contribute to good gut health and are often destroyed when cooked. The digestive tract, which is comprised mostly of the stomach and intestines, are referred to as the "gut". Gut health is very important, not just for physical health but also for mental health. The gut is sometimes called the "second brain" because some of the neurotransmitters that are known to be involved in the prevention and treatment of depression and anxiety are produced in the gut as well as in the brain. Proper digestion is important to maximize the benefits of the food we eat. If we are not digesting our food properly, many of the nutrients we consume will pass through our digestive tract without being used. The nutrients we need to produce beneficial neurotransmitters in the brain depend on those nutrients being extracted and entering the blood stream, which begins with a fully functioning digestive tract.

Probiotics are beneficial bacteria contained in fermented foods like yogurt, aged cheese, and sauerkraut. Probiotics are important for gut health because they aid in digestion. Probiotics are the "flora" in our digestive system that helps create a healthy digestive environment. Other examples of fermented foods are pickled cucumbers, pickled beets, bread, tofu, kimchi, ketchup, miso, sour cream, cottage cheese, tempeh, raw apple cider vinegar, Tabasco sauce, and soy sauce. Some examples of fermented beverages include alcoholic beverages like wine and beer. Non-alcoholic fermented beverages include root beer, kefir, cultured buttermilk, and ginger ale.

To ensure good gut health, we should eat a wide variety of both cooked and raw food every day. Fermented foods and beverages should be included in our diets regularly and frequently. Gut stress can happen as a result of sickness, use of antibiotics, overeating or undereating. Gut stress places greater demand on beneficial bacteria to maintain a healthy balance and can deplete the gut's supply of probiotics quickly. During and after any episode of gut stress, it is especially important to restore a healthy population of beneficial bacteria by eating foods rich in probiotics.

Chapter 2

WHAT IS A NEUROTRANSMITTER?
The Brain/Body connection

A neurotransmitter is a chemical substance that is produced in the brain and carries messages from one nerve cell to another.

It seems obvious that the brain is part of the body. And, yet, I think many people think of the brain as a closed system that operates separate from the body. We've probably all heard depression referred to as "a chemical imbalance" in the brain. We have chemicals in our brains that are supposed to somehow be "in balance". It follows then that if we have a "chemical imbalance" we need to take chemicals to restore that balance. That is the idea behind taking anti-depressants – to correct the "chemical imbalance" in our brains.

What many people don't realize is that nutrients are involved in creating neurotransmitters. For instance, when we eat turkey, vitamin B6 along with the amino acid, tryptophan, work together to convert the tryptophan from the turkey into the neurotransmitter, serotonin, in the brain. Serotonin is known as the "feel good" neurotransmitter and is one of the major mood regulators. Since low levels of serotonin are linked to depression, most anti-depressants target serotonin with the goal of increasing available serotonin levels in the brain. *We can increase the serotonin levels in our brains with the proper foods.* In fact, anti-depressants do not increase serotonin in the brain. Anti-depressants work to make better use of what serotonin is already there. The only way to increase serotonin is by ingesting tryptophan, which we get in significant amounts from eating protein rich foods like turkey, chicken, shrimp, salmon, halibut, milk, and beans.

How they work

The brain is the master control center of the body. The brain is where all information is processed. It is where learning and reasoning occur, where memories are made and stored, and where our emotions originate. This all happens through a rather amazing system of nerve cells, or neurons, transmitting information to each other.

There are over a hundred billion neurons in the brain. The brain and spinal cord contain over 90% of the neurons in the entire body. In addition to "thinking" and controlling our emotions, the brain is also sending and receiving messages between neurons throughout the body including our organs, muscles, and glands telling the body what to do at all times. The way it relays all of this information is by neurotransmitters. They are the chemical messengers that determine which brain cells are activated ("firing") or deactivated ("inhibited"). For instance, epinephrine is an excitatory neurotransmitter that causes nerve cells to "fire" resulting in a "fight or flight" response when in danger. Another name for it is "adrenaline" – the only difference being adrenaline is produced in the adrenal glands and is therefore considered a hormone, where epinephrine is produced in the brain. Their release in the body causes the same "fight or flight" response. The "Epi-pen" that some people carry to inject themselves in case of an allergic reaction is named for the epinephrine that it contains. Endorphins, on the other hand, are a group of neurotransmitters that act as inhibitors, particularly on nerve cells that have pain receptors. Endorphins deactivate the nerves that would tell us we are experiencing pain. Endorphins allow us to feel less pain than we would if the endorphins were not present. Each neurotransmitter has its own specific function. Some of them work by sending a signal that excites, or fires, a nerve and some of them work by sending a signal to inhibit, or *not* fire, a nerve.

A **neuron**, or **nerve**, is made up of a **cell body**, **dendrites, axon**, and **axon terminal**, or **axon "knob"**. Dendrites resemble tree branches that protrude from the cell body. Dendrites have receptor sites for neurotransmitters. The axon is like a cable coming off of the cell body. The axon can be anywhere from about 1 millimeter to about 3 feet in length. Some axons are covered with a sheath of "white matter" called the "myelin sheath". **Myelin** serves two primary purposes: it insulates and protects the nerves from touching other nerves, which can cause misfiring, and it increases the travel speed of the impulse along the axon. The end of the axon is called the axon terminal, or knob. A particular neurotransmitter is produced in the cell body, travels down the axon by an electrical impulse, and comes out at the axon knob. From there, it jumps across a gap called the *synaptic cleft*, to neighboring dendrites from other nearby cells. The neurotransmitter can only be absorbed, or received, by dendrites that have receptor sites that are compatible with that particular neurotransmitter. Not all neurotransmitters carry messages to all nerves. It is often described as a lock and key type situation with the neurotransmitter being the key and it can only fit into its matching lock on certain dendrites. The neurotransmitter is released from the terminal knob and is received by the nerve cell with compatible dendrites causing that nerve to fire, creating an electrical impulse that sends the neurotransmitter down its axon, out the terminal knob into the synaptic cleft to be received by neighboring compatible dendrites, and so on. The point at which the neurotransmitter is released from the terminal knob, crosses the synaptic cleft, and is received by the dendrite receptor site is called the *synapse*. Excess neurotransmitter that is not received by a neuron is either reabsorbed by the axon knob to be reused again or is disposed of by the body as waste.

Neurons are firing by the thousands each second. Because every time we have a thought we simultaneously experience an emotion, a physical sensation, recall a memory, or need to respond with a movement or the formation and delivery of words, the neurotransmitters involved in all of those activities are flying across synapses and along neuronal pathways in every direction. Neurons are constantly receiving and responding to information from within the body as well as receiving information from and responding to information from our environment. Our eyes perceive an object flying towards us and send the visual information to the brain where the brain interprets the object to be a baseball. The brain then sends the correct signals, via neurotransmitters, along the nerves of the arm and hand causing it to reach out and grab the ball before it hits us in the head. Neurotransmitters sent the messages along the correct synaptic pathways almost as fast as thought itself.

There are hundreds of different neurotransmitters. There are only a relative few that we know much about. We are going to be focusing primarily on the ones we know are linked to depression and anxiety.

- **Serotonin**

  Serotonin is known as "the mood molecule" or the "feel good" chemical and is an example of a neurotransmitter with a wide range of effects. It is implicated in essentially everything that involves mood. Healthy levels of serotonin are associated with feelings of happiness, security, confidence, contentment, joy, peacefulness, optimism, and overall well-being. Low levels of serotonin are associated with depression, anxiety, anger, insomnia, PMS, and addiction.

- **Norepinephrine**

  Norepinephrine affects neurons involved in increased heart rate and the slowing of intestinal activity during stress, and neurons involved in learning, memory, dreaming, waking from sleep, and emotion. Low levels of norepinephrine are associated with both depression and anxiety.

- **Dopamine**

  Dopamine is involved in voluntary movement, learning, memory, and emotions. Low levels of dopamine are associated with depression, memory problems, weight gain, Parkinson's Disease, ADHD, alcoholism, and drug addiction. High levels of dopamine are associated with schizophrenia.

- **Gamma-aminobutyric acid (GABA)**

GABA is the major inhibitory neurotransmitter in the brain and is involved with stress relief. One of GABA's functions is to prevent neurons from firing in response to stress, reducing the anxiety response. Low levels of GABA are associated with depression and anxiety.

Prescription medications such as Depakote (an anticonvulsant used to treat bipolar disorder) and benzodiazepines (used to treat anxiety) such as Xanax and Valium, affect GABA levels in the brain.

Traditional Antidepressants

Antidepressants act on certain neurotransmitters to increase their availability. There are five categories of common antidepressants: SSRI's, SNRI's, Tricyclics, MAOI's, and atypical antidepressants. All common prescription antidepressant medications are intended to work primarily on serotonin, norepinephrine, and dopamine, either singularly or in combination. Antidepressants also affect other neurotransmitters, which is what causes some of their side-effects.

Prescription medications such as Citalopram (Celexa), Escitalopram (Lexapro), Fluoxetine (Prozac, Sarafem), Paroxetine (Paxil), and Sertraline (Zoloft) are **selective serotonin reuptake inhibitors (SSRI's)**. SSRI's work by blocking the reabsorption (reuptake) of *serotonin* at the axon terminal. Remember what happens after a neurotransmitter is released from the terminal knob? It crosses the synaptic cleft and is received by the dendrites of nearby neurons that have receptor sites for that neurotransmitter. The excess neurotransmitter is then reabsorbed by the terminal knob or excreted by the body as waste. SSRI's prevent the terminal knob from reabsorbing it. The idea is to leave the neurotransmitter, in this case serotonin, available for use by nearby neurons. SSRI's don't increase the production of serotonin but they make the serotonin that is present more available.

Serotonin and norepinephrine reuptake inhibitors (SNRI's) block the reuptake of both *serotonin* and *norepinephrine* making both of those neurotransmitters more available. SNRI's include: Duloxetine (Cymbalta), Venlafaxine (Effexor), and Desvenlafaxine (Pristiq). SNRI's are also used to treat anxiety.

Tricyclic and tetracyclic medications are another class of antidepressants that work to block the reuptake of *serotonin* and *norepinephrine*. They are an older class of antidepressants and are not prescribed as frequently as the newer antidepressants like SSRI's and SNRI's due to more side effects. They include: Amitriptyline, Amoxapine, Desipramine (Norpramin), Doxepin, Imipramine (Tofranil, Tofranil-PM), Maprotiline, Nortriptyline (Pamelor), Protriptyline (Vivactil), and Trimipramine (Surmontil).

Monoamine oxidase inhibitors (MAOI's) are the original class of antidepressants and have generally been replaced by newer antidepressants with fewer side effects. Monoamine oxidase is an enzyme that is involved in destroying *serotonin*, *dopamine*, and *norepinephrine* in the brain. MAOI's inhibit that enzyme from its destructive behavior, making those neurotransmitters more available. MAOI's include: Isocarboxazid (Marplan), Phenelzine (Nardil), Selegiline (Emsam, Eldepryl, Zelapar), and Tranylcypromine (Parnate).

Atypical antidepressants are called atypical because they don't fit into any of the other categories. Each one is unique and works differently from each other. Atypical antidepressants include: Bupropion (Wellbutrin, Wellbutrin SR, Wellbutrin XL) – a *norepinephrine* and *dopamine* reuptake inhibitor, Mirtazapine (Remeron, Remeron SolTab) – a very unique antidepressant that does not involve enzyme inhibition or blockade of neurotransmitter reuptake; Mirtazapine increases the release of both *norepinephrine* and *serotonin*, Nefazodone – blocks reuptake of *serotonin* and *norepinephrine* though it is chemically unrelated to SNRI's, and Trazodone (Oleptro) – it is unclear exactly how trazodone works; it appears to block the reuptake of both *serotonin* and *norepinephrine* and is thought to possibly allow the release of a greater amount of *norepinephrine*. Trazodone is used to treat anxiety and insomnia as it has a strong sedative affect.

Antidepressants target mainly the neurotransmitters serotonin, norepinephrine, and dopamine in treating depression and anxiety. We need adequate levels of these neurotransmitters to feel good. GABA is a neurotransmitter that is more involved with controlling anxiety but low GABA levels can also contribute to depression. GABA levels are usually targeted by other types of drugs including Valium, Xanax, and Depakote.

Unlike serotonin, norepinephrine, and dopamine, which must be converted from nutrients, GABA can be taken directly as a supplement. There is currently no scientific evidence to support the effectiveness of GABA supplements. Most researchers believe that GABA cannot cross the blood/brain barrier so cannot get into the brain from the bloodstream. However, there is much anecdotal evidence to support its effectiveness. Many clinicians prescribe GABA supplements for their anxious patients and swear by its benefits.

Chapter 3

The Key Players

Each year in America an estimated 21 million people are diagnosed with depression, the highest number of any country in the world except France. Nearly twice as many, or 40 million, will be diagnosed with an anxiety disorder. Frequently, these disorders co-occur so oftentimes, if a person has one, they also have the other. About 150 million people suffer from depression worldwide and this number is increasing steadily (Sánchez-Villegas & Verberne, 2011). We can only speculate about how much depression and anxiety goes undiagnosed. The World Health Organization (WHO) estimates that by the year 2020 depression will be the second leading cause of morbidity worldwide. Nutritional deficiencies are indicated in several mental disorders, including depression and anxiety. Diets high in refined sugar that predict heart disease and diabetes are also linked to the outcome of schizophrenia and depression. The most common nutritional deficiencies seen in mental disorder patients are of omega-3 fatty acids, B vitamins, minerals, and amino acids that are precursors to neurotransmitters. Essential vitamins, minerals, and omega-3 fatty acids are often deficient in the general population in America and other developed countries; and are exceptionally deficient in patients suffering from mental disorders. A University of Calgary study compared nutrient intakes of 97 adults with bipolar or major depressive disorder against the general population. While the general population was deficient to some degree in all of the observed nutrients, a larger proportion of the depressed patients were significantly more deficient in the B vitamins thiamin, riboflavin, folate, B6, and B12 as well as phosphorous, and zinc (Davison & Kaplan, 2012).

Studies have shown that daily supplements of vital nutrients often effectively reduce patients' symptoms. Supplements that contain amino acids also reduce symptoms, because they are converted to neurotransmitters that alleviate depression and other mental disorders. Based on emerging scientific evidence, nutritional treatment may be appropriate for controlling major depression, bipolar disorder, schizophrenia, anxiety disorders, eating disorders, attention deficit disorder/attention deficit hyperactivity disorder (ADD/ADHD), addiction, and autism (Lakhan &Vierra, 2008). Researchers Davison and Kaplan (2012) at the British Columbia Centre for Excellence in Women's Health in Canada analyzed the nutritional intakes of 97 adults with mood disorders. Significant correlations were found between Global Assessment of Functioning (GAF) scores and calorie intake, carbohydrates, fiber, total fat, linoleic acid, riboflavin, niacin, folate, vitamin B6, vitamin B12, pantothenic acid, calcium, phosphorus, potassium, and iron. Their results revealed an association between higher levels of nutrient intakes and better mental health.

The benefits of good nutrition go far beyond providing the body with the nutrients it needs to grow, maintain healthy bones and fight off disease and germs. Good nutrition also contributes to proper organ function. Proper nutrition is needed for the heart and liver, as well as many other organs, even the eyes, to function optimally. We need to remember that the brain is an organ also and what we feed it will largely determine how it functions. When the brain functions as it is intended, we feel good; we have energy, clarity of thought, our memories are sharp and moods are stable. We interact with, and respond to, our environments appropriately.

Junk Food And Mental Illness

America's love of junk food and fast food and the high incidence of mental illness compared to other countries may be more than coincidence. America's 26% of the population currently diagnosed with mental illness is in stark contrast to the worldwide prevalence of 4.3% (Demyttenaere K. et al., 2004). This could, in part, be attributed to a difference in diagnostic criteria but could also be due to a lack of nutrients in processed food compared to diets richer in less processed foods in other parts of the world. People who follow a Mediterranean diet, which emphasizes fresh fruits, vegetables, whole grains, and fish, and limits red meat and dairy products have lower rates of Parkinson's Disease and Alzheimer's (Zeratsky, 2011). Researchers in Britain followed 3,000 middle-aged office workers over a period of 5 years monitoring their diets and reported levels of depression. Those who ate a diet high in junk food including processed meat, chocolate, sweet desserts, fried food, refined cereals, and high-fat dairy products were more likely to report depression. Those who ate a diet rich in fruits, vegetables, and fish were less likely to report being depressed (Akbaraly et al., 2009). In a larger European study of over 12,000 volunteers whose diets and lifestyles were followed for 6 years, researchers found that participants whose diets were high in trans-fats (present in commercially baked goods and fast-food) were 48% more likely to develop depression than those who did not consume trans-fats. Additionally, participants who consumed most of their fats in the form of fish and olive oil had a lower risk of suffering depression (Sánchez-Villegas & Toledo, 2011). Where there are trans-fats there is often sugar and a study conducted in 6 countries established a highly significant correlation

75

between sugar consumption and the prevalence of depression (Westover & Marangell, 2002.) While we are still uncertain what the relationship is, there is reason to suspect that a high intake of sugar may interfere with the balance, production or reception of neurotransmitters.

Researchers at the University of Melbourne examined over 1000 randomly selected women, ages 20-93, assessing for symptoms of depression and anxiety and comparing "traditional" diets to "western" diets. They found that the women who ate a "traditional" diet of vegetables, fruit, meat, fish, and whole grains had less depression and anxiety than those who ate a "western" diet of processed or fried foods, refined grains, sugary products, and beer (Jacka et al., 2010). A 2009 study (Sánchez-Villegas, et al.), also showed that a diet rich in vegetables, fruits, fish, and whole grains and low in red meat and dairy was associated with a lower risk of depression.

Another large study of 2579 college students over 7 cities in China found that the intake level of fresh fruit, ready-to-eat food and fast food was significantly associated with depression. Those who consumed more junk food were much more likely to be depressed than those who ate more fresh fruit (Liu & Xie, 2007). A Duke University study of 278 elderly adults (144 with depression, 134 without depression) found that fruit and vegetable intakes were lower in individuals with late-life depression than in comparison participants (Payne et al., 2012).

The Hordaland Health study looked at the association between diet quality and depression and anxiety in 5731 Norwegian adults. A traditional Norwegian diet composed of fish, meat, vegetables, fruit, and whole grains was associated with reduced depression and anxiety in women and men and a western-type diet with a higher intake of processed and unhealthy foods was associated with increased depression and anxiety in both women and men (Jacka et al., 2011).

Junk food may be a more serious problem for children, especially adolescents, due to its ready availability and cultural acceptance. Junk food as the "norm" for kids in the western world is expanding into other parts of the world. The dietary patterns of junior high school students in China compared diets high in "snack food", "animal food", and "traditional diets" to the incidence of depression and anxiety. Diets high in snacks and animal food had a higher incidence of depression and anxiety than traditional diets (Weng et al., 2012). The Australian Healthy Neighbourhoods Study examined 7114 adolescents for healthy and unhealthy diets and incidence of depression. "Our results demonstrate an association between diet quality and adolescent depression that exists over and above the influence of socioeconomic, family, and other potentially confounding factors." (Jacka et al., 2010).

Researchers at the University of South Carolina did a cross-sectional analysis of diet quality in individuals with a history of attempted suicide. Dietary information was collected from 6803 adults, aged 17 to 39 years. What they found was that men who attempted suicide had a low consumption of vegetables. Women attempters had insufficient fruit consumption. In both men and women, attempters ate less meat than non-attempters. Female attempters ate significantly less fish and seafood than non-attempters. "The data suggest that fruits, vegetables and meat were significantly under-consumed in adults who had ever attempted suicide. In clinical practice, psychiatrists should pay more attention to what patients eat." (Li, Zhang, McKeown, 2009).

A Spanish study with nearly 9000 participants showed a 40 % increase in depression among the group eating the highest amounts of junk food and commercial baked goods (Sanchez-Villegas et. al, 2012).

Processed food and its effects on mental health are reaching every corner of the globe and the results are the same. A recent study at the Tehran University of Medical Sciences in Iran looked at the relationship between eating processed food and anxiety in 1782 young adults, aged 18-35. There was a significantly higher rate of anxiety in those who ate more processed foods over those who ate a traditional, whole foods diet (Bakhtiyari et al., 2013).

A few years ago I had the opportunity for a brief visit in Amsterdam. My friend, Erin, who was born in the Netherlands, toured me around the city and explained some interesting cultural differences between the U.S. and the Netherlands. She said one of the most striking differences is in how we eat. She has occasion to visit America often on business and said it is much more difficult to make healthy food choices in the U.S., especially when dining out. She most often chooses salads but said the portions are much larger in the U.S. than in the Netherlands. I was fascinated to learn that there are no school lunch programs. Parents are expected to pack healthy lunches for their children to take to school. She said a typical child's lunch is a cucumber and cheese sandwich. She said they usually take an apple for a snack. Children are not allowed to bring sugary snacks to school and if they do, the snacks are confiscated by the teacher. They are only allowed to have healthy snacks. Also, people buy their bread and other baked goods fresh from the bakery. The bakeries there use almost exclusively whole grains so white bread is almost non-existent. In addition, they buy most of their food fresh from the local markets. Unlike Americans, they eat very little processed food, refined food, or otherwise, junk food. Is it any wonder, then, that in a recent report from UNICEF (2013) ranking children's well-being in 29 economically advanced countries, the U.S. ranked 25 out of 29 overall and 25 out of 29 specifically in the category of "Health and Safety" while the Netherlands ranked number 1?

The "Western Diet" may have originated here but its tentacles of death, disease, obesity and mental illness are fast spreading throughout the world. The seduction of processed food and fast-food is sweeping across the planet from industrialized nations to previously secluded tropical paradises. As populations forego the traditional, wholesome diets that have kept their rates of physical and mental illness far below those of the western world, we can expect to see that change. As rates of diseases and disorders grow, more and more money will be pumped into pharmaceuticals in the hopes of curing what nutritional imbalance created in the first place. The kind of nutritional imbalance that predictably occurs when we stop eating whole, natural, *real* food and substitute it with packaged, artificial food that is nutritionally deficient and full of sugar, trans-fat, artificial colors and flavors, preservatives and other substances that are toxic to our bodies. There is already a cure for all of that. Let's leave the junk food in the junkyard where it belongs and get back to eating the way we were meant to.

Omega-3 Fatty Acids

In one of the earliest experimental demonstrations of the effect of dietary substances on the structure and function of the brain, researchers compared infants who were fed milk formulas with and without the addition of omega-3 fatty acids. The results indicated that the addition of omega-3 fatty acids improved the infants' visual, cerebral, and intellectual abilities (Agnoli et al., 1976). It should be stated that breast milk is high in omega-3's and is usually the healthiest choice for feeding babies. Studies provide a strong indication of the positive effects of omega-3 fatty acids on the developing brain. It stands to reason that a deficiency in omega-3's may contribute to childhood neurodevelopmental disorders. A double-blind pilot study of 13 children with autism showed significant improvement in hyperactivity and stereotypy (repetitive movements) in the children given omega-3's as compared to the children given placebos (Amminger et al., 2007). A larger Egyptian study comparing the effects of fish oil on 30 autistic children to 30 non-autistic children as a control group showed clinical improvement in 66% of the autistic children (Meguid et al., 2008).

Autism is not the only childhood disorder that has shown significant improvement with omega-3's. A meta-analysis by Bloch and Qawasmi (2011) of ten placebo controlled trials involving 699 children with Attention Deficit Hyperactivity Disorder (ADHD) showed improvement in symptoms with treatment of omega-3's.

Accumulating evidence from demographic studies also indicates a link between high fish consumption and low incidence of mental disorders; this lower incidence rate being the direct result of omega-3 fatty acid intake (Reis & Hibbeln, 2006). Experimental studies have revealed that diets low in omega-3 fatty acids lead to considerable disturbance in neural function, which in most circumstances can be restored by the inclusion of omega-3 in the diet. It is clear from the literature that DHA is involved in a variety of processes in neural cells and that its role is far more complex than simply influencing cell membrane properties (Sinclair et al, 2007). In a controlled study of 68 medical students given fish oil or placebo, anxiety was significantly reduced in the fish oil group (Kiecolt-Glaser et. al., 2011).

Deficits in omega-3 fatty acids have been identified as a contributing factor to mood disorders and offer a potential positive treatment approach (Parker & Gibson, 2006). Case-control studies have shown that patients suffering with depression have significantly lower levels of omega-3 and clinical trials have indicated the effectiveness of omega-3 as adjunctive treatment for major depression and bipolar depression (Ross & Seguin, 2007). A review of clinical trials through September 1, 2010 of the effects of omega-3 fatty acids on bipolar disorder pooled 5 data sets involving 291 participants. The outcome of bipolar depression revealed a significant beneficial effect from omega-3's (Sarris et al., 2011). An Australian study supplemented omega-3 fatty acids in 18 children and adolescents diagnosed with bipolar disorder. Clinician ratings of mania and depression were significantly lower and global functioning significantly higher after supplementation. Parent ratings of symptomatic behaviors were also significantly lower following supplementation (Clayton et al., 2009). Three studies at the University of the Negev in Israel found highly significant improvement in both major depression and bipolar depression in children and adults treated with omega-3 fatty acids (Osher & Belmaker, 2009).

In another double-blind study comparing the effects of treatment with omega-3 fatty acid with fluoxetine (Prozac) and the effects of treatment with both, 60 participants with major depression were randomly assigned to the three groups. One group was given 1000 mg of the omega-3 eicosapentaenoic acid (EPA), one group was given 20 mg of fluoxetine, and one group was given both. 48 patients completed the 8-week trial. Results showed a 50% improvement in the group given the fluoxetine, a 56% improvement in the group given the omega-3, and 81% improvement in the group given both. So, this study suggests that treatment with omega-3 is slightly better than treatment with Prozac for depression with the greatest benefit derived from treatment with both together (Jazayeri et al., 2008).

Numerous studies, such as randomized controlled trials, cohort studies, and ecological studies, have found a positive association between low omega-3 levels and a higher incidence of maternal depression. In addition, nutrient inadequacies in pregnant women who consume a typical western diet might be much more common than researchers and clinicians realize (Leung & Kaplan, 2009).

The best way to meet our need for omega-3's, is by eating ocean fish several times a week along with flaxseed oil used daily (flaxseed oil should not be used in cooking but is excellent drizzled on cooked vegetables and in salad dressings). In order to get the most benefit from omega-3's, we must also limit omega-6's which is best accomplished by avoiding junk foods like chips and commercial baked goods, processed foods, and fried foods. Use the Nutrition Content Table to incorporate a wide variety of foods into your diet that have a positive omega-6 to omega-3 ratio.

Vitamins And Mental Health

B Vitamins

A deficiency in B vitamins can cause the psychiatric disorders of dementia and psychosis with symptoms including depression, a lack of self-control, paranoia, immodesty and hallucinations, according to Roger Simon, M.D., et al, in a 2009 article published in "Clinical Neurology." A vitamin B12 deficiency can cause dementia and psychosis, as explained by Dr. Simon. The symptoms of dementia include various memory problems, not being able to concentrate and focus, and a difficulty with mathematical calculations. People with this vitamin deficiency have manic mood swings, where they are depressed or overconfident. They are quick to anger, impulsive, paranoid, and immodest in their dress or behavior.

They may also hear voices and hallucinate. Vitamin B12 and folic acid (vitamin B9) are involved in the production of the neurotransmitters, dopamine and noradrenaline. People who are depressed often don't have enough of these chemicals. Increasing the levels of vitamin B12 and folic acid may help alleviate symptoms of depression and increase the response to medicines that treat depression.

Niacin is vitamin B3, and a deficiency in this vitamin can also lead to psychiatric disorders, explains Larry Johnson, M.D., Ph.D., attending physician at the Central Arkansas Veterans Healthcare System. People may become psychotic, have problems with their memory and create stories to fill in their gaps of memory loss, a phenomenon referred to as confabulation. They can become very confused and disoriented. Some may show signs of paranoia and depression, or become impulsive, extremely happy and full of self-importance (Coleman, 2010). Deficiencies in niacin can also cause headaches, irritability, and inability to sleep.

A deficiency in vitamin B6 has been considered rare but in a study at Tufts University, published in the May 2008 issue of the *American Journal of Clinical Nutrition,* Morris et al., discovered that it is much more common than previously thought. Of the 7822 males and females, age one year and older, in the study, four groups were found to have the biggest deficiencies; women of reproductive age, especially current and former users of oral contraceptives, male smokers, non-Hispanic African American men, and both men and women over age 65. A deficiency in vitamin B6 can be induced by certain drugs, including antidepressants. A vitamin B6 deficiency is characterized by mental changes such as fatigue, nervousness, irritability, depression, insomnia, dizziness, confusion, and nerve changes. These mental changes are related to the body's decreased ability to manufacture neurotransmitters. Vitamin B6 is needed by the body to produce most of the brain's neurotransmitters including serotonin, dopamine, norepinephrine, and GABA.

Although it is actually more closely related to carbohydrate (glucose), inositol is informally referred to as vitamin B8. It differs from the other B-vitamins because the body can produce its own inositol. However, similar to some other nutrients and amino acids, things like poor diet and stress can interfere with our ability to produce adequate amounts of inositol. Inositol has been successfully used to treat depression (Levine, et al., 1995) and has been shown to be as effective as fluvoxamine (Prozac) for the treatment of panic disorder with none of the side effects (Palatnik, et al., 2001). It is present in a variety of foods but is more bioavailable in some foods than others. While it is present in beans and seeds, it is more available, or breaks down better, in the body in foods such as egg yolks, dairy products, meat, vegetables such as cauliflower, and fruits, especially cantaloupe and oranges. Like some of the other "non-essential" nutrients, we can become depleted and fail to produce optimum amounts of what we need to keep us healthy. Eating a variety of nutrient dense foods helps insure that we give our bodies what they need to manufacture these very essential, "non-essential" nutrients.

Because B vitamins are water soluble, they leech out of food into cooking water. They are also damaged by high, as well as prolonged, heat and freezing. Eating raw foods and foods that are minimally cooked will provide the most benefit.

Vitamin C

A deficiency in vitamin C, also called ascorbic acid, can cause neurological damage and the addition of vitamin C to the diet can improve or reverse symptoms of anxiety, depression and bipolar disorder.

A recent study at the Vanderbilt University Medical Center, Department of Neuroscience in Nashville, Tennessee and published in the *Journal of Neurochemistry* (Ward, et al., 2013) deprived mice of vitamin C. The deprivation caused depressive and submissive behaviors as well as an increased preference for sugar. More importantly, there were decreases in dopamine and serotonin in the brain.

Another interesting study with mice was recently conducted in Brazil and published in the *Journal of Psychiatric Research* (Moretti et al., 2012). The mice were subjected to "chronic unpredictable stress" (CUS) for 14 days. This CUS produced depressive behaviors and neurochemical alterations. From the 8th to the 14th day, half of the mice were treated with fluoxetine (Prozac) and half were treated with vitamin C. The results were as powerful with the vitamin C as with the fluoxetine. In other words, the vitamin C reversed the detrimental effects and helped the mice cope with the ongoing stress as well as the Prozac did. The researchers concluded, "These findings indicate a rapid and robust effect of ascorbic acid in reversing behavioral and biochemical alterations induced by CUS in mice, suggesting that this vitamin may be an alternative approach for the management of depressive symptoms."

Researchers at the Global Neuroscience Initiative Foundation in Los Angeles, California (Amr et al., 2013), studied the effects of fluoxetine (Prozac) alone and in combination with vitamin C in depressed children. Their results showed a significantly more positive effect in the group treated with both fluoxetine and vitamin C as compared to the group given fluoxetine and a placebo. The results suggest that vitamin C may be an effective adjunctive treatment in depressed children treated with Prozac.

Eighty psychiatric patients at a private hospital in India, 40 suffering from depression and 40 suffering from anxiety, were found to have much lower levels of vitamins A, C, and E than a healthy population. Half of each group was given 600 mg/day of vitamin A, 1000 mg/day of vitamin C, and 800 mg/day of vitamin E in addition to their regular anti-depressant or antianxiety medication. After 6 weeks of treatment with vitamins A, C, and E, a significant reduction in both depression and anxiety was observed in those treated with the vitamins than in those treated with medication alone. It's hard to say in a study that combines nutrients whether the improvement was due to one or more of the vitamins but in another study done with rats in New Zealand, groups of stressed rats were treated with vitamin C and vitamin E separately and one group was treated with both vitamins C and E together. There were no significant differences between the groups. Vitamins C and E were effective in reducing anxiety whether given separately or together (Hughes et. al., 2010).

In a double-blind study by Naylor and Smith (1981), both manic and depressed patients were significantly better following a single 3000 mg dose of vitamin C than following a placebo. Likewise, a German study found an increase in sexual intercourse and decrease in depression in 42 young adults given 3000 mg of vitamin C per day for 14 days (Brody, 2002).

Vitamin D

While there has been some evidence linking Vitamin D deficiency to anxiety in mice (Kalueff et al., 2004, Kalueff et al., 2006) and in fibromyalgia patients (Armstrong et al., 2007), until recently very little evidence has linked vitamin D to depression, although it has long been suspected.

A few recent studies probably have merit but as with all correlational studies, even though we can see there is a relationship, we can't be completely sure what the relationship is. One such study was done in the Indian Antarctic. Blood levels of vitamin D were checked in 20 healthy males on a year long arctic expedition that lasted from November 2010 to December 2011. Since the sun's rays would not provide adequate vitamin D, researchers were interested to see if the incidence of depression increased among the subjects. Indeed they did find a significant increase in depressive symptoms after 6 months and at the end of 1 year as well as decreased levels of vitamin D (Premkumar et al., 2013). Since the sun's rays would not provide vitamin D and their dietary intake was not adequate, it would stand to reason that their vitamin D levels would drop. The fact that depressive symptoms also increased could be due to low levels of vitamin D but could also be due to being relatively isolated in Antarctica for a year! I'm only including this study because, along with others showing similar associations, it *may* be evidence of a link between vitamin D and depression and, specifically, as the authors conclude, between vitamin D and seasonal affective disorder.

Another is a small pilot study of children hospitalized with cystic fibrosis that found low levels of vitamin D corresponding with significantly more depressive symptoms increasing with length of stay (Smith, et al., 2013). Again, this *could* be evidence of a connection between vitamin D and depression or it could just be that children who are hospitalized with cystic fibrosis are depressed for that reason alone and the longer they are hospitalized, the more depressed they become.

A more convincing association was made by researchers in London (Maddock et al., 2013), who screened 7400 middle-aged individuals for vitamin D levels and depressive symptoms. They found a significant link between low levels of vitamin D and depression.

One of the most supportive connections is a recent study in the Netherlands (Milaneschi et al., 2013) involving over 2000 adults aged 18-65, which found a strong link between vitamin

D and depression. In fact, what they found was a consistent relationship between the amount of vitamin D in the blood and severity of depressive symptoms. So, a mild deficiency was consistent with mild depression and severe deficiency was consistent with severe depression. Similarly, researchers from the University of Antwerp in Belgium looked at depression and vitamin D levels in 589 elderly nursing home residents. "Almost our entire study population appeared to be vitamin D deficient. Comparison of the most severely and least deficient subgroups showed a consistent tendency towards more depressive symptoms and more use of antidepressants in the group with the lowest vitamin D level" (Verhoeven, et al., 2012).

An encouraging experiment at the Tehran University of Medical Sciences in Iran compared the therapeutic effects of treating depression with fluoxetine (Prozac) alone or with a combination of fluoxetine and vitamin D. In the double-blind, randomized, placebo controlled study, involving 42 patients over a period of 8 weeks, they found that treatment with fluoxetine combined with vitamin D was superior to treatment with fluoxetine alone (Khoraminya, et al., 2013). So, this is good evidence that vitamin D can enhance traditional pharmaceutical treatment of depression.

Another recent study in Iran using Vitamin D alone as a treatment for depression involved 120 depressed patients, who were also shown to be deficient in vitamin D. The patients were randomly divided into 3 groups of 40 each. One group was given no treatment, one group was given a single injection of 150,000 IU of vitamin D and one group was given a single injection of 300,000 IU of vitamin D. When tested 3 months later, researchers found significant improvement in both treatment groups with the most significant improvement occurring in the group receiving the higher dose (Mozaffari-Khosravi et al., 2013). While 300,000 IU is an unusually high experimental dose, a study of over 36,000 postmenopausal U.S. women found that supplementing with 400 IU per day of vitamin D had no effect on depression (Bertone-Johnson, 2012). What we don't know about these women is how much vitamin D they were consuming from food and/or from sun. If they were, as many Americans are, deficient in vitamin D, 400 IU per day may not have been enough to correct the deficiency.

Anglin et al., (2013) at the Department of Psychiatry and Behavioural Neurosciences at St Joseph's Hospital in Ontario, Canada performed a systematic assessment of the available literature and concluded that, "Our analyses are consistent with the hypothesis that low vitamin D concentration is associated with depression, and highlight the need for randomised controlled trials of vitamin D for the prevention and treatment of depression to determine whether this association is causal."

Enough information is currently available to make us reasonably confident that there is a connection between vitamin D and depression. What we don't know for sure is if low levels of vitamin D *cause* depression. We know that depressed people tend to have low levels of vitamin D and non-depressed people tend to have higher levels of vitamin D. And there is good evidence from the recent Tehran University of Medical Sciences study that vitamin D has a positive effect when used to treat depression, at least in conjunction with a traditional anti-depressant. What this tells me is that vitamin D is something that should be considered when we are talking about preventing and treating depression. I am confident that many more studies will be forthcoming soon that will settle the question of causality and demonstrate how vitamin D may be used to treat depression alone, or in conjunction with other nutrients. Meanwhile, it makes sense, given the evidence regarding the association between vitamin D and depression, to maintain adequate levels of vitamin D.

This comes with some good news and some bad news. The bad news is that it is very difficult to get enough vitamin D from food alone. This is why vitamin D is added to a number of foods including milk, soymilk and fortified cereals. About the only things vitamin D occurs in naturally are fatty fish like salmon, sardines, and tuna, eggs, and mushrooms. Some mushrooms are higher in vitamin D than others. It depends on how they were grown and if they were exposed to sunlight. Mushrooms convert sunshine or UVB rays to vitamin D like we do. Which brings me to the good news; our main source of vitamin D is the sun! We convert ultraviolet B (UVB) rays from the sun to vitamin D through our skin. The bad news here is that if you live north of 42 degrees latitude, as I do in Montana, the angle and distance of the sun make it impossible to get enough UVB rays from November to March. The 42nd parallel is the southern border of both Oregon and Idaho and runs through the states of Wyoming, Nebraska, Iowa, Illinois, Michigan, Pennsylvania, New York, Connecticut, Rhode Island, and Massachusetts.

South of the 42nd parallel year-round and north of the 42nd parallel from March through October, the amount of vitamin D you will get from the sun will depend on several things. More UVB rays are available in the middle of the day than they are in the morning or evening. Lighter skinned people will absorb more UVB rays for conversion to vitamin D than dark skinned people in the same amount of exposure time. How much skin you have exposed will affect how much vitamin D you get from the sun. Clouds and air pollution can also block UVB rays.

Basically, a light skinned person with arms, legs, and face exposed to the sun (without sunscreen) in the middle of the day, will get about 10,000 units of vitamin D in about 10 minutes. That is very good news because you probably don't need anywhere near that much vitamin D in one day. Darker skinned people need to be in the sun longer to absorb the same amount as light skinned people because the melanin in darker skin helps to block UVB rays. People of Hispanic origin, for instance, probably need to be in the sun nearly twice as long and very dark skinned people of African origin may need to be in the sun 6 times as long. Recommendations for vitamin D vary from the FDA's Percent Daily Value (%DV) of 400 IU's (International Units) per day for most people to prescription doses of 50,000 IU's per week with an upper limit recommendation of 10,000 units per day. The Vitamin D Council recommends 5000 units per day.

Since we store vitamin D in our bodies, we will use what we need and any excess will be saved for use later. A relatively short time in the sun a few times a week will give us plenty of vitamin D. The more time we spend in the sun, the more vitamin D reserves we will have for use later. What we store in the summer months can help those of us in the northern latitudes get through some of the winter months without being completely depleted. I spend a lot of time outdoors in the summer. However most of that time, I have on sunscreen, especially in the middle of the day because I am very fair-skinned and burn easily. I try to make sure to spend some amount of time in the sun without sunscreen nearly every day right through October if it doesn't get too cold. Later in the winter I take 2000 units of vitamin D each day that I remember.

It is possible to get some vitamin D from tanning beds. How much you are able to get varies because tanning beds use lights with different rays and in different strengths from each other. Some tanning beds have stronger UVB rays than others. A very rough estimate would be 20%. So, 10 minutes in a tanning bed for a light skinned person might give you about 2000 units of vitamin D.

Vitamin E

Vitamin E is an especially powerful antioxidant involved in the protection and regeneration of skin cells. Used topically and orally, it is very effective at preventing and reducing scarring and discolorations of the skin. Research has also shown that vitamin E possesses anti-inflammatory effects that can combat arthritis, asthma, and other inflammatory disorders linked to chronic inflammation. Recent research suggests that eating foods high in vitamin E may lower the risk of Alzheimer's Disease and other cognitive decline (Morris et. al., 2002, Devore et. al. 2010). Interestingly, while these results have been found when subjects obtained vitamin E from food, they have not been replicated when using vitamin E supplements in clinical trials. This may be another of those cases where there are multiple nutrients, or forms of nutrients, working together when consumed in food that is impossible to simulate with a nutrient in isolation.

A study by the Department of Agricultural Chemistry at the Meiji University, Kawasaki, Kanagawa Japan found that a deficiency in Vitamin E increased anxiety in both juvenile and adult rats (Terada et al., 2011). In a 2009 study at the same university, Okura et al., discovered that they could induce anxiety behaviors in rats by making them deficient in vitamin E.

When compared to healthy Australians, researchers at the University of Wollongong found 49 patients suffering from major depression to have significantly lower levels of vitamin E (Owen et al., 2005). A similar study at the Clinical Research Center for Mental Health in Antwerp, Belgium compared blood samples of 49 depressed patients to 26 healthy volunteers and found significantly lower vitamin E in the depressed patients (Maes et al., 2000).

In another study in Italy, researchers tested groups of adult rats whose mothers had been given elevated doses of vitamin E during pregnancy against those whose mothers had not been given additional vitamin E. The rats whose mothers had been given vitamin E performed much better in stressful situations, demonstrating less anxiety and fear than the other group (Ambrogini et al., 2011). Prenatal exposure to vitamin E while in the womb had lasting effects in decreasing anxious responses to stress into adulthood.

The potential effects of vitamin E as a treatment for stress induced depression was tested in a group of mice and compared to a group treated with fluoxetine (Prozac). They found the vitamin E to be more effective than Prozac (Lobato et al., 2010).

Researchers looking at a low-income elderly population in central Israel found that a deficiency in vitamin E was associated with depression. They found that an increase in as little as 1 mg per day of vitamin E decreased the risk of depression (German et al., 2011).

Minerals And Mental Health

Calcium

Calcium is another of Nature's sedatives with calming and relaxing effects. It has recently been shown to be significantly more effective than acetaminophen in long-term pain reduction in orthodontic treatment (Yassaei et al., 2012). So, in addition to relaxation and stress relief, calcium also provides relief from pain.

People who have depression and anxiety have been found to be deficient in calcium. A negative association was found in 105 middle-aged Korean women between dietary intake of calcium and depression; the less calcium they consumed in their diets, the more depressed they were (Bae & Kim, 2012).

While there has been little research on the benefits of treating anxiety or depression with calcium alone, it has been shown to enhance treatment with prescription drugs like diazepam (Hiremath et al., 2010).

Calcium is a key player in both depression relief and stress reduction, working closely with magnesium, vitamin D, potassium and other nutrients to maximize its benefits. Foods that are high in magnesium, like dark green leafy vegetables, also tend to be good sources of calcium. Foods that are high in calcium tend to also be good sources of potassium, as well as other important nutrients, because all of these things work together. The best way to ensure consuming adequate amounts of calcium, along with the other nutrients calcium needs to do its job properly, is to eat a wide variety of whole, healthy foods including dairy products and dark green leafy vegetables.

Iron

Depression, fatigue, excessive sleepiness, poor concentration, irritability and nervousness are considered to be symptoms of iron deficiency. Iron deficiency can also cause Restless Leg Syndrome. Iron deficiency is fairly common among women of childbearing age. The requirements for iron are higher for premenopausal women.

Female soldiers participated in a study published in the

American Journal of Clinical Nutrition (McClung et al., 2009) that measured both physical performance and mood. In the double-blind study, half of the 219 participants were given 100 mg iron, half were given a placebo. Both physical performance and mood were improved in the group given iron compared to the placebo group.

The link between iron deficiency and depression is linked to older people as well. Data from the 2005 Health Survey for England from 1875 participants 65 years and older found that iron deficiency commonly co-occurs with depressive symptoms in older people (Stewart & Hirani, 2012).

An interesting study published in Women's Health (Aubuchon-Endsley et al., 2012) looked at the relationship between iron levels, depression, and parenting styles. 105 breastfeeding mothers were interviewed when their babies were 3 months old. Participants completed questionnaires for 2 years regarding their depressive symptoms and parenting styles. Iron levels were assessed from blood samples. Significant interactions were found between iron status and depressive symptoms and authoritarian parenting style (low warmth and nurturing, high punishment and directiveness). The women with low iron levels were more depressed and more authoritarian in their parenting styles.

Childbearing age and elderly women are not the only ones suffering depression that is linked to iron deficiency. A study of middle-aged municipal workers in Japan found an increased prevalence of depressive symptoms in men who had decreased iron levels. In fact, the lower the iron level, the greater the depressive symptoms (Yi et al., 2011).

Iron deficiency in children causes cognitive impairment and prevents millions of young children from attaining their developmental potential (Walker et al., 2011). Poor children around the world are at greater risk of nutritional deficiencies, perhaps especially iron deficiency as the most bioavailable iron comes from meat. A randomized controlled trial of 2730 elementary school students, mostly aged 10-12 years, from 54 schools in 8 of the poorest counties in Northwest China found over 42% of the children deficient in iron. Half of the schools received no treatment and the children in the other half of the schools received 5 mg of iron each day. Anxiety was significantly reduced in the children receiving iron (Zhang et al., 2013).

Iron deficiency is linked to depression and anxiety across genders and in all age groups. Since anxiety is associated with lack of concentration and difficulty learning, an iron deficiency puts a child at a disadvantage in a learning environment, both academically and socially. Young mothers who are iron deficient have an increased likelihood of becoming a harsher, less nurturing parent. Iron has been shown to effectively decrease depression and anxiety and improve mood in people who were iron deficient.

Iron is present in many plant-based foods like beans and green leafy vegetables. But our bodies can utilize the iron we get from meat more readily than iron we get from plants. We will utilize some of the iron from plants, just not as much of it as what we get from meat.

Magnesium

Magnesium is Nature's original relaxer. Magnesium has long been used for calming nerves and relaxing muscles and as a natural laxative. Its therapeutic role in both anxiety and depression is well supported.

Our ancestors would have had a ready supply from food grown on magnesium rich soil. Modern farming practices have diminished magnesium levels in some soils. Magnesium is present in many natural water sources – the "harder" the water, the more minerals like calcium and magnesium it contains. Magnesium is removed in municipal water treatments and in "soft" water systems used in many homes and offices. Foods that contain magnesium like seafood, whole grains, Brazil nuts, and dark green leafy vegetables are not consumed in great quantities in the Western diet. For all of those reasons, and because stress depletes our magnesium levels quickly, the average American is deficient in magnesium.

The Hordaland Health Study in Norway of over 5700 individuals found that magnesium intake was definitely related to depression. Those who had less magnesium in their diets had higher rates of depression (Jacka et al., 2009).

An article in Neuropharmacology (Sartori et al., 2012) describes a study with mice at the University of Innsbruck in Austria. They found that anxiety-related behaviors can be induced by making mice deficient in magnesium. Magnesium had already been shown to be an effective treatment for both depression and anxiety in mice (Poleszak et al., 2004). A Russian study demonstrated that both anxiety and depression could be induced in mice by making them deficient in magnesium. They also found that the symptoms could be significantly relieved by adding magnesium back into the diet and that even better results were obtained when the mice were treated with both magnesium and vitamin B6 together (Spasov et al., 2008). Another study on Russian children aged 6-12 with ADHD found a very strong difference between the control group and the children given magnesium and vitamin B6. The children given magnesium and vitamin B6 showed improvements in behavior, decreased anxiety and aggression, and increased characteristics of attention (Nogovitsina & Levitina, 2006).

George and Karen Eby have done extensive research on the effects of magnesium on depression and anxiety at their nutritional research center in Austin, Texas. In a paper they wrote titled, "Rapid recovery from major depression using magnesium treatment" (2006), they present numerous case histories showing rapid recovery (less than 7 days) from major depression using 125-300 mg of magnesium with each meal and at bedtime.

Exactly how magnesium works to alleviate anxiety and depression is not fully understood but there is some evidence to suggest that it acts on GABA receptors, increasing GABA levels which decreases anxiety and stress-related depression (Poleszak, 2008). It appears to also assist in blocking the production of adrenaline (the hormone involved in our "fight or flight" response) allowing us to remain calmer under stress (Murck, 2002).

Magnesium is a good example of why I would recommend choosing foods high in a particular nutrient over taking supplements. There are many types of magnesium available to take as supplements. Some are more "bioavailable" than others. In other words, your body is better able to utilize some types more than others. Some magnesium supplements are going to be a good investment and some are going to be a near waste of money. The magnesium available in food is going to be magnesium that your body can use. Another reason is because you may have noticed by now that many of the nutrients implicated in depression and anxiety share foods in common. When we eat foods high in magnesium, for instance, we are also eating foods containing vitamin B6, folate, calcium and other nutrients that are beneficial in treating depression and anxiety. Each time you eat these foods, it's like taking a super pack depression and anxiety supplement – but without the risk of taking too much or wasting money on the wrong kind.

Potassium

Low potassium levels have been associated with greater risk for mood disturbances and depression. A study published in the "British Journal of Nutrition" (Torres et al., 2008) examined the relationship between potassium and mood, and found that a high-potassium diet helped to relieve symptoms of depression and tension among study subjects. These findings suggest both that potassium may be useful in the treatment of mood disturbances and that low potassium levels may be linked to symptoms of depression.

Potassium deficiency can cause irritability, fatigue, muscle weakness, cramps, Restless Leg Syndrome, and chronic pain. Depression often accompanies these symptoms. Depression and pain are intimately intertwined. "Pain is depressing, and depression causes and intensifies pain. People with chronic pain have three times the average risk of developing psychiatric symptoms — usually mood or anxiety disorders — and depressed patients have three times the average risk of developing chronic pain" (Harvard Mental Health Letter, 2004).

A study in the journal "Nature Neuroscience" (Heurteaux et al., 2006) investigated the role of potassium in the regulation of serotonin, the neurotransmitter primarily targeted by antidepressants. The researchers speculated that potassium channels in the brain may play an important role in serotonin regulation. Potassium appears to act as a facilitator in ensuring the brain's ability to properly utilize serotonin. Depression is often characterized by negative thoughts such as guilt, feelings of helplessness and hopelessness, low self-worth, and suicide. Potassium is required to activate neurons involved in positive thoughts and feelings. Without the electrical charge sparked by potassium, neurotransmitters like serotonin cannot be utilized to make us feel better. This may explain why even a slight decrease in potassium levels can result in significant feelings of anxiety (McCleane & Waters, 2007).

Potassium deficiency can be caused by bulimia, chronic diarrhea, diuretics, and Crohn's disease. One of the biggest causes of potassium deficiency is excessive consumption of cola drinks (Tsimihodimos et al., 2009). This is one of many good reasons to limit cola drinks or, better yet, to not drink them at all.

The Canadian Mental Health Association reports that low levels of potassium, caused by hormonal imbalances that contribute to premenstrual syndrome, can lead to depression. In addition, they explain that consuming excessive quantities of caffeine, sodium, and alcohol can contribute to deficiency and lead to depression. Women who have recently given birth also may experience a drop in potassium associated with a decrease in progesterone. This can result in postpartum depression.

Most people probably associate bananas with potassium and while bananas are a source of potassium, there are better ones. One of the top things on the list – you can probably guess by now - dark green leafy vegetables, especially spinach and chard. White beans are also an excellent source, as are potatoes, sweet potatoes, yoghurt, salmon, mushrooms, and avocados.

Selenium

There has probably been more research on selenium and its relationship to depression and anxiety than any other nutrient. Back in 1991, Benton & Cook's study, "The impact of selenium supplementation on mood" published in Biological Psychiatry showed a strong correlation between depressive symptoms and selenium in 50 British subjects. In their double-blind study, subjects received either a placebo or 100 mcg selenium daily. A food frequency questionnaire was used to estimate the intake of selenium in the diet. The subjects consuming the highest amounts of selenium had the highest elevation of mood and lower anxiety. The lower the level of selenium in the diet the more reports of anxiety, depression, and tiredness, which were all reversed following 5 weeks of selenium therapy. Ongoing studies have continued to confirm that lower dietary selenium intakes are associated with an increased risk of depression (Pasco et al., 2012).

Recently, researchers at the University of Calgary in Canada studied 475 pregnant women to see if selenium played a role in preventing postpartum depression. They found that prenatal supplementation with selenium decreased the risk of postpartum depression (Leung et al., 2013). A 2011 study of 166 pregnant women in Iran reached the same conclusion; selenium supplementation during pregnancy significantly decreased the risk of postpartum depression. While selenium supplementation reduces the risk of depression, deficiencies in vitamin D, zinc, and selenium all contribute to the development of postpartum depression (Ellsworth-Bowers & Corwin, 2012).

Selenium has improved depressive symptoms among the elderly living in nursing and residential homes (Gosney et al., 2008). This is very good news since it is estimated that one third of older people in elderly care facilities have significant symptoms of depression, although I suspect that number is actually higher. Since the elderly are no longer able to cook for themselves, they are at the mercy of the facilities for their meals. It is too often the case that dietary regimens in institutions of all kinds are woefully lacking in nutrients necessary for good mental health.

A study in Russia examined 59 patients with cardiovascular disease and obesity. The researchers looked at quality of life, overall health, level of anxiety, and the dynamics of mental processes. The 36 patients put on a diet enriched with selenium showed an increase in activity, improvement of overall health and cognitive functions, mood stabilization, reduction of anxiety and increased emotional stability. The biggest difference between the two groups was the decreased anxiety level in the selenium group (Derbeneva et al., 2012).

Selenium has also significantly reduced anxiety in HIV/AIDS patients. A randomized, double-blind trial of 32 men and 31 women where half were given placebo and half were given selenium for 12 months showed a significant reduction in anxiety in the selenium treated group. At the 12-month evaluation, participants who received selenium reported increased vigor as well as less anxiety compared to the placebo-treated group. In fact, the risk for trait anxiety (anxiety that is considered a personality trait rather than anxiety resulting from a stressful situation) was nine times greater in the placebo-treated group (Shor-Posner et al., 2003).
Ongoing research is also showing some potential for the use of selenium in preventing and treating Alzheimer's disease (Kryscio et al., 2013, Broersen et al., 2013).

Adequate selenium levels are crucial for the prevention of depression and anxiety. Consuming the recommended amount of selenium has been demonstrated to relieve depression and anxiety caused by major life stressors. Numerous studies have supported its effectiveness at preventing postpartum depression and research on its use in preventing Alzheimer's disease and other types of cognitive decline is promising.

Zinc

Clinical studies and experimental work using animals have both revealed a link between zinc and neuropsychological disorders like depression and anxiety. Not only has zinc deficiency been shown to induce depression and anxiety (Tassabehji et al., 2008, Whittle et al., 2009), supplementation with zinc has been used as an effective treatment for major depression. Zinc also improves the effect of antidepressants in depressed patients (Cope & Levenson, 2010).

A double-blind study with 674 school children in Guatemala gave half of them 10 mg of zinc 5 days per week for 6 months and the other half were given a placebo. Significant decreases in depression and anxiety were seen in the group given zinc compared to the group given the placebo (DiGirolamo et al., 2010).

Zinc not only reduces anxiety and depression in mice (Partyka et al., 2011), but also psychosis (Joshi et al., 2012).

Traumatic brain injury is associated with a wide variety of behavioral deficits, including memory loss, depression, and anxiety. While treatments for these outcomes are currently limited, human clinical data suggest that zinc can be used during recovery to improve cognitive and behavioral deficits associated with brain injury. Additionally, zinc may increase resilience to traumatic brain injury, making it potentially useful in populations at risk for injury (Cope et al., 2012).

Zinc may have another role in protecting the brain from damage. Most people probably know that cancer and other diseases are linked to environmental toxins but depression can also be caused from toxic chemicals in the environment like pesticides. Malathion is a widely used pesticide in agriculture that is linked to depression. Malathion residue, like many other pesticides, can remain on fruits and vegetables that have not been grown organically. Researchers in Brazil (Brocardo et al., 2007) exposed a group of rats to malathion for 3 days to induce depression. A second group was given zinc while exposed to the malathion. Neurochemical damage including disruption of neurotransmitters and depressive behavior was evident in both groups but the malathion had less damaging effects in the group given the zinc. The damage done in both groups was completely reversed when treated with zinc.

It appears that zinc acts as a protector of the brain, mediating the effects of traumatic brain injury as well as the damaging effects of environmental toxins. Beyond protecting the brain, zinc can also reverse some kinds of damage. Zinc deficiency can cause depression and anxiety, which is quickly relieved when adequate zinc levels are restored.

From Food To Neurotransmitter

Up to this point we have covered some of the vitamins and minerals that are major players in depression and anxiety. They all work in different ways, including facilitating the transmission of neurotransmitters that make us feel calm and happy or by blocking neurotransmitters that make us feel anxious or sad. Now we are going to talk about the nutrients that convert directly, or indirectly, into the neurotransmitters that make us feel good. It won't matter how well the "helper" nutrients do their job if we don't have enough of the right kind of neurotransmitters to begin with.

Remember the neurotransmitters primarily involved in anxiety and depression, are:

- **Serotonin**
- **Norepinephrine**
- **Dopamine**
- **Gamma-aminobutyric acid (GABA)**

The amino acids that convert to these neurotransmitters are:

- **Tryptophan**
- **Tyrosine**
- **Phenylalanine**
- **Glutamine**

Which neurotransmitter do you need?

Depression can symptomize differently in different people. Sometimes the symptoms of depression can be characterized as more lethargic with low energy and little interest in things that would normally bring pleasure. Depression can also be primarily an agitated type with irritability, insomnia, and restlessness.

Low **serotonin** levels are associated with:

- Insomnia
- Anxiety

- Irritability
- Low stress tolerance
- Sugar cravings
- Obsessive-compulsive tendencies
- Anger
- Weight gain

Low levels of **norepinephrine** are associated with:

- Excessive sleep
- Sadness
- Fatigue
- Lethargy
- Difficulty concentrating
- Memory problems
- Apathy

Low levels of **dopamine** are associated with:

- Sadness
- Excessive sleep
- Weight gain
- Loss of pleasure
- Low energy
- Addictive behaviors

Low levels of **gamma-aminobutyric acid (GABA)** are associated with:

- Anxiety

- Irritability
- Fatigue
- Panic attacks
- Insomnia
- Restlessness
- Low stress tolerance
- Feelings of dread
- Short temper

Tryptophan To Serotonin

Tryptophan is an amino acid that is present in a variety of protein-rich foods. Tryptophan is the only substance that can make serotonin. Men typically have higher levels of serotonin than women, which could be one explanation for why women have higher rates of depression.

Foods high in tryptophan include:

- Chicken
- Turkey
- Dairy products
- Nuts
- Wild Game and fowl
- Tuna
- Salmon
- Lobster
- Crab
- Cod
- Sardines
- Beans
- Eggs

- Pumpkin seeds
- Wheat germ

Tryptophan converts to serotonin with the help of other nutrients, most notably vitamin B6. Vitamin B6 is also present in the foods that contain tryptophan. Tryptophan competes with other amino acids in protein-rich foods fighting for entry into the brain. Tryptophan will often get beat out by other amino acids and get left behind unless it is eaten together with starchy food. Whether this is because the starch causes the body to release insulin and the insulin aids in carrying the tryptophan from the bloodstream to the brain or whether it is because the starch itself or the fiber in the starchy food slows the digestive process giving the tryptophan more time to reach the brain is not entirely clear. But, if you eat foods containing tryptophan together with starchy carbohydrates, you are more likely to be able to utilize the tryptophan. Beans, like kidney beans or navy beans, are a good choice because they have both tryptophan and starch. You can also combine the protein foods containing tryptophan with starchy vegetables like corn, squash, potatoes, and sweet potatoes or with whole grains.

Tryptophan-rich foods should be eaten with all 3 daily meals as well as 2 snacks. If you are consuming 60-80 grams of tryptophan-containing protein per day, you should be getting enough tryptophan for adequate serotonin levels. Nuts, cheese, and hard-boiled eggs are all good snack choices for tryptophan. Remember you need to have some starch with that so adding some carrot sticks, whole grain crackers or granola bars made without refined sugar make good combinations.

Another noteworthy thing about tryptophan is that a certain amount of it will convert to niacin (vitamin B3) before it converts to serotonin. It is usually a small amount, approximately 3%. However, if you are deficient in niacin, tryptophan will meet the need for niacin first, which may not leave enough for adequate serotonin. Because niacin is also present in foods containing tryptophan, you should get these nutrients from food rather than taking them separately as supplements.

Phenylalanine and tyrosine to norepinephrine and dopamine

Phenylalanine can convert to norepinephrine and it can also convert to tyrosine, which converts to both norepinephrine and dopamine. But the two amino acids function a little bit differently. Phenylalanine can make norepinephrine without first converting to tyrosine. Also, phenylalanine can convert to a substance called phenylethylamine (PEA). Low levels of PEA are associated with some cases of depression and only phenylalanine can restore PEA levels. PEA is an amphetamine-like alkaloid stimulant found in cocoa, which may be one reason why chocolate is one of the most sought-after foods when depressed. PEA is naturally released in the body when you are in love.

Food high in phenylalanine include:

- Soybeans
- Lentils
- Chickpeas
- Flaxseed
- Sesame seed
- Pork
- Beef

- Shrimp
- Salmon
- Chicken
- Eggs
- Peanuts
- Almonds
- Wild game
- Crab
- Parmesan cheese
- Liver
- Halibut
- Tuna

Recommended amounts of phenylalanine range from about 3000-4000 mg per day, which is not difficult if you are eating the right things. A half-cup of Italian salami made with pork has about 1000 mg of phenylalanine. A half-cup of soybeans has about 2000 mg. and a half-cup of peanuts has about 1500 mg.

Tyrosine converts to both norepinephrine and dopamine. It is a "non-essential" amino acid, meaning the body can manufacture it on its own. However, tyrosine levels can become diminished with stress and with demands for norepinephrine and dopamine. We can increase our levels of tyrosine by eating tyrosine-rich foods.

Foods high in tyrosine include:

- Almonds
- Cottage cheese (low fat is best)

- Parmesan cheese
- Salmon
- Turkey
- Eggs
- Fish (both fresh and saltwater)
- Beans
- Peanuts
- Tofu
- Pumpkin seeds
- Chicken
- Wild game
- Beef
- Pork

Daily recommendations for tyrosine are the same as for phenylalanine – about 3000-4000 mg per day. One medium salmon steak, 3 eggs, or 1 cup of 2% cottage cheese will each provide about 2000 mg of tyrosine.

Glutamine to GABA

GABA is one of the body's most calming neurotransmitters. Like serotonin, norepinephrine, and dopamine, GABA is not directly available in food. But the amino acid glutamine is present in food and converts to GABA. GABA is available as a supplement but most medical professionals do not believe it can cross the blood-brain barrier to enter the brain. However, there are many people who take GABA as a supplement and report that it relieves their anxiety. It is possible that due to malnutrition or inflammation the blood-brain barrier could weaken, allowing a substance to cross. Glutamine is an amino acid that can cross the blood-brain barrier and can convert to GABA in the brain. Glutamine is found in many different foods.

Foods high in glutamine are:

- Grass-fed beef
- Bison
- Free range chicken
- Free range eggs
- Whey protein
- Yogurt
- Cheese
- Cottage cheese
- Red cabbage
- Beets
- Beans

There is no established daily recommendation for glutamine. The body can make its own glutamine but it is diminished under stressful conditions, including mental stress or physical stress like intensive exercise. Because of this, sometimes the body is not able to keep up with glutamine production making it a "conditionally essential" amino acid, so it becomes "essential" during these times to obtain glutamine from the diet. Supplementation of 10 grams per day has been found to be safe. An individual's actual needs are difficult to determine because it will depend on stress levels, physical exertion, or mental or physical trauma, all of which can cause a deficiency in glutamine. While it is not recommended for people with neurological disorders to take supplements containing glutamine, consumption of glutamine from food sources is not known to cause any harmful effects. A whole foods organic diet rich in protein should supply all the building blocks needed for the body to produce its own needed glutamine.

Ensuring that your glutamine levels are adequate will help

your brain make the GABA it needs to prevent or correct the anxiety and depression that can result from low levels of GABA. Eating good quality protein several times a day should provide adequate glutamine.

There are also 2 other amino acids that have a positive impact on GABA levels: these are *taurine* and *theanine.* **Taurine** is a potent activator of GABA receptor cells in the brain. When we experience fear and/or anxiety, GABA receptor sites shut down or turn off. The presence of taurine will cause more GABA receptor sites to remain available for the absorption of GABA. Increasing utilization of GABA during times of fear and stress will allow a person to remain more calm and less anxious. Taurine has been successfully used to treat seizure disorders, insomnia, agitation, restlessness, irritability, anxiety and depression. Taurine itself is probably not directly responsible for the improvement in these conditions but more likely is due to its effect on GABA levels.

Foods that contain taurine are:

- Fish
- Red meat
- Poultry
- Dairy products
- Eggs

Monosodium glutamate (MSG) is a food additive that is used to enhance flavor in processed foods and is an enemy of taurine because MSG degrades taurine and inhibits its function. Unfortunately, food labeling does not require MSG to be labeled as such so may be hidden in many processed foods and listed only as "natural flavors". This is one more probable link between processed food and anxiety and depression. Ingredients, like MSG, that are added to processed foods interfere with the processes and production of neurotransmitters that promote feelings of joy, peacefulness, and calm.

Theanine is found naturally in tea, both green tea and black tea, though black tea seems to have considerably more than green tea. Darjeeling tea has some of the highest concentrations of theanine. In addition to the many physical health benefits of tea, theanine has been demonstrated to relieve depression, anxiety, and insomnia.

Exactly how theanine works to increase GABA levels is currently debated. Some researchers believe it is converted to GABA but most believe it either inhibits excitatory receptors involved with neurotransmitters, like glutamate, that counteract GABA's calming effects or it opens pathways for GABA in a similar way as taurine, or both. However it does it, theanine does appear to increase GABA levels. A typical dose of theanine is 50 mg to 200 mg per day. A standard cup of black tea brewed for 30 minutes has about 25-30 mg of theanine. Since it would be difficult to drink enough tea to achieve the higher ends of those recommendations, a more sensible approach would be to combine drinking tea for the theanine along with eating good quality protein foods for the glutamine and taurine while avoiding processed foods because of the likelihood of their containing MSG.

In addition to decreased anxiety, numerous studies have linked theanine to increased creativity, increased performance under stress, and improved learning and concentration. Theanine also raises levels of **dopamine.**

And let's not forget that **magnesium** relieves anxiety and depression by increasing GABA levels. Magnesium, glutamine, taurine, and theanine give us an array of things to choose from in our nutrition toolbox to maintain healthy levels of GABA.

Chapter 4

The Real Food Solution

Hopefully by now you have begun to see some patterns. The nutrients that are known to be involved in mental health occur, oftentimes together in "teams", in good, whole food. The amino acids we need to make the beneficial neurotransmitters along with their helpers, vitamins and minerals, are in **fish, red meat, poultry, eggs, green leafy vegetables, colorful vegetables and fruits, whole grains, nuts and seeds, beans, and dairy products.** These whole, "real" foods keep appearing over and over again as the sources of what we need to eat to be healthy, both physically and mentally and should be the mainstay of our regular diet. The key to a nutritional approach to mental health is in eating foods containing the nutrients that help our brains function optimally and *not* eating foods that are depleted of those nutrients or, worse yet, actively working against the good foods we are eating. We can break the vicious cycle of relying on processed and fast-foods that are causing the nutritional deficiencies that result in depression and anxiety, robbing us of our energy and joy. Eating processed and fast-food perpetuates the cycle of eating more foods laden in trans-fats, refined grains and sugar in an attempt to make ourselves, momentarily, feel better, or just for the sake of convenience. We are beginning to see the toll this dietary lifestyle has taken on our health. The best solution for fixing a problem is to discover the cause of the problem and correct it. Anything else is nothing more than treating symptoms or, at the very least, trying to fix a problem that could have been prevented. Avoiding processed food while eating nutrient rich "real" food can act as both prevention and cure of problems associated with nutritional deficiencies.

There can be little argument that our Western diet has created a plethora of physical and mental problems. Americans spend $11.3 *billion* dollars annually on antidepressants. More and more children are taking antidepressants at younger and younger ages. Antidepressants can have serious side effects, sometimes they don't help very much and sometimes they don't work at all. When they do work, research has shown that they work better in combination with nutrients like B-vitamins and omega-3 fatty acids. So, even if you are taking antidepressants, they may be more effective if you eat more whole grains, grass-fed meat, and fish.

Americans are beginning to understand the connections between diet and health. There is growing concern about the link between our diet and diseases like diabetes, heart disease, hypertension, neurological disorders, and obesity, among others. It is well past time for us to make the connection between our diets and our mental health. It is time for us to understand that eating too much of the things that are bad for us and not enough of the things that are good for us can make us anxious and depressed.

So, how do we know what to eat? The good news is, it isn't as hard as you might think! On the following pages you will find a Daily Value (DV) table showing the US FDA recommendations for each nutrient. This used to be called the US RDA (Recommended Daily Allowance). According to the DV, meeting the daily requirements for each nutrient will insure that you are not deficient. In some cases, there will also be a "suggested" daily allowance (SDA), based on the current research in preventing and treating depression and anxiety. The rule of thumb would be that if you are generally somewhere between the DV and the SDA, you should be in good shape. If you are currently depressed or anxious, you may want to try to meet the SDA until the symptoms subside. Remember that it is possible to get too much of some nutrients when taking supplements. It is nearly impossible to get too much of any particular nutrient from eating food. Also remember that all whole foods contain many nutrients that are working together to make you feel your best.

The DV table will tell you how much of all the nutrients you need each day. After the DV table you will find the Nutrition Content table. This will help you track all of the nutrients known to be linked to depression and anxiety and choose the specific foods you need to meet your nutritional requirements. This will be your reference for knowing how much and which nutrients are contained in nearly 300 different foods.

Finally, you will find the Recipes section. The recipes will not only give you some new ideas for using real food in your everyday meals, this section is also intended to show you, with the included nutritional breakdown in each recipe, how many nutrients you can obtain with common dishes that are familiar to you. You don't have to change everything about the way you eat. You just need to know how to meet your nutritional needs. These recipes will help you do that and to see what kinds of nutrients are in things you already make. They are divided into Main Courses, Salads, Vegetables, and Desserts and Snacks so you can mix and match, using the DV and Nutritional Content Table, to meet your daily requirements. It takes a little effort at first, but once you get the hang of it, knowing how to combine things to get all the nutrients you need becomes second nature.

There were several considerations that went into the recipes. They had to have readily available ingredients, not too many ingredients, be good sources of nutrients, score favorably on the Glycemic Index, and be fairly simple to make. You will also find that the recipes are gluten free because there is some evidence to suggest a link between gluten and depression. The evidence is far from conclusive at this point but since there is some evidence of a link, and because more and more people are developing sensitivity to gluten, it seemed a good idea to only include recipes that don't contain gluten. Since consuming grain is not necessary for life, and because as a species we probably consume way too much of it, very little grain is included in these recipes. You will find some oats and brown rice. I don't recommend eating a lot of grain but when you do eat grain, I recommend you eat whole grains. Whole grains are much more nutritious than processed grains. White rice and white flour should be avoided because they have been stripped of the hulls and bran that contain most of the beneficial nutrients and fiber.

You may also notice a conspicuous absence of soy in the recipes. While soybeans and soy-based products, like tofu, have some benefits, there are detrimental things about soy that makes it best to mostly avoid it, in my opinion. The high estrogen content in soy that has been linked to some cancers as well as the high omega-6 content that makes it an inflammatory food are two major considerations. In addition, over 90% of soy grown in the U.S. is genetically modified (GMO). What that means is that DNA from other living organisms (we don't know what) is added to the soybeans to make them resistant to powerful herbicides. Soybeans are then heavily sprayed with herbicides that are linked to various cancers, neurological disorders, and other diseases. So, if you choose to eat soy products, limit the amount you eat and make sure you eat only organic and non-GMO soy. A couple of the recipes in this book call for soy sauce in which case I recommend organic, GMO-free Tamari, which is a wheat-free soy sauce. If you choose to avoid soy completely, coconut aminos is a very good substitute for soy sauce and is soy and wheat-free.

At the time of this writing, at least 20 countries have full country or regional bans on genetically modified foods. Unfortunately, the U.S. is not one of them, although several states currently have anti-GMO legislation in process. In addition to soybeans, much of our wheat and corn is genetically modified now and rice may not be far behind. We don't know yet how genetically modified foods will affect us. But there is enough concern to cause a rapidly growing number of countries to ban their growth or import.

Food should be our medicine. It should nourish us and give us strong immune systems, stamina, strength, and mental acuity. Food should provide the chemical balance we need to approach life with joy, energy, and enthusiasm. Food should be grown with care, then chosen and prepared thoughtfully, cooked with love, savored and enjoyed with loved ones. Food deserves to be a central part of our lives. The more important we make it, the more benefit we will derive from it. Good food makes good bodies and good minds.

DAILY VALUE TABLE

NUTRIENT	DAILY VALUE (DV)*	SDA***
Protein	50 g	60-80 g
Fat	65 g	**
Carbohydrate	300 g	**
Fiber	25 g	**
Niacin	20 mg	100-3000 mg
Vitamin B6	2 mg	20-150 mg
Folate	400 mcg	800-3000 mcg
Vitamin B12	6 mcg	20-100 mcg
Inositol	**	100 mg-18 g
Vitamin C	60 mg	1000-3000 mg
Vitamin D	400 IU	5000 IU
Vitamin E	30 IU	400-800 IU
Calcium	1000 mg (1g)	1000-1500 mg
Iron	18 mg	30-50 mg
Magnesium	400 mg	500-1000 mg
Potassium	3500 mg	2-6 g
Selenium	70 mcg	100-400 mcg
Zinc	15 mg	10-50 mg
Tryptophan	**	1000-4000 mg
Tyrosine	**	3000-4000 mg
Phenylalanine	**	3000-4000 mg
Glutamine	**	1000-3000 mg
Omega-3	**	1000-3000 mg
Omega-6	**	1000-3000 mg

*Based on caloric intake of 2000 calories for adults and children 4 or more years of age.
** No recommended daily amount
***Suggesteded daily amount for adults

NUTRIENT CONTENT TABLE

The Nutrient Content Table is a collection of nearly 300 foods listing all of the nutrients we have discussed that are known to play a part in depression and anxiety. This allows you to track any and all of the key nutrients to help ensure that you are getting all of them that you need in order to feel your best. You can use the table to plan meals and menus. You can also use it to calculate your nutritional intake at the end of each day or week to see how you have done. It is a very useful tool to use along with the recipes included in this book when deciding what to add to meals for side dishes or between meal snacks.

It is important to understand that the nutritional information given in the Nutrient Content Table and in the nutritional breakdown in the recipes is intended as an approximation. Nutritional content is not an absolute science. The nutritional content of food depends on many things. Nutritional content can vary depending on the soil the food was grown in, the stage of maturity in which it was picked, how much time has passed between when it is picked and when it is consumed, and how the food is prepared, to name just a few. Even different varieties of the same fruit or vegetable can have widely varying nutritional content. So, the best we can do is to get an approximate amount and the tables should be used accordingly. Fortunately, our nutritional needs are not exact either. Our bodies are designed with a great deal of resilience. What we are aiming for is to spend most of our time in the general ballpark of adequate nutrition. This is not something we need to be rigid about. These tools are provided to act as guides to help steer us on our nutritional path.

Another important thing to keep in mind is that everyone's body is different and will have different nutritional needs. Also, every individual will have varying nutritional needs to some degree depending on changes in lifestyle, stressors, etc. Many nutrients are depleted quickly during times of stress and need to be replenished in greater amounts or more frequently to avoid deficiency. It's probably most helpful to think of our needs for each nutrient being in a range rather than a static amount. The Nutrient Content Table and the nutritional breakdowns for the recipes are provided to help give you a general idea of how much of the key nutrients are contained in a variety of foods.

Using these tools will help you identify specific foods that are generally high in particular nutrients so you will know which foods to incorporate into your diet. The basic rules are, eat a wide variety of whole, natural foods, including high quality protein, avoid processed food, and be conscious of increasing omega-3 fatty acids and decreasing omega-6 fatty acids. Taking those steps will have you well on your way to optimum physical and mental health. The Nutrient Content Table will help you refine your efforts in making the choices that are best for you.

If you would like to view the table on a computer screen, you can download a copy of the Nutritient Content Table found on the following pages at MentalHealthFood.net.

FOOD	approx amt	Calories	Protein_(g)	Fat_Tot_(g)	Carbohydrt_(g)	Fiber(g)	Sugar_Tot_(g)	Calcium_(mg)	Iron_(mg)
DAIRY									
BUTTER, STICK	1 TBSP	102.0	0.1	11.5	0.0	0.0	0.0	3.0	0.0
CHEESE,BLUE	1 OZ (3 TBS)	117.7	7.1	9.6	0.8	0.0	0.2	176.0	0.1
CHEESE,CHEDDAR	1 OZ (3 TBS)	114.0	6.2	8.3	0.3	0.0	0.1	180.0	0.2
CHEESE,COTTAGE,CREAMED,LARGE OR SMALL CURD	1/2 CUP	98.0	11.1	4.3	3.4	0.0	2.7	83.0	0.1
CHEESE,COTTAGE,LOWFAT,2% MILKFAT	1/2 CUP	86.0	11.8	2.5	3.7	0.0	3.7	91.0	0.2
CHEESE,COTTAGE,LOWFAT,1% MILKFAT	1/2 CUP	72.0	12.4	1.0	2.7	0.0	2.7	61.0	0.1
CHEESE,CREAM	1/4 CUP	171.0	3.0	17.1	2.0	0.0	1.6	49.0	0.2
CHEESE,FETA	3 TBSP	66.0	3.6	5.3	1.0	0.0	1.0	123.3	0.2
CHEESE,MOZZARELLA,PART SKIM MILK	1/3 CUP	127.0	12.1	8.0	1.4	0.0	0.6	391.0	0.1
CHEESE,PARMESAN,GRATED	1/2 CUP	216.0	19.2	14.3	2.0	0.0	0.5	554.5	0.5
CREAM,FLUID,HALF AND HALF	1/2 CUP	130.0	3.0	11.5	4.3	0.0	0.2	105.0	0.1
CREAM,SOUR,REDUCED FAT,CULTURED	1/2 CUP	135.0	2.9	12.0	4.3	0.0	0.2	104.0	0.1
CREAM,SOUR,CULTURED	1/2 CUP	193.0	2.1	19.7	2.9	0.0	2.9	110.0	0.2
EGG,WHITE,RAW,FRESH	2 WHITES	52.0	10.9	0.2	0.7	0.0	0.7	7.0	0.1
EGG,WHOLE,COOKED,HARD-BOILED	2 LARGE	155.0	12.6	10.6	1.1	0.0	1.1	50.0	1.2
EGG,WHOLE,RAW,FRESH	2 LARGE	143.0	12.6	9.5	0.7	0.0	0.4	56.0	1.8
EGG,WHOLE,COOKED,SCRAMBLED	2 LARGE	149.0	10.0	11.0	1.6	0.0	1.4	66.0	1.3
ICE CREAM,VANILLA	1/2 CUP	207.0	3.5	11.0	23.6	0.7	21.2	128.0	0.1
MILK,WHOLE,3.25% MILKFAT,W/ ADDED VITAMIN D	1/2 CUP	61.0	3.2	3.3	4.8	0.0	5.1	113.0	0.0
MILK,WHOLE,3.25% MILKFAT,WO/ ADDED VIT A & VIT D	1/2 CUP	61.0	3.2	3.3	4.8	0.0	5.1	113.0	0.0
MILK,FLUID,2% MILKFAT,W/ ADDED VIT A & VITAMIN D	1/2 CUP	50.0	3.3	2.0	4.8	0.0	5.1	120.0	0.0
MILK,FLUID,2% MILKFAT,WO/ ADDED VIT A & VIT D	1/2 CUP	50.0	3.3	2.0	4.8	0.0	5.1	120.0	0.0
MILK,NONFAT,FLUID,W/ ADDED VIT A & VIT D	1/2 CUP	34.0	3.4	0.1	5.0	0.0	5.1	122.0	0.0
MILK,BUTTERMILK,FLUID,CULTURED,LOWFAT	1/2 CUP	40.0	3.3	0.9	4.8	0.0	4.8	116.0	0.1
MILK,DRY,NONFAT,INSTANT,W/ ADDED VIT A & VIT D	1 1/2 CUPS	358.0	35.1	0.7	52.2	0.0	52.2	1231.0	0.3
YOGURT, GREEK, PLAIN, NONFAT	1/2 CUP	59.0	10.2	0.4	3.6	0.0	3.2	110.0	0.1
YOGURT,PLAIN,WHOLE MILK	1/2 CUP	61.0	3.5	3.3	4.7	0.0	4.7	121.0	0.1
YOGURT,PLAIN,LOWFAT	1/2 CUP	63.0	5.3	1.6	7.0	0.0	7.0	183.0	0.1
YOGURT,PLAIN,SKIM MILK	1/2 CUP	56.0	5.7	0.2	7.7	0.0	7.7	199.0	0.1
OILS									
FISH OIL,COD LIVER	1 TBSP	123.0	0.0	13.6	0.0	0.0	0.0	0.0	0.0
OIL, COCONUT	1 TBSP	117.0	0.0	13.6	0.0	0.0	0.0	0.0	0.0
OIL,FLAXSEED,COLD PRESSED	1 TBSP	120.0	0.0	13.6	0.0	0.0	0.0	0.0	0.0
OIL,OLIVE,SALAD OR COOKING	1 TBSP	119.0	0.0	13.5	0.0	0.0	0.0	0.0	0.1
MEAT AND FISH									
ANCHOVY,EUROPEAN,CANNED IN OIL,DRAINED	1 CAN	105.0	14.4	4.9	0.0	0.0	0.0	116.0	2.3
BEEF,GRASS-FED,STRIP STEAKS,LEAN,RAW	4 OZ	117.0	23.1	2.7	0.0	0.0	0.0	9.0	1.9
BEEF,GRASS-FED,GROUND,RAW	4 OZ	192.0	19.4	12.7	0.0	0.0	0.0	12.0	2.0
BEEF LIVER,COOKED,PAN-FRIED	4 OZ	193.0	27.4	6.5	4.5	0.0	0.0	7.0	6.0
BEEF,RIB,SHORTRIBS,LN&FAT,BRAISED	4 OZ	471.0	21.6	42.0	0.0	0.0	0.0	12.0	2.3
BEEF,TOP SIRLOIN,STEAK,LEAN,BROILED	4 OZ	219.0	29.0	10.5	0.0	0.0	0.0	19.0	2.0
BEEF,TOP SIRLOIN,STEAK,LN & FAT,1/8" FAT,BROILED	4 OZ	257.0	26.8	15.8	0.0	0.0	0.0	18.0	1.8
BISON,GROUND,GRASS-FED,COOKED	4 OZ	179.0	25.5	8.6	0.0	0.0	0.0	14.0	3.2
CHICKEN,BREAST,MEAT ONLY,ROASTED	4 OZ	165.0	31.0	3.6	0.0	0.0	0.0	15.0	1.0
CHICKEN,BREAST,MEAT&SKIN,ROASTED	4 OZ	197.0	29.8	7.8	0.0	0.0	0.0	14.0	1.1
CHICKEN,THIGH,MEAT ONLY,ROASTED	4 OZ	177.0	24.0	8.3	0.0	0.0	0.0	10.0	1.1
CHICKEN,THIGH,MEAT&SKIN,ROASTED	4 OZ	229.0	22.6	14.8	0.0	0.0	0.0	10.0	1.1
CLAM,MIXED SPECIES,COOKED,MOIST HEAT	4 OZ	148.0	25.6	2.0	5.1	0.0	~	92.0	28.0
COD,ATLANTIC,COOKED,DRY HEAT	4 OZ	105.0	22.8	0.9	0.0	0.0	0.0	14.0	0.5
CRAB,ALASKA KING,COOKED,MOIST HEAT	4 OZ	97.0	19.4	1.5	0.0	0.0	~	59.0	0.8
CRAB,ALASKA KING,RAW	4 OZ	84.0	18.3	0.6	0.0	0.0	~	46.0	0.6
GAME MEAT,ANTELOPE,COOKED,ROASTED	4 OZ	150.0	29.5	2.7	0.0	0.0	~	4.0	4.2
GAME MEAT,DEER,COOKED,ROASTED	4 OZ	158.0	30.2	3.2	0.0	0.0	~	7.0	4.5
GAME MEAT,MOOSE,LIVER,BRAISED	4 OZ	155.0	24.4	4.9	3.4	~	~	7.0	6.8
GAME MEAT,ELK,COOKED,ROASTED	4 OZ	146.0	30.2	1.9	0.0	0.0	~	5.0	3.6
GAME MEAT,MOOSE,RAW	4 OZ	103.0	22.3	1.5	0.0	0.0	0.0	5.0	3.3
HADDOCK,COOKED,DRY HEAT	4 OZ	90.0	20.0	0.6	0.0	0.0	0.0	14.0	0.2
HALIBUT,ATLANTIC&PACIFIC,COOKED,DRY HEAT	4 OZ	111.0	22.5	1.6	0.0	0.0	0.0	9.0	0.2
HAM,SLICED,REG (APPROX 11% FAT)	4 OZ	163.0	16.6	8.6	3.8	1.3	0.0	24.0	1.0
LAMB,CUBED FOR STEW OR KABOB,LEAN,1/4"FAT,RAW	4 OZ	134.0	20.2	5.3	0.0	0.0	~	9.0	1.8

Magnesium_ (mg)	Potassium_ (mg)	Selenium_ (µg)	Zinc_ (mg)	Niacin_ (mg)	Vit_B6_ (mg)	Folate_Tot_ (µg)	Vit_B12_ (µg)	Vit_C_ (mg)	Vit_D_ (IU)	Vit_E_ (mg)	Tryptophan (mg)	Phenylalanine (mg)	Tyrosine (mg)	Inositol (mg)	tot Omega-3 (mg)	tot Omega-6 (mg)
0.0	3.0	0.0	0.0	0.0	0.0	0.0	0.0	0.0	9.0	0.3	1.7	5.7	5.7	~	44.1	382.0
7.7	85.3	4.8	0.9	0.3	0.1	12.0	0.4	0.0	7.0	0.1	87.4	304.0	363.0	~	73.9	150.0
7.0	24.5	3.5	0.8	0.0	0.0	4.5	0.2	0.0	6.0	0.1	89.6	367.0	337.0	2.5	102.0	162.0
8.0	104.0	9.7	0.4	0.1	0.0	12.0	0.4	0.0	3.0	0.1	154.5	606.0	634.0	2.1	17.9	110.5
7.0	84.0	9.9	0.4	0.1	0.0	10.0	0.5	0.0	0.0	0.0	176.5	694.0	726.5	1.1	11.3	68.0
5.0	86.0	9.0	0.4	0.1	0.1	12.0	0.6	0.0	0.0	0.0	156.0	755.0	746.0	~	10.2	24.9
4.5	69.0	1.2	0.3	0.1	0.0	5.5	0.1	0.0	12.5	0.1	40.0	168.8	175.8	4.1	100.3	598.5
4.8	15.5	3.8	0.7	0.2	0.1	8.0	0.4	0.0	4.0	0.0	56.3	189.8	187.9	~	74.6	91.7
11.5	42.0	7.2	1.4	0.1	0.0	4.5	0.4	0.0	6.0	0.1	169.9	633.7	703.5	2.5	68.7	167.9
19.0	62.5	8.9	1.9	0.1	0.0	5.0	1.1	0.0	10.5	0.1	259.0	1040.5	1164.0	3.0	95.0	471.5
10.0	130.0	1.8	0.5	0.1	0.0	3.0	0.3	0.9	8.0	0.3	51.0	173.0	173.0	~	202.0	314.5
10.0	129.0	2.1	0.5	0.1	0.0	11.0	0.3	0.9	9.0	0.3	49.6	172.0	172.0	~	212.0	328.0
10.0	141.0	2.6	0.4	0.1	0.1	7.0	0.3	0.9	14.0	0.4	~	~	~	87.4	92.8	700.0
11.0	163.0	20.0	0.0	0.1	0.0	4.0	0.1	0.0	0.0	0.0	82.4	452.0	302.0	3.3	0.0	0.0
10.0	126.0	30.8	1.1	0.1	0.1	44.0	1.1	0.0	87.0	1.0	153.0	668.0	514.0	~	78.0	1188.0
12.0	138.0	30.7	1.3	0.1	0.2	47.0	0.9	0.0	82.0	1.1	167.0	682.0	500.0	9.0	74.0	1148.0
11.0	132.0	23.5	1.0	0.1	0.1	36.0	0.8	0.0	72.0	1.2	166.0	712.0	558.0	9.8	141.6	2338.0
14.0	199.0	1.8	0.7	0.1	0.0	5.0	0.4	0.0	8.0	0.3	29.7	104.0	102.0	5.9	117.0	182.0
10.0	132.0	3.7	0.4	0.1	0.0	5.0	0.5	0.0	51.0	0.1	91.5	179.5	185.5	4.9	91.5	146.5
10.0	132.0	3.7	0.4	0.1	0.0	5.0	0.5	0.0	2.0	0.1	91.5	179.5	185.5	4.9	91.5	146.5
11.0	140.0	2.5	0.5	0.1	0.0	5.0	0.5	0.2	49.0	0.0	48.8	197.5	186.5	~	9.8	75.5
11.0	140.0	2.5	0.5	0.1	0.0	5.0	0.5	0.2	1.0	0.0	48.8	197.5	186.5	~	9.8	75.5
11.0	156.0	3.1	0.4	0.1	0.0	5.0	0.5	0.0	47.0	0.0	59.0	202.0	202.0	4.9	2.5	6.2
11.0	151.0	2.0	0.4	0.1	0.0	5.0	0.2	1.0	1.0	0.1	44.1	213.0	170.5	~	16.0	24.5
117.0	1705.0	27.3	4.4	0.9	0.3	50.0	4.0	5.6	440.0	0.0	505.5	1728.0	1728.0	~	11.3	18.3
11.0	141.0	9.7	0.5	0.2	0.1	7.0	0.8	0.0	0.0	0.0	~	~	~	~	~	~
12.0	155.0	2.2	0.6	0.1	0.0	7.0	0.4	0.5	2.0	0.1	24.5	231.5	214.5	7.4	33.1	79.5
17.0	234.0	3.3	0.9	0.1	0.0	11.0	0.6	0.8	1.0	0.0	36.8	350.5	324.5	~	16.0	38.0
19.0	255.0	3.6	1.0	0.1	0.1	12.0	0.6	0.9	0.0	0.0	39.2	383.5	354.0	~	1.3	4.9
0.0	0.0	0.0	0.0	0.0	0.0	0.0	0.0	0.0	1360.0	~	0.0	0.0	0.0	~	2664.0	126.0
0.0	0.0	0.0	0.0	0.0	0.0	0.0	0.0	0.0	0.0	0.0	0.0	0.0	0.0	~	~	243.0
0.0	0.0	0.0	0.0	0.0	0.0	0.0	0.0	0.0	0.0	0.1	0.0	0.0	0.0	~	7196.0	1715.0
0.0	0.0	0.0	0.0	0.0	0.0	0.0	0.0	0.0	0.0	1.9	0.0	0.0	0.0	~	103.0	1318.0
34.5	272.0	34.1	1.2	10.0	0.1	6.5	0.4	0.0	34.5	1.7	146.0	508.0	439.0	~	951.0	163.0
23.0	342.0	21.1	3.6	6.7	0.7	13.0	1.3	0.0	~	0.2	~	~	~	~	23.6	89.6
19.0	289.0	14.2	4.6	4.8	0.4	6.0	2.0	0.0	~	0.4	~	~	~	~	98.4	480.0
23.0	353.0	24.9	11.9	14.4	0.9	350.0	72.5	0.7	~	0.6	375.2	1548.0	1152.0	71.7	11.2	23.6
15.0	224.0	20.8	4.9	2.5	0.2	5.0	2.6	0.0	27.0	0.3	159.2	956.0	768.0	~	560.0	1096.0
24.0	355.0	31.5	5.2	7.9	0.6	9.0	1.9	0.0	~	0.4	222.8	1340.0	1080.0	33.6	21.2	214.0
22.0	327.0	29.0	4.8	7.3	0.5	8.0	1.8	0.0	~	0.5	206.0	1240.0	1000.0	33.6	156.8	456.0
23.0	353.0	31.1	5.3	6.0	0.4	16.0	2.4	0.0	0.0	0.2	215.2	1212.0	968.0	~	50.4	350.4
29.0	256.0	27.6	1.0	13.7	0.6	4.0	0.3	0.0	5.0	0.3	404.0	1380.0	1172.0	33.6	78.4	660.0
27.0	245.0	24.7	1.0	12.7	0.6	4.0	0.3	0.0	5.0	0.3	380.8	1308.0	1096.0	33.6	123.2	1580.0
24.0	277.0	26.1	1.8	6.2	0.5	5.0	0.4	0.0	7.0	0.2	339.2	1152.0	980.0	43.7	212.8	2352.0
22.0	260.0	24.5	1.6	5.8	0.4	4.0	0.4	0.0	7.0	0.2	314.8	1092.0	908.0	43.7	246.4	3348.0
18.0	628.0	64.0	2.7	3.4	0.1	29.0	98.9	22.1	~	~	320.4	1024.0	916.0	3.4	444.0	36.0
42.0	244.0	37.6	0.6	2.5	0.3	8.0	1.1	1.0	46.0	0.8	286.8	996.0	864.0	~	192.8	6.8
63.0	262.0	40.0	7.6	1.3	0.2	51.0	11.5	7.6	~	~	301.2	916.0	720.0	5.6	512.0	22.4
49.0	204.0	36.4	6.0	1.1	0.2	44.0	9.0	7.0	~	~	285.6	864.0	684.0	5.6	~	~
28.0	372.0	12.9	1.7	~	0.2	9.0	~	0.0	~	~	~	1308.0	1144.0	~	112.0	369.6
24.0	335.0	12.9	2.8	6.7	~	~	~	0.0	~	~	~	1380.0	1196.0	~	100.8	448.0
20.0	235.0	~	6.1	10.7	0.9	217.0	71.0	22.6	~	~	~	~	~	~	504.0	~
24.0	328.0	13.0	3.2	~	~	9.0	~	0.0	~	~	~	1076.0	916.0	~	33.6	156.8
23.0	317.0	10.8	2.8	5.0	~	~	~	4.0	~	~	612.0	1340.0	1212.0	~	67.2	257.6
26.0	351.0	31.7	0.4	4.1	0.3	13.0	2.1	0.0	23.0	0.6	304.8	1060.0	916.0	~	296.8	13.6
28.0	528.0	55.4	0.4	7.9	0.6	14.0	1.3	0.0	231.0	0.7	334.8	1168.0	1008.0	~	748.0	42.4
22.0	287.0	20.7	1.4	2.9	0.3	7.0	0.4	4.0	29.0	0.1	173.6	556.0	472.0	16.0	67.2	772.0
26.0	284.0	22.8	4.2	6.0	0.2	23.0	2.7	0.0	~	0.2	264.4	920.0	760.0	~	78.4	404.0

FOOD	approx amt	Calories	Protein_(g)	Fat_Tot_(g)	Carbohydrt_(g)	Fiber(g)	Sugar_Tot_(g)	Calcium_(mg)	Iron_(mg)
MEAT AND FISH (Continued)									
LAMB,LIVER,COOKED,PAN-FRIED	4 OZ	238.0	25.5	12.7	3.8	0.0	~	9.0	10.2
LOBSTER,NORTHERN,COOKED,MOIST HEAT	4 OZ	89.0	19.0	0.9	0.0	0.0	0.0	96.0	0.3
LOBSTER,NORTHERN,RAW	4 OZ	77.0	16.5	0.8	0.0	0.0	0.0	84.0	0.3
OCEAN PERCH,ATLANTIC,COOKED,DRY HEAT	4 OZ	96.0	18.5	1.9	0.0	0.0	0.0	34.0	0.3
OYSTER,EASTERN,WILD,COOKED,MOIST HEAT	4 OZ	102.0	11.4	3.4	5.5	0.0	1.2	116.0	9.2
OYSTER,EASTERN,WILD,RAW	4 OZ	51.0	5.7	1.7	2.7	0.0	0.6	59.0	4.6
PORK,CURED,BACON,BROILED,PAN-FRIED OR ROASTED	4 OZ	541.0	37.0	41.8	1.4	0.0	0.0	11.0	1.4
PORK,FRESH,BACKRIBS,LN&FAT,ROASTED	4 OZ	292.0	23.0	21.5	0.0	0.0	0.0	46.0	0.9
PORK,CENTER LOIN (CHOPS),BONE-IN,LN&FAT,BROILED	4 OZ	209.0	25.6	11.1	0.0	0.0	0.0	24.0	0.8
PORK,CENTER LOIN (ROASTS),BONE-IN,LEAN,ROASTED	4 OZ	194.0	28.6	8.0	0.0	0.0	0.0	30.0	0.9
PORK,LOIN,COUNTRY-STYLE RIBS,LEAN,BONE-IN,ROASTED	4 OZ	227.0	29.2	11.4	0.0	0.0	0.0	31.0	1.0
PORK SAUSAGE,FRESH,COOKED	4 OZ	339.0	19.4	28.4	0.0	0.0	0.0	13.0	1.4
SALAMI COOKED BEEF	4 OZ	261.0	12.6	22.2	1.9	0.0	1.5	6.0	2.2
SALMON,COHO,WILD,COOKED,MOIST HEAT	4 OZ	184.0	27.4	7.5	0.0	0.0	~	46.0	0.7
SALMON,PINK,CANNED,TOTAL CAN CONTENTS	4 OZ	129.0	19.7	5.0	0.0	0.0	0.0	215.0	0.6
SALMON,PINK,RAW	4 OZ	127.0	20.5	4.4	0.0	0.0	0.0	7.0	0.4
SALMON,SOCKEYE,COOKED,DRY HEAT	4 OZ	169.0	25.4	6.7	0.0	0.0	0.0	12.0	0.5
SARDINE,ATLANTIC,CANNED IN OIL,DRAINED SOLIDS W/BO	4 OZ	208.0	24.6	11.5	0.0	0.0	0.0	382.0	2.9
SCALLOP,MIXED SPECIES,RAW	4 OZ	69.0	12.1	0.5	3.2	0.0	0.0	6.0	0.4
SHRIMP,MIXED SPECIES,COOKED,MOIST HEAT	4 OZ	119.0	22.8	1.7	1.5	0.0	0.0	91.0	0.3
SHRIMP,MIXED SPECIES,RAW	4 OZ	71.0	13.6	1.0	0.9	0.0	0.0	54.0	0.2
TILAPIA,COOKED,DRY HEAT	4 OZ	128.0	26.2	2.7	0.0	0.0	0.0	14.0	0.7
TROUT,RAINBOW,WILD,COOKED,DRY HEAT	4 OZ	150.0	32.9	5.8	0.0	0.0	~	86.0	0.4
TUNA,FRESH,BLUEFIN,COOKED,DRY HEAT	4 OZ	184.0	29.9	6.3	0.0	0.0	~	10.0	1.3
TUNA,FRESH,BLUEFIN,RAW	4 OZ	144.0	23.3	4.9	0.0	0.0	0.0	8.0	1.0
TUNA,LIGHT,CANNED IN H2O,DRAINED	4 OZ	86.0	19.4	1.0	0.0	0.0	0.0	17.0	1.6
TURKEY,BREAST,MEAT ONLY,ROASTED	4 OZ	135.0	30.1	0.7	0.0	0.0	0.0	12.0	1.5
TURKEY,BREAST,MEAT&SKIN,ROASTED	4 OZ	189.0	28.7	7.4	0.0	0.0	~	21.0	1.4
VEAL,GROUND,BROILED	4 OZ	172.0	24.4	7.6	0.0	0.0	0.0	17.0	1.0
FRUIT									
APPLES,RAW,WITH SKIN	1/2 LARGE	52.0	0.3	0.2	13.8	2.4	10.4	6.0	0.1
APPLESAUCE,CANNED,UNSWEETENED,WO/ADDED VIT C	1/2 CUP	42.0	0.2	0.1	11.3	1.1	9.4	4.0	0.2
APRICOTS,RAW	1/2 CUP	48.0	1.4	0.4	11.1	2.0	9.2	13.0	0.4
AVOCADOS,RAW,CALIFORNIA	1 SMALL	167.0	2.0	15.4	8.6	6.8	0.3	13.0	0.6
BANANAS,RAW	1 SMALL	89.0	1.1	0.3	22.8	2.6	12.2	5.0	0.3
BLUEBERRIES,RAW	1/2 CUP	57.0	0.7	0.3	14.5	2.4	10.0	6.0	0.3
CHERRIES,SWEET,RAW	1/2 CUP	63.0	1.1	0.2	16.0	2.1	12.8	13.0	0.4
CRANBERRIES,RAW	1/2 CUP	23.0	0.2	0.1	12.2	2.3	2.0	4.0	0.1
DATES,DEGLET NOOR	1/4 CUP	93.0	0.8	0.1	24.8	2.6	20.9	12.9	0.3
DATES,MEDJOOL	1/4 CUP	91.0	0.6	0.1	24.7	2.2	21.9	21.1	0.3
FIGS,DRIED,UNCOOKED	1/4 CUP	82.0	1.1	0.3	21.1	3.2	15.8	53.5	0.7
GRAPEFRUIT,RAW,PINK&RED,ALL AREAS	1/2 MED	42.0	0.8	0.1	10.7	1.6	6.9	22.0	0.1
GRAPES,RED OR GREEN,RAW	10 GRAPES	34.5	0.4	0.1	9.1	0.5	7.7	5.0	0.2
LEMON JUICE,RAW	1/2 CUP	22.0	0.4	0.2	6.9	0.3	2.5	6.0	0.1
LEMON PEEL,RAW	1 TBSP	3.0	0.1	0.0	1.0	0.6	0.3	8.0	0.1
MANGOS,RAW	1/2 MED	60.0	0.8	0.4	15.0	1.6	13.7	11.0	0.2
MELONS,CANTALOUPE,RAW	1/2 CUP	34.0	0.8	0.2	8.2	0.9	7.9	9.0	0.2
NECTARINES,RAW	1/2 CUP	44.0	1.1	0.3	10.6	1.7	7.9	6.0	0.3
OLIVES,PICKLED,CANNED OR BOTTLED,GREEN	5 OLIVES	20.0	0.1	1.9	0.5	0.4	0.1	6.5	0.1
OLIVES,RIPE,CANNED (SMALL-EXTRA LRG)	5 OLIVES	38.0	0.3	3.5	2.1	1.1	0.0	29.0	1.1
ORANGE PEEL,RAW	1 TBSP	5.8	0.1	0.0	1.5	0.6	0.0	9.7	0.0
ORANGES,RAW,ALL COMMERCIAL VARIETIES	1 SMALL	47.0	0.9	0.1	11.8	2.4	9.4	40.0	0.1
PEACHES,RAW	1/2 CUP	39.0	0.9	0.3	9.5	1.5	8.4	6.0	0.3
PEARS,RAW	1/2 LARGE	57.0	0.4	0.1	15.2	3.1	9.8	9.0	0.2
PINEAPPLE,RAW,ALL VARIETIES	1/2 CUP	50.0	0.5	0.1	13.1	1.4	9.9	13.0	0.3
POMEGRANATES,RAW	1/2 CUP	83.0	1.7	1.2	18.7	4.0	13.7	10.0	0.3
PRUNES,DEHYDRATED (LOW-MOISTURE),UNCOOKED	3/4 CUP	339.0	3.7	0.7	89.1	~	~	72.0	3.5
RAISINS,SEEDLESS	1/4 CUP	98.7	1.0	0.2	26.1	1.2	19.5	16.5	0.6
RASPBERRIES,RAW	3/4 CUP	52.0	1.2	0.7	11.9	6.5	4.4	25.0	0.7
STRAWBERRIES,RAW	1/2 C SLICED	32.0	0.7	0.3	7.7	2.0	4.9	16.0	0.4

128

Magnesium_ (mg)	Potassium_ (mg)	Selenium_ (µg)	Zinc_ (mg)	Niacin_ (mg)	Vit_B6_ (mg)	Folate_Tot_ (µg)	Vit_B12_ (µg)	Vit_C_ (mg)	Vit_D_ (IU)	Vit_E_ (mg)	Tryptophan (mg)	Phenylalanine (mg)	Tyrosine (mg)	Inositol (mg)	tot Omega-3 (mg)	tot Omega-6 (mg)
23.0	352.0	116.1	5.6	16.7	1.0	400.0	85.7	13.0	~	~	331.6	1276.0	1020.0	~	190.4	908.0
43.0	230.0	73.1	4.1	1.8	0.1	11.0	1.4	0.0	1.0	1.0	319.2	968.0	764.0	~	96.4	5.6
38.0	200.0	63.6	3.5	1.6	0.1	10.0	1.3	0.0	1.0	0.9	293.6	888.0	700.0	~	~	~
27.0	226.0	34.6	0.4	1.2	0.1	10.0	1.7	0.0	58.0	0.9	299.2	1044.0	904.0	~	532.0	40.4
35.0	139.0	39.5	78.6	1.9	0.1	14.0	17.5	0.0	2.0	1.7	176.8	564.0	504.0	28.0	1508.0	131.2
18.0	156.0	19.7	39.3	0.9	0.0	7.0	8.8	0.0	1.0	0.9	88.4	283.2	253.2	28.0	752.0	64.8
33.0	565.0	62.0	3.5	11.1	0.3	2.0	1.2	0.0	42.0	0.3	359.6	1704.0	1344.0	25.8	224.0	217.2
17.0	240.0	32.2	3.1	7.6	0.4	0.0	0.7	0.0	48.0	0.3	344.8	1084.0	948.0	~	100.8	2296.0
25.0	344.0	43.6	2.1	8.1	0.7	0.0	0.6	0.0	30.0	0.1	302.4	1208.0	1092.0	15.7	57.2	1340.0
21.0	370.0	45.2	3.7	7.7	0.5	0.0	0.9	0.0	21.0	0.2	392.0	1232.0	1076.0	33.6	22.4	704.0
22.0	390.0	47.6	3.9	7.8	0.5	0.0	0.9	0.0	42.0	0.3	378.4	1188.0	1040.0	~	33.6	1076.0
17.0	294.0	0.0	2.1	6.3	0.3	3.0	1.2	0.7	27.0	0.6	173.6	728.0	628.0	~	154.4	3896.0
13.0	188.0	14.6	1.8	3.2	0.2	2.0	3.1	0.0	48.0	0.2	153.6	604.0	548.0	47.0	424.0	740.0
35.0	455.0	46.2	0.5	7.8	0.6	9.0	4.5	1.0	~	~	342.8	1196.0	1036.0	~	2092.0	291.2
30.0	344.0	33.2	0.8	6.5	0.3	15.0	4.4	0.0	547.0	0.6	248.8	864.0	748.0	~	1968.0	64.8
27.0	366.0	31.4	0.4	8.0	0.6	4.0	4.2	0.0	435.0	0.4	249.6	872.0	752.0	~	1272.0	56.0
36.0	408.0	36.5	0.5	9.7	0.7	9.0	5.7	0.0	526.0	1.1	342.8	1196.0	1032.0	~	1596.0	126.4
39.0	397.0	52.7	1.3	5.2	0.2	10.0	8.9	0.0	193.0	2.0	309.2	1076.0	932.0	13.4	1656.0	3968.0
22.0	205.0	12.8	0.9	0.7	0.1	16.0	1.4	0.0	1.0	0.0	210.4	672.0	600.0	~	240.8	4.4
37.0	170.0	49.5	1.6	2.7	0.2	24.0	1.7	0.0	4.0	2.2	326.0	988.0	780.0	7.8	388.8	23.6
22.0	113.0	29.6	1.0	1.8	0.0	19.0	1.1	0.0	2.0	1.3	316.8	960.0	756.0	7.8	604.0	31.2
34.0	380.0	54.4	0.4	4.7	0.1	6.0	1.9	0.0	150.0	0.8	296.8	1176.0	976.0	~	268.8	336.0
31.0	448.0	13.2	0.5	5.8	0.3	19.0	6.3	2.0	~	~	288.0	1004.0	868.0	12.3	1316.0	322.4
64.0	323.0	46.8	0.8	10.5	0.5	2.0	10.9	0.0	~	~	375.2	1308.0	1132.0	~	1864.0	76.0
50.0	252.0	36.5	0.6	8.7	0.5	2.0	9.4	0.0	227.0	1.0	292.4	1020.0	880.0	~	1452.0	59.2
23.0	179.0	70.6	0.7	10.1	0.3	4.0	2.6	0.0	47.0	0.3	320.4	1116.0	964.0	16.8	314.8	10.0
29.0	292.0	32.1	1.7	7.5	0.6	6.0	0.4	0.0	8.0	0.1	383.2	1336.0	1332.0	9.0	22.4	145.6
27.0	288.0	29.1	2.0	6.4	0.5	6.0	0.4	0.0	~	~	356.0	1260.0	1228.0	25.8	156.8	1624.0
24.0	337.0	13.7	3.9	8.0	0.4	11.0	1.3	0.0	0.0	0.2	276.8	1100.0	872.0	~	56.0	472.0
5.0	107.0	0.0	0.0	0.1	0.0	3.0	0.0	4.6	0.0	0.2	1.1	6.7	1.1	~	10.1	48.0
3.0	74.0	0.3	0.0	0.1	0.0	3.0	0.0	1.0	0.0	0.2	2.5	6.1	3.7	22.0	3.7	14.7
10.0	259.0	0.1	0.2	0.6	0.1	9.0	0.0	10.0	0.0	0.9	14.8	51.5	28.7	51.5	~	76.2
29.0	507.0	0.4	0.7	1.9	0.3	89.0	0.0	8.8	0.0	2.0	34.0	310.0	65.3	62.6	150.0	2298.0
27.0	358.0	1.0	0.2	0.7	0.0	20.0	0.0	8.7	0.0	0.1	9.1	49.5	9.1	~	27.3	46.5
6.0	77.0	0.1	0.2	0.4	0.1	6.0	0.0	9.7	0.0	0.6	2.2	19.3	6.7	~	42.9	65.0
11.0	222.0	0.0	0.1	0.2	0.0	4.0	0.0	7.0	0.0	0.1	9.0	24.1	14.0	14.0	26.0	27.0
3.0	42.0	0.1	0.1	0.1	0.1	1.0	0.0	13.3	0.0	1.2	1.5	18.0	16.0	7.5	11.0	16.5
14.2	216.5	1.0	0.1	0.4	0.1	6.3	0.0	0.1	0.0	0.0	4.4	18.4	5.5	55.9	1.1	5.9
17.8	229.7	0.2	0.5	0.5	0.1	5.0	~	0.0	0.0	0.0	2.3	15.7	5.3	65.4	~	~
22.4	224.4	0.0	0.2	0.2	0.0	3.0	0.0	0.4	0.0	11.5	7.5	28.3	15.3	33.9	~	128.5
9.0	135.0	0.1	0.1	0.2	0.1	13.0	0.0	31.2	0.0	0.1	9.8	56.6	9.8	244.8	9.8	35.7
3.5	95.5	0.0	0.1	0.1	0.0	1.0	0.0	1.6	0.0	0.1	5.4	9.3	4.9	7.8	5.4	18.1
6.0	103.0	0.1	0.1	0.1	0.0	20.0	0.0	38.7	0.0	0.2	~	~	~	36.6	0.0	0.0
0.9	9.6	0.0	0.0	0.0	0.0	0.8	0.0	7.7	0.0	0.0	~	~	~	2.0	1.6	3.8
10.0	168.0	0.6	0.1	0.7	0.1	43.0	0.0	36.4	0.0	0.9	8.3	17.6	10.4	102.5	38.3	14.5
12.0	267.0	0.4	0.2	0.7	0.1	21.0	0.0	36.7	0.0	0.1	1.8	20.4	12.4	~	40.7	31.0
9.0	201.0	0.0	0.2	1.1	0.0	5.0	0.0	5.4	0.0	0.8	3.6	7.9	5.0	84.4	1.5	79.5
1.4	5.3	0.1	0.0	0.0	0.0	0.4	0.0	0.0	0.0	0.5	~	~	~	0.6	11.5	152.0
1.3	2.6	0.3	0.1	0.0	0.0	0.0	0.0	0.3	0.0	0.5	~	9.1	7.6	3.0	20.5	273.6
1.3	12.7	0.1	0.0	0.1	0.0	1.8	0.0	8.2	0.0	0.0	~	~	~	~	0.7	1.7
10.0	181.0	0.5	0.1	0.3	0.1	30.0	0.0	53.2	0.0	0.2	9.6	34.2	17.5	244.1	12.7	35.0
9.0	190.0	0.1	0.2	0.8	0.0	4.0	0.0	6.6	0.0	0.7	7.7	14.7	10.8	~	1.6	64.5
7.0	116.0	0.1	0.1	0.2	0.0	7.0	0.0	4.3	0.0	0.1	2.3	12.7	2.3	84.0	~	33.4
12.0	109.0	0.1	0.1	0.5	0.1	18.0	0.0	47.8	0.0	0.0	4.2	17.4	15.7	27.2	14.1	19.0
12.0	236.0	0.5	0.4	0.3	0.1	38.0	0.0	10.2	0.0	0.6	~	~	~	~	~	68.7
64.0	1058.0	~	0.8	3.0	0.7	2.0	0.0	0.0	0.0	~	~	~	~	465.3	~	157.5
10.6	247.2	0.2	0.1	0.3	0.1	1.7	0.0	0.0	0.0	0.0	18.1	50.8	4.4	14.5	2.6	10.5
22.0	151.0	0.2	0.4	0.6	0.1	21.0	0.0	26.2	0.0	0.9	~	~	~	~	116.3	229.5
13.0	153.0	0.4	0.1	0.4	0.0	24.0	0.0	58.8	0.0	0.3	6.7	15.8	18.3	10 8	54.0	74.5

FOOD	approx amt	Calories	Protein_(g)	Fat_Tot_(g)	Carbohydrt_(g)	Fiber(g)	Sugar_Tot_(g)	Calcium_(mg)	Iron_(mg)
FRUIT (Continued)									
VINEGAR,APPLE CIDER	1 TBSP	3.0	0.0	0.0	0.1	0.0	0.1	1.0	0.0
VINEGAR,BALSAMIC	1 TBSP	14.0	0.1	0.0	2.7	0.0	2.4	4.3	0.1
WATERMELON,RAW	3/4 CUP	30.0	0.6	0.2	7.6	0.4	6.2	7.0	0.2
VEGETABLES									
ALFALFA SEEDS,SPROUTED,RAW	1 CUP	8.0	1.3	0.2	0.7	0.6	0.1	10.6	0.3
ARROWROOT FLOUR	1 CUP	357.0	0.3	0.1	88.2	3.4	~	40.0	0.3
ARROWROOT,RAW	1 ROOT	21.0	1.4	0.1	4.4	0.4	0.0	2.0	0.7
ARTICHOKES,(GLOBE OR FRENCH),RAW	1 SMALL	47.0	3.3	0.2	10.5	5.4	1.0	44.0	1.3
ARUGULA,RAW	1 CUP	2.5	0.3	0.1	0.4	0.2	0.2	16.0	0.1
ASPARAGUS,RAW	1 CUP	20.0	2.2	0.1	3.9	2.1	1.9	24.0	2.1
ASPARAGUS,COOKED,BOILED,DRAINED	1/2 CUP	22.0	2.4	0.2	4.1	2.0	1.3	23.0	0.9
BEANS,SNAP,GREEN,RAW	1 CUP	31.0	1.8	0.2	7.0	2.7	3.3	37.0	1.0
BEANS,SNAP,GREEN,MICROWAVED	1 CUP	39.0	2.3	0.5	6.4	3.4	3.2	55.0	0.8
BEETS,COOKED,BOILED,DRAINED	2 MEDIUM	44.0	1.7	0.2	10.0	2.0	8.0	16.0	0.8
BEET GREENS,RAW	1 CUP	8.0	0.7	0.0	1.4	1.2	0.2	38.6	0.8
BEET GREENS,COOKED,BOILED,DRAINED	3/4 CUP	27.0	2.6	0.2	5.5	2.9	0.6	114.0	1.9
BROCCOLI,RAW	1 CUP	34.0	2.8	0.4	6.6	2.6	1.7	47.0	0.7
BROCCOLI,COOKED,BOILED,DRAINED	1/2 CUP	35.0	2.4	0.4	7.2	3.3	1.4	40.0	0.7
BRUSSELS SPROUTS,COOKED,BOILED,DRAINED	3/4 CUP	36.0	2.6	0.5	7.1	2.6	1.7	36.0	1.2
CABBAGE,RAW	1 CUP	25.0	1.3	0.1	5.8	2.5	3.2	40.0	0.5
CABBAGE,COOKED,BOILED,DRAINED	3/4 CUP	23.0	1.3	0.1	5.5	1.9	2.8	48.0	0.2
CABBAGE,RED,RAW	1 CUP	31.0	1.4	0.2	7.4	2.1	3.8	45.0	0.8
CABBAGE,RED,COOKED,BOILED,DRAINED	1/2 CUP	29.0	1.5	0.1	6.9	2.6	3.3	42.0	0.7
CARROTS,RAW	3/4 CUP	41.0	0.9	0.2	9.6	2.8	4.7	33.0	0.3
CARROTS,COOKED,BOILED,DRAINED	3/4 CUP	35.0	0.8	0.2	8.2	3.0	3.5	30.0	0.3
CAULIFLOWER,RAW	1 CUP	25.0	1.9	0.3	5.0	2.0	1.9	22.0	0.4
CAULIFLOWER,COOKED,BOILED,DRAINED	1 CUP	23.0	1.8	0.5	4.1	2.3	2.1	16.0	0.3
CELERY,RAW	1 CUP	16.0	0.7	0.2	3.0	1.6	1.8	40.0	0.2
CHARD,SWISS,RAW	1 CUP	6.0	0.6	0.1	1.2	0.5	0.4	16.8	0.6
CHARD,SWISS,COOKED,BOILED,DRAINED	1/2 CUP	20.0	1.9	0.1	4.1	2.1	1.1	58.0	2.3
CHIVES,RAW	1 TBSP	1.0	0.1	0.0	0.1	0.1	0.1	3.1	0.1
COLLARDS,RAW	1 CUP	11.0	1.0	0.2	1.8	1.3	0.2	76.6	0.2
COLLARDS,COOKED,BOILED,DRAINED	1/2 CUP	33.0	2.7	0.7	5.7	4.0	0.4	141.0	1.1
CORN,SWEET,YELLOW,RAW	1 EAR MED	86.0	3.3	1.4	18.7	2.0	6.3	2.0	0.5
CORN,SWEET,YELLOW,FROZEN,ON COB,BOILED,DRAINED	1 EAR MED	94.0	3.1	0.7	22.3	2.8	3.6	3.0	0.6
CUCUMBER,WITH PEEL,RAW	1/3 CUKE	15.0	0.7	0.1	3.6	0.5	1.7	16.0	0.3
DANDELION GREENS,RAW	1 CUP	45.0	2.7	0.7	9.2	3.5	0.7	187.0	3.1
DANDELION GREENS,COOKED,BOILED,DRAINED	1 CUP	33.0	2.0	0.6	6.4	2.9	0.5	140.0	1.8
EDAMAME,FROZEN,PREPARED	2/3 CUP	122.0	10.9	5.2	9.9	5.2	2.2	63.0	2.3
EGGPLANT,COOKED,BOILED,DRAINED	1 CUP	35.0	0.8	0.2	8.7	2.5	3.2	6.0	0.3
FIDDLEHEAD FERNS,RAW	1 CUP	34.0	4.6	0.4	5.5	~	~	32.0	1.3
GARLIC,RAW	1 tsp/1 CLVE	4.0	0.2	0.0	1.0	0.1	0.0	5.4	0.1
GINGER ROOT,RAW	1 tsp	2.0	0.1	0.0	0.5	0.1	0.1	0.5	0.0
JERUSALEM-ARTICHOKES,RAW	3/4 CUP	73.0	2.0	0.0	17.4	1.6	9.6	14.0	3.4
KALE,RAW	1 CUP	33.0	2.9	0.6	5.9	0.0	0.0	100.5	1.0
KALE,COOKED,BOILED,DRAINED	3/4 CUP	28.0	1.9	0.4	5.6	2.0	1.3	72.0	0.9
LAMBSQUARTERS,RAW	3/4 CUP	43.0	4.2	0.8	7.3	4.0	~	309.0	1.2
LAMBSQUARTERS,COOKED,BOILED,DRAINED	1/2 CUP	32.0	3.2	0.7	5.0	2.1	0.6	258.0	0.7
LEEKS,(BULB&LOWER LEAF-PORTION),BOILED,DRAINED	1 LEEK	31.0	0.8	0.2	7.6	1.0	2.1	30.0	1.1
LETTUCE,GREEN LEAF,RAW	1 CUP	5.0	0.4	0.0	0.9	0.4	0.3	11.9	0.3
LETTUCE,ICEBERG (INCL CRISPHEAD TYPES),RAW	2 CUPS	14.0	0.9	0.1	3.0	1.2	2.0	18.0	0.4
LETTUCE,RED LEAF,RAW	1 CUP	4.0	0.3	0.1	0.6	0.2	0.1	8.3	0.3
LETTUCE, ROMAINE,RAW	2 CUPS	17.0	1.2	0.3	3.3	2.1	1.2	33.0	1.0
MUNG BNS,MATURE SEEDS,SPROUTED,RAW	1 CUP	30.0	3.0	0.2	5.9	1.8	4.1	13.0	0.9
MUSHROOMS,PORTABELLA,EXPOSED TO UV LIGHT,RAW	1 CUP	22.0	2.1	0.4	3.9	1.3	2.5	3.0	0.3
MUSHROOMS,PORTABELLA,GRILLED	3/4 CUP	29.0	3.3	0.6	4.4	2.2	2.3	3.0	0.4
MUSHROOMS,WHITE,RAW	1 C WHOLE	22.0	3.1	0.3	3.3	1.0	2.0	3.0	0.5
MUSTARD GREENS,RAW	2 CUPS	27.0	2.9	0.4	4.7	3.2	1.3	115.0	1.6
MUSTARD GREENS,BOILED,DRAINED	3/4 CUP	26.0	2.6	0.5	4.5	2.0	1.4	118.0	0.9

130

Magnesium_(mg)	Potassium_(mg)	Selenium_(µg)	Zinc_(mg)	Niacin_(mg)	Vit_B6_(mg)	Folate_Tot_(µg)	Vit_B12_(µg)	Vit_C_(mg)	Vit_D_(IU)	Vit_E_(mg)	Tryptophan_(mg)	Phenylalanine_(mg)	Tyrosine_(mg)	Inositol_(mg)	tot_Omega-3_(mg)	tot_Omega-6_(mg)
0.7	10.2	0.0	0.0	0.0	0.0	0.0	0.0	0.0	0.0	0.0	0.0	0.0	0.0	~	0.0	0.0
1.9	17.9	0.0	0.0	0.0	0.0	0.0	0.0	0.0	0.0	0.0	~	~	~	~	0.0	0.0
10.0	112.0	0.4	0.1	0.2	0.0	3.0	0.0	8.1	0.0	0.1	8.1	17.3	13.9	35.8	~	57.8
8.9	26.1	0.2	0.3	0.2	0.0	11.9	0.0	2.7	0.0	0.0	~	~	~	~	57.8	77.2
3.0	11.0	~	0.1	0.0	0.0	7.0	0.0	0.0	0.0		5.1	15.4	11.5	~	11.5	46.1
8.3	149.8	0.2	0.2	0.6	0.1	111.5	0.0	0.6	0.0	0.0	~	~	~	~	5.9	24.4
60.0	370.0	0.2	0.5	1.0	0.1	68.0	0.0	11.7	0.0	0.2	~	~	~	59.9	17.0	45.9
4.7	36.9	0.0	0.0	0.0	0.0	9.7	0.0	1.5	0.0	0.0	~	~	~	~	34.0	26.0
14.0	202.0	2.3	0.5	1.0	0.1	52.0	0.0	5.6	0.0	1.1	36.2	100.0	69.7	38.9	13.4	53.6
14.0	224.0	6.1	0.6	1.1	0.1	149.0	0.0	7.7	0.0	1.5	26.1	73.8	51.3	25.2	26.1	68.4
25.0	211.0	0.6	0.2	0.7	0.1	33.0	0.0	12.2	0.0	0.4	20.9	73.7	46.2	192.5	39.6	25.3
28.0	323.0	~	0.4	0.8	0.1	47.0	~	7.3	~	~	21.1	73.3	46.6	192.5	73.3	45.5
23.0	305.0	0.7	0.4	0.3	0.1	80.0	0.0	3.6	0.0	0.0	35.0	58.0	52.0	16.0	4.0	41.0
23.1	251.5	0.3	0.1	0.1	0.0	5.0	0.0	9.9	0.0	0.5	5.1	8.4	7.5	~	0.6	5.9
68.0	909.0	0.9	0.5	0.5	0.1	14.0	0.0	24.9	0.0	1.8	43.2	73.4	65.9	~	6.5	70.2
21.0	316.0	2.5	0.4	0.6	0.2	63.0	0.0	89.2	0.0	0.8	30.0	106.0	45.5	27.3	19.1	15.5
21.0	293.0	1.6	0.5	0.6	0.2	108.0	0.0	64.9	0.0	1.5	26.5	90.5	46.8	9.4	92.8	39.8
20.0	317.0	1.5	0.3	0.6	0.2	60.0	0.0	62.0	0.0	0.4	32.7	86.6	~	94.8	202.5	92.4
12.0	170.0	0.3	0.2	0.2	0.1	43.0	0.0	36.6	0.0	0.2	9.8	28.5	16.9	18.7	~	15.1
15.0	196.0	0.6	0.2	0.2	0.1	30.0	0.0	37.5	0.0	0.1	12.5	36.0	21.3	~	15.8	10.1
16.0	243.0	0.6	0.2	0.4	0.2	18.0	0.0	57.0	0.0	0.1	10.7	32.0	19.6	8.0	40.0	30.3
17.0	262.0	2.3	0.3	0.4	0.2	24.0	0.0	34.4	0.0	0.1	9.8	28.5	17.3	~	18.0	14.2
12.0	320.0	0.1	0.2	1.0	0.1	19.0	0.0	5.9	0.0	0.7	~	~	~	11.5	2.0	110.3
10.0	235.0	0.7	0.2	0.6	0.2	14.0	0.0	3.6	0.0	1.0	~	~	~	~	1.2	101.9
15.0	299.0	0.6	0.3	0.5	0.2	57.0	0.0	48.2	0.0	0.1	26.0	71.0	43.0	18.0	37.0	11.0
9.0	142.0	0.6	0.2	0.4	0.2	44.0	0.0	44.3	0.0	0.1	29.8	81.8	49.6	~	208.0	62.0
11.0	260.0	0.4	0.1	0.3	0.1	36.0	0.0	3.1	0.0	0.3	9.1	20.2	9.1	5.1	~	79.8
26.7	125.1	0.3	0.1	0.1	0.0	4.6	0.0	9.9	0.0	0.6	6.1	39.6	~	~	2.5	22.7
86.0	549.0	0.9	0.3	0.4	0.1	9.0	0.0	18.0	0.0	1.9	15.8	100.0	~	~	2.7	21.9
1.4	9.9	0.0	0.0	0.0	0.0	3.5	0.0	1.9	0.0	0.0	1.1	3.2	2.8	~	0.4	7.6
8.9	70.3	0.4	0.1	0.2	0.1	42.6	0.0	11.6	0.0	0.7	11.2	31.3	23.8	23.0	38.9	29.5
21.0	117.0	0.5	0.2	0.6	0.1	16.0	0.0	18.2	0.0	0.9	25.7	71.0	53.0	4.3	88.5	66.5
37.0	270.0	0.6	0.5	1.8	0.0	42.0	0.0	6.8	0.0	0.1	20.7	135.0	111.0	~	14.4	488.0
29.0	251.0	0.7	0.6	1.5	0.2	31.0	0.0	4.8	0.0	0.1	13.9	91.3	75.0	6.9	6.3	213.0
13.0	147.0	0.3	0.2	0.1	0.0	7.0	0.0	2.8	0.0	0.0	5.0	19.1	11.0	15.0	5.0	28.1
36.0	397.0	0.5	0.4	0.8	0.3	27.0	0.0	35.0	0.0	3.4	~	~	~	~	24.2	144.0
24.0	232.0	0.3	0.3	0.5	0.2	13.0	0.0	18.0	0.0	2.4	~	~	~	~	39.9	235.0
64.0	436.0	~	1.4	0.9	0.1	311.0	~	6.1	~	0.7	130.0	504.0	347.3	~	373.3	1854.0
11.0	123.0	0.1	0.1	0.6	0.1	14.0	0.0	1.3	0.0	0.4	7.9	34.7	21.8	83.2	14.8	77.2
34.0	370.0	~	0.8	5.0	~	~	0.0	26.6	0.0	~	~	~	~	~	~	~
0.8	12.0	0.4	0.0	0.0	0.0	0.1	0.0	0.9	0.0	0.0	1.8	5.0	2.2	~	0.6	6.3
1.3	12.5	0.0	0.0	0.0	0.0	0.3	0.0	0.2	0.0	0.0	0.2	0.9	0.4	~	0.7	2.4
17.0	429.0	0.7	0.1	1.3	0.1	13.0	0.0	4.0	0.0	0.2	~	~	~	~	~	1.1
31.5	329.0	0.6	0.4	0.7	0.2	20.8	0.0	80.4	0.0	0.0	26.8	113.0	78.4	~	121.0	92.4
18.0	228.0	0.9	0.2	0.5	0.1	13.0	0.0	41.0	0.0	0.9	22.4	94.5	65.3	~	100.5	77.3
34.0	452.0	0.9	0.4	1.2	0.3	30.0	0.0	80.0	0.0	~	38.0	166.0	175.0	~	36.0	313.0
23.0	288.0	0.9	0.3	0.9	0.2	14.0	0.0	37.0	0.0	1.9	26.1	113.5	120.5	~	28.8	246.5
14.0	87.0	0.5	0.1	0.2	0.1	24.0	0.0	4.2	0.0	0.5	7.4	37.2	27.3	~	81.8	55.8
4.3	64.0	0.2	0.1	0.1	0.0	12.5	0.0	3.0	0.0	0.1	3.2	19.8	11.5	~	20.9	8.6
7.0	141.0	0.1	0.2	0.1	0.0	29.0	0.0	2.8	0.0	0.2	13.0	33.2	10.0	~	74.8	30.2
3.0	46.8	0.4	0.1	0.1	0.0	9.0	0.0	0.9	0.0	0.0	6.2	18.8	8.1	6.2	~	~
14.0	247.0	0.4	0.2	0.3	0.1	136.0	0.0	4.0	0.0	0.1	9.4	61.2	23.4	16.0	106.2	44.2
21.0	149.0	0.6	0.4	0.7	0.1	61.0	0.0	13.2	0.0	0.1	38.5	122.0	54.1	~	16.6	43.7
10.0	364.0	18.6	0.5	4.5	0.0	28.0	0.1	0.0	446.0	0.0	26.7	47.3	37.0	~	0.9	64.5
13.0	437.0	21.9	0.7	6.3	0.1	19.0	0.0	0.0	14.0	0.0	45.4	82.5	64.4	~	~	181.5
9.0	318.0	9.3	0.5	3.6	0.1	17.0	0.0	2.1	7.0	0.0	33.6	81.6	42.2	8.6	~	133.0
32.0	384.0	0.9	0.3	0.8	0.2	12.0	0.0	70.0	0.0	2.0	33.6	80.6	160.2	25.8	20.2	22.4
13.0	162.0	0.6	0.2	0.4	0.1	9.0	0.0	25.3	0.0	1.8	26.3	63.0	125.3	9.5	23.1	25.2

FOOD	approx amt	Calories	Protein_(g)	Fat_Tot_(g)	Carbohydrt_(g)	Fiber(g)	Sugar_Tot_(g)	Calcium_(mg)	Iron_(mg)
VEGETABLES (Continued)									
ONIONS,RAW	1 MED	40.0	1.1	0.1	9.3	1.7	4.2	23.0	0.2
PARSLEY,FRESH	1 TBSP	1.0	0.1	0.0	0.2	0.1	0.0	3.8	0.2
PEAS,EDIBLE-PODDED,RAW	1 CUP	42.0	2.8	0.2	7.6	2.6	4.0	43.0	2.1
PEAS,GREEN,COOKED,BOILED,DRAINED	1/2 CUP	84.0	5.4	0.2	15.6	5.9	5.9	27.0	1.5
PEPPERS,SWEET,GREEN,RAW	1 MED	20.0	0.9	0.2	4.6	1.7	2.4	10.0	0.3
PEPPERS,SWEET,GREEN,BOILED,DRAINED	3/4 CUP	28.0	0.9	0.2	6.7	1.2	3.2	9.0	0.5
PEPPERS,SWEET,YELLOW,RAW	1/2 LARGE	27.0	1.0	0.2	6.3	0.9	~	11.0	0.5
POTATOES,RUSSET,FLESH & SKIN,BAKED	1/3 LARGE	97.0	2.6	0.1	21.4	2.3	1.1	18.0	1.1
POTATOES,RED,FLESH & SKIN,BAKED	1/3 LARGE	89.0	2.3	0.2	19.6	1.8	1.4	9.0	0.7
PUMPKIN FLOWERS,RAW	1 CUP	5.0	0.3	0.0	1.1	0.0	0.0	12.9	0.2
PUMPKIN FLOWERS,COOKED,BOILED,DRAINED	3/4 CUP	15.0	1.1	0.1	3.3	0.9	2.4	37.0	0.9
PUMPKIN,COOKED,BOILED,DRAINED	1/2 CUP	20.0	0.7	0.1	4.9	1.1	2.1	15.0	0.6
RADICCHIO,RAW	1 CUP	8.0	0.5	0.1	1.5	0.3	0.2	6.3	0.2
RUTABAGAS,RAW	1/2 SMALL	37.0	1.1	0.2	8.6	2.3	4.5	43.0	0.4
RUTABAGAS,COOKED,BOILED,DRAINED	1/2 CUP	30.0	0.9	0.2	6.8	1.8	4.0	18.0	0.2
SEAWEED,AGAR,RAW	2 TBSP	3.0	0.1	0.0	0.8	0.1	0.0	6.8	0.2
SEAWEED,KELP,RAW	2 TBSP	4.0	0.2	0.1	1.0	0.1	0.1	16.8	0.3
SPINACH,RAW	1 CUP	7.0	0.9	0.1	1.2	0.7	0.1	32.7	0.9
SPINACH,COOKED,BOILED,DRAINED	1/2 CUP	23.0	3.0	0.3	3.8	2.4	0.4	136.0	3.6
SQUASH,SUMMER,YELLOW,BOILED,DRAINED	1/2 CUP	23.0	1.0	0.4	3.8	1.1	2.5	22.0	0.4
SQUASH,ZUCCHINI,INCL SKIN,COOKED,BOILED,DRAINED	1/2 CUP	15.0	1.1	0.4	2.7	1.0	1.7	18.0	0.4
SQUASH,WINTER,ACORN,COOKED,BAKED	1/2 CUP	56.0	1.1	0.1	14.6	4.4	~	44.0	0.9
SQUASH,WINTER,BUTTERNUT,COOKED,BAKED	1/2 CUP	40.0	0.9	0.1	10.5	3.2	2.0	41.0	0.6
SQUASH,WINTER,SPAGHETTI,BOILED,DRAINED,OR BAKED	1/2 CUP	27.0	0.7	0.3	6.5	1.4	2.5	21.0	0.3
SWEET POTATO,COOKED,BAKED IN SKIN	1 MED	90.0	2.0	0.2	20.7	3.3	6.5	38.0	0.7
TOMATOES,RED,RIPE,RAW,YEAR ROUND AVERAGE	1 MED	18.0	0.9	0.2	3.9	1.2	2.6	10.0	0.3
TOMATOES,RED,RIPE,COOKED	1/2 CUP	18.0	1.0	0.1	4.0	0.7	2.5	11.0	0.7
TOMATOES,SUN-DRIED	1/2 CUP	70.0	3.8	0.8	15.1	3.3	10.1	29.8	2.5
TURNIPS,RAW	3/4 CUP	28.0	0.9	0.1	6.4	1.8	3.8	30.0	0.3
TURNIPS,COOKED,BOILED,DRAINED	1/2 CUP	22.0	0.7	0.1	5.1	2.0	3.0	33.0	0.2
TURNIP GREENS,RAW	2 CUPS	32.0	1.5	0.3	7.1	3.2	0.8	190.0	1.1
TURNIP GREENS,COOKED,BOILED,DRAINED	1 CUP	20.0	1.1	0.2	4.4	3.5	0.5	137.0	0.8
WATERCRESS,RAW	1 CUP	4.0	0.8	0.0	0.4	0.2	0.1	39.6	0.1
NUTS AND SEEDS									
ALMONDS	23 ALMNDS	164.0	6.1	14.1	6.2	3.5	1.1	75.4	1.1
ALMOND BUTTER,PLAIN,WO/SALT	1 TBSP	98.0	3.4	8.9	3.0	1.6	0.7	55.5	0.6
ALMONDS,DRY ROASTED,WO/SALT	23 ALMNDS	167.0	6.0	15.0	6.0	3.0	1.4	75.0	1.1
BRAZILNUTS,DRIED,UNBLANCHED	6 NUTS	184.0	4.0	18.6	3.4	2.1	0.7	44.8	0.7
CASHEW NUTS,DRY ROASTED,WO/SALT	1 OZ	160.0	4.3	13.0	9.0	0.8	1.4	12.6	1.7
CASHEW NUTS,RAW	1 OZ	155.0	5.0	12.2	8.5	0.9	1.6	10.4	1.9
CHIA SEEDS,DRIED	1 TBSP	49.0	1.6	3.0	4.2	3.4	0.0	63.1	0.8
COCONUT MEAT,DRIED (DESICCATED),UNSWEETENED	1/4 CUP	46.0	0.5	4.5	1.6	1.1	0.5	1.8	0.2
COCONUT MEAT,RAW	1C SHRED	283.0	2.6	26.7	12.2	7.2	5.0	11.2	1.9
COCONUT MILK,CANNED	1/2 CUP	223.0	2.3	24.0	3.2	0.0	0.0	20.3	3.7
FLAXSEED	1 TBSP	54.0	1.8	4.2	2.9	2.7	0.2	25.5	0.6
HAZELNUTS OR FILBERTS	10 NUTS	88.0	2.0	8.5	2.3	1.4	0.6	16.0	0.7
MACADAMIA NUTS,RAW	10-12 NUTS	201.0	2.2	21.2	3.9	2.4	1.3	23.8	1.0
MIXED NUTS,DRY ROASTED,W/PEANUTS	3/4 CUP	594.0	17.3	51.5	25.4	9.0	~	70.0	3.7
PEANUTS,ALL TYPES,DRY-ROASTED	3/4 CUP	585.0	23.7	49.7	21.5	8.0	4.2	54.0	2.3
PEANUTS,ALL TYPES,RAW*	3/4 CUP	567.0	25.8	49.2	16.1	8.5	4.0	92.0	4.6
PEANUT BUTTER,SMOOTH STYLE	2 TBSP	194.0	8.3	16.6	6.5	2.0	3.0	14.2	0.6
PECANS	19 HALVES	194.0	2.6	20.2	3.9	2.7	1.1	19.6	0.7
PINE NUTS,DRIED	1/4 CUP	222.0	4.5	22.6	4.3	1.2	1.2	5.3	1.8
PISTACHIO NUTS,DRY ROASTED	1/4 CUP	176.0	6.5	13.9	9.1	3.1	2.4	33.2	1.2
PUMPKIN&SQUASH SEED KERNELS,ROASTED	1/4 CUP	166.0	8.7	14.2	4.3	1.9	0.4	15.1	2.3
SESAME SEEDS,WHOLE,DRIED	1 TBSP	52.0	1.6	4.5	2.1	1.1	0.0	87.8	1.3
SUNFLOWER SEED KERNELS,TOASTED	1/4 CUP	204.0	5.7	18.7	6.8	3.8	0.0	18.8	2.2
WALNUTS,ENGLISH	14 HALVES	183.0	4.3	18.3	3.8	1.9	0.7	27.4	0.8

*peanuts are a legume but listed here as they are commonly thought of as a nut

132

Magnesium_ (mg)	Potassium_ (mg)	Selenium_ (µg)	Zinc_ (mg)	Niacin_ (mg)	Vit_B6_ (mg)	Folate_Tot_ (µg)	Vit_B12_ (µg)	Vit_C_ (mg)	Vit_D_ (IU)	Vit_E_ (mg)	Tryptophan (mg)	Phenylalanine (mg)	Tyrosine (mg)	Inositol (mg)	tot Omega-3 (mg)	tot Omega-6 (mg)
10.0	146.0	0.5	0.2	0.1	0.1	19.0	0.0	7.4	0.0	0.0	15.4	27.5	15.4	~	4.4	14.3
1.3	15.3	0.0	0.0	0.0	0.0	4.2	0.0	3.7	0.0	0.0	1.7	5.4	3.1	0.9	0.3	4.3
24.0	200.0	0.7	0.3	0.6	0.2	42.0	0.0	60.0	0.0	0.4	26.5	88.2	97.0	~	12.7	73.5
39.0	271.0	1.9	1.2	2.0	0.2	63.0	0.0	14.2	0.0	0.1	29.6	158.5	89.5	60.8	15.2	65.5
10.0	175.0	0.0	0.1	0.5	0.2	10.0	0.0	80.4	0.0	0.4	14.3	109.0	14.3	~	9.5	64.3
10.0	166.0	0.3	0.1	0.5	0.2	16.0	0.0	74.4	0.0	0.5	12.2	29.3	19.2	~	10.1	97.5
12.0	212.0	0.3	0.2	0.9	0.2	26.0	0.0	183.5	0.0	~	12.1	28.9	19.6	~	~	~
30.0	550.0	0.5	0.4	1.3	0.4	26.0	0.0	8.3	0.0	0.1	24.9	174.3	69.7	~	10.0	31.9
28.0	545.0	~	0.4	1.6	0.2	27.0	0.0	12.6	0.0	0.1	23.9	160.3	61.7	~	10.0	31.9
7.9	57.1	0.2	0.0	0.2	0.0	19.5	0.0	9.2	0.0	0.0	~	~	~	~	0.7	0.7
25.0	106.0	0.7	0.1	0.3	0.1	41.0	0.0	5.0	0.0	0.0	~	~	~	~	2.0	2.0
9.0	230.0	0.2	0.2	0.4	0.0	9.0	0.0	4.7	0.0	0.8	11.0	28.2	36.8	76.0	2.5	2.5
4.3	99.7	0.3	0.2	0.1	0.0	19.8	0.0	2.6	0.0	0.7	10.4	13.6	~	~	6.4	37.2
20.0	305.0	0.7	0.2	0.7	0.1	21.0	0.0	25.0	0.0	0.3	12.5	29.8	22.1	23.0	51.0	33.6
10.0	216.0	0.7	0.1	0.7	0.1	15.0	0.0	18.8	0.0	0.2	11.9	28.9	21.3	214.2	48.5	32.3
8.4	28.3	0.1	0.1	0.0	0.0	10.6	0.0	0.0	0.0	0.1	~	~	~	~	0.8	~
12.1	8.9	0.1	0.1	0.0	0.0	18.0	0.0	0.3	0.0	0.1	4.8	4.3	2.6	~	0.8	2.0
26.1	184.1	0.3	0.2	0.2	0.0	64.0	0.0	9.3	0.0	0.7	11.7	38.7	32.4	2.4	41.4	7.8
87.0	466.0	1.5	0.8	0.5	0.2	146.0	0.0	9.8	0.0	2.1	36.0	120.5	101.5	22.5	83.0	15.3
16.0	177.0	0.2	0.2	0.5	0.1	23.0	0.0	11.6	0.0	0.1	7.2	28.8	21.6	~	73.8	44.1
19.0	264.0	0.2	0.3	0.5	0.1	28.0	0.0	12.9	0.0	0.1	5.4	19.8	15.3	~	11.7	7.2
43.0	437.0	0.7	0.2	0.9	0.2	19.0	0.0	10.8	0.0	~	16.4	45.1	39.0	~	38.0	22.6
29.0	284.0	0.5	0.1	1.0	0.1	19.0	0.0	15.1	0.0	1.3	13.4	35.9	30.8	~	24.6	14.4
11.0	117.0	0.3	0.2	0.8	0.1	8.0	0.0	3.5	0.0	0.1	7.0	18.6	15.5	~	60.5	36.4
27.0	475.0	0.2	0.3	1.5	0.3	6.0	0.0	19.6	0.0	0.7	45.6	130.0	50.2	104.9	4.6	68.4
11.0	237.0	0.0	0.2	0.6	0.1	15.0	0.0	13.7	0.0	0.5	7.4	82.4	17.2	66.4	3.7	98.4
9.0	218.0	0.5	0.1	0.5	0.1	13.0	0.0	22.8	0.0	0.6	9.6	33.6	21.6	40.8	2.4	50.5
52.5	928.7	1.5	0.5	2.5	0.1	18.4	0.0	10.6	0.0	0.0	28.1	99.0	65.5	~	3.0	298.0
11.0	191.0	0.7	0.3	0.4	0.1	15.0	0.0	21.0	0.0	0.0	8.8	16.6	12.7	~	39.0	11.7
9.0	177.0	0.2	0.1	0.3	0.0	9.0	0.0	11.6	0.0	0.0	8.1	16.1	12.7	~	36.8	10.4
31.0	296.0	1.2	0.2	0.6	0.3	194.0	0.0	60.0	0.0	2.9	28.6	101.2	63.8	47.3	92.4	39.6
22.0	203.0	0.9	0.1	0.4	0.2	118.0	0.0	27.4	0.0	1.9	28.8	101.0	63.4	17.3	92.1	40.3
6.9	108.9	0.3	0.0	0.1	0.0	3.0	0.0	14.2	0.0	0.3	10.2	38.8	21.4	~	7.8	4.1
76.5	201.4	0.7	0.9	1.0	0.0	14.3	0.0	0.0	0.0	7.5	48.3	257.6	103.5	63.9	2.3	2783.0
44.6	119.7	0.4	0.5	0.5	0.0	8.5	0.0	0.0	0.0	3.9	43.4	135.0	85.3	~	67.7	1901.0
78.7	199.4	0.6	0.9	1.0	0.0	14.8	0.0	0.0	0.0	6.7	58.8	352.3	163.1	66.7	~	3735.4
105.3	184.5	536.8	1.1	0.1	0.0	6.2	0.0	0.2	0.0	5.7	39.8	178.0	119.0	~	5.1	5809.0
72.8	158.2	3.3	1.6	0.4	0.1	19.3	0.0	0.0	0.0	0.3	66.4	221.0	137.0	22.7	45.1	2145.0
81.8	184.8	5.6	1.6	0.3	0.0	7.0	0.0	0.1	0.0	0.3	80.4	266.0	142.0	22.7	17.4	2179.0
33.5	40.7	5.5	0.5	0.9	0.0	4.9	0.0	0.2	0.0	0.1	72.7	103.7	50.8	~	1769.4	583.2
6.3	38.0	1.3	0.1	0.0	0.0	0.6	0.0	0.1	0.0	0.0	5.7	24.4	14.9	2.3	~	49.5
25.6	284.8	8.1	0.9	0.4	0.0	20.8	0.0	2.6	0.0	0.2	31.2	135.0	82.4	~	~	293.0
52.0	248.6	0.0	0.6	0.7	0.0	15.8	0.0	1.1	0.0	0.0	27.1	115.0	70.0	~	~	263.5
39.2	81.3	2.5	0.4	0.3	0.0	8.7	0.0	0.1	0.0	0.0	30.4	98.1	50.5	~	2338.0	606.0
22.8	95.2	0.3	0.3	0.3	0.1	15.8	0.0	0.9	0.0	2.1	27.0	92.8	50.7	~	12.2	1097.0
36.4	103.0	1.0	0.4	0.7	0.1	3.1	0.0	0.3	0.0	0.2	18.9	188.0	144.0	~	58.2	366.0
225.0	597.0	~	3.8	4.7	0.3	50.0	0.0	0.4	0.0	~	271.5	979.5	694.5	~	195.0	10825.5
176.0	658.0	7.5	3.3	13.5	0.3	145.0	0.0	0.0	0.0	6.9	252.0	1344.0	1054.5	146.7	3.3	17181.8
168.0	705.0	7.2	3.3	12.1	0.3	240.0	0.0	0.0	0.0	8.3	273.8	1464.0	1149.0	145.6	3.3	17033.3
50.8	214.2	1.8	1.0	4.4	0.2	24.4	0.0	0.0	0.0	3.0	73.0	379.0	262.0	97.3	26.6	4709.0
33.9	114.8	1.1	1.3	0.3	0.1	6.2	0.0	0.3	0.0	0.4	26.3	120.0	60.7	~	279.0	5828.0
82.8	197.0	0.2	2.1	1.4	0.0	11.2	0.0	0.3	0.0	3.1	36.0	176.8	171.8	~	37.8	11342.3
33.8	312.2	3.1	0.7	0.4	0.3	15.8	0.0	0.9	0.0	0.8	87.3	339.5	132.8	~	80.5	4193.0
159.5	228.5	2.7	2.2	1.3	0.0	16.5	0.0	0.5	0.0	0.2	328.0	931.8	776.3	~	94.3	10793.8
31.6	42.1	3.1	0.7	0.4	0.1	8.7	0.0	0.0	0.0	0.0	34.9	84.6	66.9	~	33.8	1924.0
42.6	162.0	0.0	1.7	1.4	0.3	78.5	0.0	0.5	0.0	0.0	88.0	295.8	168.5	4.0	26.5	12525.3
44.2	123.5	1.4	0.9	0.3	0.2	27.4	0.0	0.4	0.0	0.2	48.0	201.0	115.0	55.4	2565.0	10761.0

FOOD	approx amt	Calories	Protein_(g)	Fat_Tot_(g)	Carbohydrt_(g)	Fiber(g)	Sugar_Tot_(g)	Calcium_(mg)	Iron_(mg)
BEVERAGES									
BEER,REGULAR,ALL	1 CAN	150.0	1.6	0.0	12.4	0.0	0.0	14.0	0.1
COFFEE,BREWED FROM GROUNDS,PREPARED W/ TAP H2O	1 CUP	2.0	0.2	0.0	0.0	0.0	0.0	4.0	0.0
TEA,BLACK,BREWED,PREPARED W/ TAP H2O	1 CUP	2.0	0.0	0.0	0.6	0.0	0.0	0.0	0.0
TEA,HERB,CHAMOMILE,BREWED	1 CUP	2.0	0.0	0.0	0.4	0.0	0.0	4.0	0.2
TEA,HERB,OTHER THAN CHAMOMILE,BREWED	1 CUP	2.0	0.0	0.0	0.4	0.0	0.0	4.0	0.2
WINE,TABLE,RED,CABERNET SAUVIGNON	5 OZ	124.0	0.1	0.0	3.9	0.0	0.0	0.0	0.0
WINE,TABLE,WHITE,PINOT GRIS (GRIGIO)	5 OZ	124.0	0.1	0.0	3.1	0.0	0.0	0.0	0.0
BEANS (LEGUMES)									
BEANS,BLACK,COOKED,BOILED	1 CUP	227.0	15.2	0.9	40.8	15.0	0.0	46.4	3.6
BEANS,KIDNEY,ALL TYPES,COOKED,BOILED	1 CUP	225.0	15.3	0.9	40.4	11.3	0.6	62.0	3.9
BEANS,PINTO,COOKED,BOILED	1 CUP	245.0	15.4	1.1	44.8	15.4	0.6	78.7	3.6
BEANS,NAVY,MATURE SEEDS,COOKED,BOILED	1 CUP	255.0	15.0	1.1	47.4	19.1	0.7	125.6	4.3
CAROB FLOUR	1 CUP	222.0	4.6	0.7	88.9	39.8	49.1	348.0	2.9
CHICKPEAS (GARBANZOS) ,MATURE SEEDS,CKD,BLD	1/2 CUP	134.0	7.3	2.1	22.5	6.2	3.9	40.2	2.4
LENTILS,COOKED,BOILED	1/2 CUP	116.0	9.0	0.4	20.1	7.9	1.8	19.0	3.3
NOODLES, CHINESE,DEHYDRATED	3/4 CUP	351.0	0.2	0.1	86.1	0.5	0.0	25.0	2.2
PEAS,SPLIT,COOKED,BOILED	1/2 CUP	118.0	8.3	0.4	21.1	8.3	2.9	14.0	1.3
SOYMILK,ORIGINAL & VANILLA,W/ ADDED CALC,VIT A & D	1/2 CUP	43.0	2.6	1.5	4.9	0.2	3.7	123.0	0.4
SOY SAUCE MADE FROM SOY (TAMARI)	1 TBSP	12.0	2.1	0.0	1.1	0.2	0.3	4.0	0.5
TOFU,FIRM,PREPARED W/CAL&MAG CHLORIDE (NIGARI)	1/5 BLOCK	70.0	8.2	4.2	1.7	0.9	0.6	201.0	1.6
GRAINS									
BAGEL,WHEAT	1 BAGEL	250.0	10.2	1.5	48.9	4.1	6.1	20.0	2.8
BARLEY,HULLED	1/2 CUP	354.0	12.5	2.3	73.5	17.3	0.8	33.0	3.6
BREAD,MULTI-GRAIN (INCLUDES WHOLE-GRAIN)	1 Slice Large	108.7	5.5	1.7	17.8	3.0	2.6	42.2	1.0
BREAD,RICE BRAN	1 SLICE	66.0	2.4	1.2	11.7	1.3	1.3	18.6	1.0
BREAD,RYE	1 SLICE	83.0	2.7	1.1	15.5	1.9	1.2	23.4	0.9
BUCKWHEAT FLOUR	3/4 CUP	343.0	13.3	3.4	71.5	10.0	~	18.0	2.2
BULGUR,COOKED	1/2 CUP	83.0	3.1	0.2	18.6	4.5	0.1	10.0	1.0
CORN FLOUR,WHOLE-GRAIN,YELLOW	1 CUP	422.0	8.1	4.5	89.9	8.5	0.7	8.2	2.8
COUSCOUS,COOKED	1/2 CUP	112.0	3.8	0.2	23.2	1.4	0.1	8.0	0.4
DANISH PASTRY,CHEESE	1 PASTRY	266.0	5.7	15.5	26.4	0.7	4.9	24.9	1.3
DOUGHNUTS,CAKE-TYPE,WHEAT,SUGARED OR GLAZED	2 Doughnuts	360.0	6.3	19.3	42.6	2.2	21.6	49.0	1.1
ENGLISH MUFFINS,WHOLE-WHEAT	1 MUFFIN	134.0	5.8	1.4	26.7	4.4	5.3	174.9	1.6
MUFFINS,BLUEBERRY,COMMERCIALLY PREPARED	1 LARGE	524.0	6.3	22.0	75.0	1.4	45.6	63.9	1.8
OATS, ROLLED, DRY	1/2 CUP	303.0	13.2	5.4	51.7	8.3	0.0	42.1	3.7
PANCAKES,PLAIN,DRY MIX,COMPLETE (INC BUTTERMILK)	3/4 C. DRY	368.0	9.8	3.1	73.7	2.9	16.0	344.0	3.6
QUINOA,COOKED	1/2 CUP	120.0	4.4	1.9	21.3	2.8	0.9	17.0	1.5
RICE,BROWN,LONG-GRAIN,COOKED	1/2 CUP	111.0	2.6	0.9	23.0	1.8	0.4	10.0	0.4
RICE FLOUR,BROWN	2/3 CUP	363.0	7.2	2.8	76.5	4.6	0.9	11.0	2.0
RICE,WHITE,LONG-GRAIN,REGULAR,COOKED	2/3 CUP	130.0	2.7	0.3	28.2	0.4	0.1	10.0	1.2
RICE,WILD, COOKED	2/3 CUP	101.0	4.0	0.3	21.3	1.8	0.7	3.0	0.6
RYE FLOUR, DARK	3/4 CUP	338.0	10.3	1.6	75.9	15.1	1.0	24.0	2.6
TORTILLAS,CORN,WO/ SALT	1 Tortilla	58.0	1.5	0.7	12.1	1.4	0.0	45.5	0.4
TORTILLAS,FLOUR,WO/ ADDED CALCIUM	1 Large 12"	325.0	8.7	7.1	55.6	3.3	~	39.0	3.3
TORTILLAS,FLOUR,SHELF STABLE	2 Tort 7-8"	297.0	8.0	7.6	49.3	2.4	2.7	163.0	3.3
WHEAT,DURUM	1/2 CUP	339.0	13.7	2.5	71.1	~	~	34.0	3.5
WHEAT FLOUR,WHOLE-GRAIN	1 CUP	408.0	15.9	3.0	86.4	12.8	0.5	40.8	4.3
WHEAT GERM,CRUDE	1 CUP	360.0	23.2	9.7	51.8	13.2	~	39.0	6.3
WHEAT,HARD RED WINTER	1/2 CUP	327.0	12.6	1.5	71.2	12.2	0.4	29.0	3.2

134

Magnesium_ (mg)	Potassium_ (mg)	Selenium_ (µg)	Zinc_ (mg)	Niacin_ (mg)	Vit_B6_ (mg)	Folate_Tot_ (µg)	Vit_B12_ (µg)	Vit_C_ (mg)	Vit_D_ (IU)	Vit_E_ (mg)	Tryptophan (mg)	Phenylalanine (mg)	Tyrosine (mg)	Inositol (mg)	tot Omega-3 (mg)	tot Omega-6 (mg)
21.0	94.5	2.1	0.0	1.8	0.2	21.0	0.1	0.0	0.0	0.0	0.0	0.0	0.0	~	0.0	0.0
6.0	98.0	0.0	0.0	0.4	0.0	4.0	0.0	0.0	0.0	0.0	0.0	2.4	7.1	11.9	~	2.4
6.0	74.0	0.0	0.0	0.0	0.0	10.0	0.0	0.0	0.0	0.0	0.0	0.0	0.0	7.1	7.1	2.4
2.0	18.0	0.0	0.1	0.0	0.0	2.0	0.0	0.0	0.0	0.0	0.0	0.0	0.0	~	~	~
2.0	18.0	0.0	0.1	0.0	0.0	2.0	0.0	0.0	0.0	0.0	0.0	0.0	0.0	~	~	~
0.0	0.0	0.0	0.0	0.0	0.0	0.0	0.0	0.0	0.0	0.0	~	~	~	~	0.0	0.0
0.0	0.0	0.0	0.0	0.0	0.0	0.0	0.0	0.0	0.0	0.0	~	~	~	~	0.0	0.0
120.4	610.6	2.1	1.9	0.9	0.1	256.3	0.0	0.0	0.0	0.0	181.0	824.0	430.0	~	181.0	217.0
74.3	716.9	1.9	1.8	1.0	0.2	230.1	0.0	2.1	0.0	0.1	184.0	905.0	363.0	~	301.0	191.0
85.5	745.6	10.6	1.7	0.5	0.4	294.1	0.0	1.4	0.0	1.6	185.0	908.0	364.0	106.0	234.0	168.0
96.5	708.0	5.3	1.9	1.2	0.3	254.8	0.0	1.6	0.0	0.0	182.0	857.0	358.0	118.3	322.0	248.0
54.0	827.0	5.3	0.9	1.9	0.4	29.0	0.0	0.2	0.0	0.6	49.4	156.0	124.0	~	4.1	218.0
39.4	238.6	3.0	1.3	0.4	0.1	141.0	0.0	1.1	0.0	0.3	69.5	389.5	180.5	~	35.3	912.5
36.0	369.0	2.8	1.3	1.1	0.2	181.0	0.0	1.5	0.0	0.1	80.0	440.5	238.5	~	36.7	135.5
3.0	10.0	7.9	0.4	0.2	0.1	2.0	0.0	0.0	0.0	0.1	2.1	10.5	5.3	~	1.1	17.9
36.0	362.0	0.6	1.0	0.9	0.0	65.0	0.0	0.4	0.0	0.0	91.0	376.5	237.0	~	27.5	134.5
15.0	122.0	2.3	0.3	0.4	0.0	9.0	0.9	0.0	43.0	0.1	26.8	79.0	62.0	~	91.0	709.5
8.0	42.4	0.2	0.1	0.8	0.0	3.6	0.0	0.0	0.0	0.0	32.6	96.1	61.6	~	0.9	7.0
37.0	148.0	9.9	0.8	0.1	0.1	19.0	0.0	0.2	0.0	0.0	112.0	398.0	334.0	~	165.0	1458.0
51.0	165.0	28.7	1.1	3.4	0.1	76.0	0.0	0.0	0.0	0.3	113.1	474.2	274.9	~	32.9	602.9
133.0	452.0	37.7	2.8	4.6	0.3	19.0	0.0	0.0	0.0	0.6	191.5	644.0	329.5	~	101.0	919.0
32.0	94.3	13.5	0.7	1.7	0.1	30.8	0.0	0.0	0.0	0.2	50.8	159.0	96.8	19.3	84.0	684.0
21.6	58.1	7.7	0.4	1.8	0.1	23.2	0.0	0.0	0.0	0.2	28.6	119.0	73.2	~	28.6	447.0
12.8	53.1	9.9	0.4	1.2	0.0	35.2	0.0	0.1	0.0	0.1	30.7	132.0	68.2	15.0	19.2	236.0
231.0	460.0	8.3	2.4	7.0	0.2	30.0	0.0	0.0	0.0	~	165.0	445.5	207.0	~	63.9	789.0
32.0	68.0	0.6	0.6	1.0	0.1	18.0	0.0	0.0	0.0	0.0	43.7	132.0	82.0	~	3.7	85.5
108.8	368.6	18.0	2.0	2.2	0.4	29.3	0.0	0.0	0.0	0.5	57.3	398.0	330.0	~	62.0	1996.0
8.0	58.0	27.5	0.3	1.0	0.1	15.0	0.0	0.0	0.0	0.1	38.5	144.5	78.5	~	2.4	47.1
10.7	69.6	13.4	0.5	1.4	0.0	42.6	0.1	0.1	1.4	0.2	63.2	285.0	208.0	~	123.0	1705.0
22.0	148.0	19.4	0.7	1.9	0.1	20.0	0.2	0.2	0.0	1.7	79.2	266.0	192.6	~	436.0	5908.0
46.9	138.6	26.6	1.1	2.3	0.1	32.3	0.0	0.0	0.0	0.3	85.1	275.0	180.0	~	30.4	519.0
13.9	159.9	12.6	0.5	1.8	0.1	66.7	0.2	1.3	5.6	2.5	84.8	368.0	209.0	~	1715.0	11771.0
138.1	334.6	0.0	3.1	0.7	0.1	43.7	0.0	0.0	0.0	0.0	73.5	269.5	160.0	~	40.5	891.0
28.0	191.0	21.6	0.7	4.4	0.2	~	0.3	~	~	~	111.0	481.5	343.5	~	93.8	1447.5
64.0	172.0	2.8	1.1	0.4	0.1	42.0	0.0	0.0	0.0	0.6	48.1	171.0	77.0	~	~	~
43.0	43.0	9.8	0.6	1.5	0.1	4.0	0.0	0.0	0.0	0.0	32.2	129.5	94.5	29.3	13.7	301.5
112.0	289.0	~	2.5	6.3	0.7	16.0	0.0	0.0	0.0	1.2	96.7	392.7	285.3	~	44.3	1004.7
12.0	35.0	7.5	0.5	1.5	0.1	58.0	0.0	0.0	0.0	0.2	32.7	152.0	94.7	15.8	13.7	65.3
32.0	101.0	0.8	1.3	1.3	0.1	26.0	0.0	0.0	0.0	0.2	53.6	213.3	184.7	29.5	104.0	130.0
110.0	510.0	13.9	2.7	4.3	0.3	38.0	0.0	0.0	0.0	0.9	152.3	681.8	266.3	~	162.0	990.0
16.9	40.0	0.0	0.2	0.4	0.1	29.6	0.0	0.0	0.0	0.0	10.9	74.1	61.4	~	8.8	283.0
26.0	131.0	23.4	0.7	3.6	0.1	123.0	0.0	0.0	~	~	124.0	509.0	311.0	~	63.2	1181.0
21.0	133.0	21.9	0.6	4.2	0.0	118.0	0.0	0.0	0.0	0.9	~	~	~	~	~	~
144.0	431.0	89.4	4.2	6.7	0.4	43.0	0.0	0.0	0.0	~	169.0	654.0	342.5	~	46.1	893.0
164.4	435.6	74.2	3.1	5.9	0.5	52.8	0.0	0.0	0.0	0.9	254.0	775.0	480.0	~	45.6	886.0
239.0	892.0	79.2	12.3	6.8	1.3	281.0	0.0	0.0	0.0	~	365.0	1067.0	810.0	~	831.0	6081.0
126.0	363.0	70.7	2.7	5.5	0.3	38.0	0.0	0.0	0.0	1.0	153.5	568.5	371.5	~	25.9	576.0

FOOD	approx amt	Calories	Protein_(g)	Fat_Tot_(g)	Carbohydrt_(g)	Fiber(g)	Sugar_Tot_(g)	Calcium_(mg)	Iron_(mg)
CHOCOLATE									
BAKING CHOCOLATE,UNSWEETENED,SQUARES	3/4 C. gratec	501.0	12.9	52.3	29.8	16.6	0.9	101.0	17.4
CANDIES,SPECIAL DARK CHOCOLATE BAR	2.6 OZ BAR	406.0	4.0	23.7	44.2	4.7	34.7	21.9	1.6
COCOA,DRY POWDER,UNSWEETENED	1/2 CUP	98.0	8.4	5.9	24.9	14.3	0.8	55.0	6.0
SWEETENERS									
HONEY	1/3 CUP	340.0	0.3	0.0	92.3	0.2	92.0	6.7	0.5
MOLASSES	1/3 CUP	290.0	0.0	0.1	74.7	0.0	74.7	205.0	4.7
SUGARS,BROWN	1/3 C. pckd	277.0	0.1	0.0	71.6	0.0	70.8	60.6	0.5
SUGARS,GRANULATED	1/2 CUP	387.0	0.0	0.0	100.0	0.0	99.8	1.0	0.1
SYRUPS,MAPLE	1/3 CUP	260.0	0.0	0.1	67.0	0.0	67.9	102.0	0.1
SYRUPS,CORN,HIGH-FRUCTOSE	1/3 CUP	281.0	0.0	0.0	76.0	0.0	75.7	0.0	0.0

sources: 1. http://ndb.nal.usda.gov 2. http://ajcn.nutrition.org/content/33/9/1954.full.pdf   ~ insufficient information available

Magnesium_(mg)	Potassium_(mg)	Selenium_(ug)	Zinc_(mg)	Niacin_(mg)	Vit_B6_(mg)	Folate_Tot_(ug)	Vit_B12_(ug)	Vit_C_(mg)	Vit_D_(IU)	Vit_E_(mg)	Tryptophan (mg)	Phenylalanine (mg)	Tyrosine (mg)	Inositol (mg)	tot Omega-3 (mg)	tot Omega-6 (mg)
327.0	830.0	8.1	9.6	1.4	0.0	28.0	0.0	0.0	0.0	0.4	129.0	519.8	420.8	~	115.5	1422.8
22.6	366.5	0.2	0.0	0.0	0.0	0.0	0.0	0.0	0.0	0.0	~	~	~	~	~	~
214.6	655.3	6.1	2.9	0.9	0.1	13.8	0.0	0.0	0.0	0.0	126.0	404.5	316.0	~	~	378.0
2.2	58.2	0.9	0.2	0.1	0.0	2.2	0.0	0.6	0.0	0.0	4.5	12.4	9.0	37.3	0.0	0.0
242.0	1464.0	17.8	0.3	0.9	0.7	0.0	0.0	0.0	0.0	0.0	0.0	0.0	0.0	~	~	56.0
6.6	97.1	0.9	0.0	0.1	0.0	0.7	0.0	0.0	0.0	0.0	~	~	~	~	0.0	0.0
0.0	2.0	0.6	0.0	0.0	0.0	0.0	0.0	0.0	0.0	0.0	0.0	0.0	0.0	~	0.0	0.0
21.0	212.0	0.6	1.5	0.1	0.0	0.0	0.0	0.0	0.0	0.0	0.0	0.0	0.0	~	~	107.3
0.0	0.0	0.7	0.0	0.0	0.0	0.0	0.0	0.0	0.0	0.0	0.0	0.0	0.0	~	0.0	0.0

Chapter 5

Recipes

In the following section you will find easy to make, nutritious dishes. I've tried to incorporate a variety of common, healthful ingredients including raw, cooked, and fermented foods. They are separated into Main Courses, Salads, Vegetables, and Desserts and Snacks. I've left room for your personal notes and I have added a few of my own!

With only one exception, the Main Courses have a minimum of 20 grams of protein per serving. It is recommended that you have 20-30 grams of protein with each meal for a total of 60-80 grams per day. You will find that in addition to a primary protein source, many of the main courses also incorporate many different nutrient rich vegetables.

Several of the Salads contain 20 grams of protein or more. Those are considered to be full-meal salads that would be suitable for lunch or dinner. The ones containing less than 20 grams of protein are considered to be side dishes.

Vegetables are so important for the nutrients they provide, including fiber. Consuming adequate amounts of fiber is crucial to good gut health and for our digestive systems to effectively deliver nutrients into our bloodstream. Cooking vegetables properly will help ensure that their nutrients aren't wasted.

Some vegetables are more "nutrient dense" than others and I've tried to focus primarily on some of those containing the most nutrients per serving. It is recommended that you eat at least 4 cups of a combination of raw and cooked vegetables every day.

Desserts and Snacks can be interchangeable so I included them together. Sometimes we snack in the evening for instance, sometimes we have dessert. I recommend snacks and desserts that have nutritional value instead of empty calories. They should add to your nutritional wellbeing. Traditional snacks and desserts can be laden with trans-fats and refined sugar with little to no redeeming nutritional value. The desserts and snacks you will find here have no refined sugar, no trans-fats, and lots of nutritional value! They use a variety of fruits, vegetables, raw cacao, and nuts that provide healthy fats, important vitamins and minerals, and rely on their own sweetness with only honey, maple syrup, or stevia added as sweeteners.

Fruit, especially citrus and berries, are very high in antioxidants and other nutrients vital to mental health. They have been included in several of the salads as well as desserts and snacks. Recipes, however, are not necessary to enjoy fresh fruit. We should have fruit every day and it is one of the easiest things to eat "as is". A variety of different colored fruits are highly recommended for snacks or desserts either singularly or mixed together in a simple fruit compote. 100% fruit juices can also be nutrient rich but should be limited because they have a more concentrated sugar to fiber ratio than the whole fruits.

Each recipe has a nutritional breakdown of the nutrients to track for preventing and treating depression. This table does not include all of the nutrients that are important to good health, just the "key players" that we know are indicated in depression and anxiety. Information for "non-essential" nutrients, like inositol and glutamine, are not available in the recipe nutrient breakdowns but inositol is included in the Nutrition Content Table where reliable information for its content was available. The table is included so we can track these particular nutrients where a deficiency is known to contribute to or cause depression or anxiety. This provides a way for us to be sure we are meeting those particular nutritional needs. The bonus is that if you are meeting 100% of the DV of each by eating a wide variety of foods, you will be meeting your needs for the other nutrients that aren't listed on this table. That is the beauty of attaining nutritional balance by eating real, whole food. Eating a variety of real, whole unprocessed food will ensure that we meet our nutritional needs for maximum physical and mental health.

Enjoy your time in the kitchen. Share meal making with your family members and other loved ones. Make meal preparation a time to gather and create something for all to enjoy together. Prepare your food in a loving environment with a loving attitude. Being directly involved in handling, washing, chopping, dicing and cooking creates an intimate connection with food that will make consuming the meal much more satisfying and nourishing. Sharing that food connection with others is at the core of our most basic and primal social bonds. Food, growing it, making it, cooking it, and eating it, should be a family affair. It should be shared with neighbors and friends. It should be shared with strangers. Enjoy the comforting and healing power of food.

*M*ain Courses

The main courses are not separated into "breakfast", "lunch" and "dinner" because some main courses are interchangeable. Omelettes, for instance, are appropriate for any meal of the day. The primary criterion for a main course is that it contains 20 to 30 grams of good quality "useable" protein. That is enough protein for an entire meal so your side dishes don't need to contain any protein.

Don't be afraid to play around with the recipes to make them your own. The recipes should all be fairly easy and are not intended to be followed rigidly. They are included to show you some simple ways of using whole foods, using the nutritional information as a guide.

This is very garlicky. You can cut down on the garlic if you don't love it as much as I do. Basically, I don't think there can ever be too much garlic.
Also, instead of the lemon pepper seasoning, you can use 1 tsp. of black pepper and the zest of 1 organic lemon.

LEMON GARLIC ROAST CHICKEN

Servings: 6

1 whole chicken, about 4 lbs.
3 Tbsp. garlic, minced
1 medium onion
1 Tbsp. olive oil
½ tsp. sea salt
1 Tbsp. lemon pepper seasoning (make sure it is gluten and MSG-free)

Slice onion into ¼" rounds and place in bottom of covered roasting pan. Place chicken on top of onions, breast side up. Rub olive oil over chicken. Spread garlic evenly over chicken. Sprinkle lemon pepper seasoning over chicken and rub in lightly. Sprinkle with salt. Bake, covered, at 350º until nicely browned – about 2 to 2 ½ hours. Baste once about halfway through bake time by spooning juices over chicken. When finished, remove chicken from pan and pour pan juices into gravy boat. Serve with the juice to pour on top of each serving.

Lemon Garlic Roast Chicken

Amounts per serving		%DV	Amounts per serving		%DV
Calories	272	14%	Vitamin B12	0.3 mcg	5%
Carbohydrates	3 g	1%	Vitamin C	3 mg	5%
Fiber	9 g	8%	Vitamin D	0 IU	0 %
Fat	0.4 g	2%	Vitamin E	0.6 mg	3%
Protein	28 g	55%	Calcium	28 mg	3%
Tryptophan	310 mg	*	Iron	1.4 mg	8%
Tyrosine	882 mg	*	Magnesium	26 mg	6%
Phenylalanine	1071 mg	*	Potassium	268 mg	8%
Niacin	8.5 mg	43%	Zinc	2 mg	13%
Vitamin B6	0.5 mg	24%	Omega-3	198 mg	*
Folate	9 mcg	2%	Omega-6	2794mg	*
Selenium	25 mcg	35%			

* No recommended DV

1 bunch of kale will cook down to about 2 cups when it is steamed. You can use any kind of cooked greens so this is a great way to use up any leftover greens. These are super high in omega-3's!

SALMON VEGGIE PATTIES

Servings: 4

2 15 oz. cans salmon, drained
1 large egg, beaten
1 clove garlic
2 cups steamed kale, chopped fine
2 tsp. mustard, Dijon or spicy brown
1 tsp. olive oil
¼ c. onion, diced
2 cooked sweet potatoes, skins removed
½ tsp. sea salt
1tsp. smoked paprika

Cook onion and garlic in olive oil until onions are caramelized and beginning to brown. Place cooked onions and garlic in a large bowl and add remaining ingredients. Mix well with hands and divide into 8 patties. Cook the patties in a skillet over medium heat with just enough olive or coconut oil to brown. Brown on both sides making sure the patties are heated through.

Salmon Veggie Patties

Amounts per serving		%DV	Amounts per serving		%DV
Calories	254	13%	Vitamin B12	5 mcg	85%
Carbohydrates	20 g	8%	Vitamin C	68 mg	112%
Fiber	3.4 g	13%	Vitamin D	470 IU	118%
Fat	8 g	12%	Vitamin E	2 mg	9%
Protein	27 g	55%	Calcium	364 mg	36%
Tryptophan	296 mg	*	Iron	2.4 mg	14%
Tyrosine	976 mg	*	Magnesium	65 mg	16%
Phenylalanine	1157 mg	*	Potassium	916 mg	26%
Niacin	8 mg	42%	Zinc	2 mg	11%
Vitamin B6	0.4 mg	21%	Omega-3	1340mg	*
Folate	35 mcg	9%	Omega-6	494 mg	*
Selenium	45 mcg	65%			

* No recommended DV

CRUSTLESS QUICHE

Servings: 4

1 c. broccoli flowerets
1 c. cheddar cheese, grated
3 large eggs
2 cups milk, 2% milkfat
½ c. mushrooms, sliced
¼ c. onion, chopped
½ c. ham, chopped
1 tsp. olive oil
dash salt and pepper

Saute onion, mushrooms, broccoli and ham in oil until they are beginning to brown. Place sautéed veggies and ham in oiled pie pan. Spread cheese over veggies. In a medium size bowl, mix together eggs, milk, salt and pepper. Pour milk mixture over the top and bake at 350º until golden brown, about 30-45 minutes.

Crustless Quiche

Amounts per serving		%DV	Amounts per serving		%DV
Calories	200	10%	Vitamin B12	0 mcg	0%
Carbohydrates	9 g	3%	Vitamin C	32 mg	52%
Fiber	0.2 g	1%	Vitamin D	0 IU	0%
Fat	9 g	14%	Vitamin E	1.7 mg	9%
Protein	20 g	40%	Calcium	60 mg	6%
Tryptophan	246 mg	*	Iron	1.8 mg	10%
Tyrosine	816 mg	*	Magnesium	82 mg	20%
Phenylalanine	969 mg	*	Potassium	591 mg	17%
Niacin	2 mg	13%	Zinc	1.2 mg	8%
Vitamin B6	0.3 mg	5%	Omega-3	90 mg	*
Folate	115 mcg	29%	Omega-6	654 mg	*
Selenium	24 mcg	34%			

*No recommended DV

This is classic comfort food. It is very filling but low in calories and a good source of zinc.

STUFFED CABBAGE ROLLS

Servings: 6

12 cabbage leaves
1-1/2 lbs. lean grass-fed ground beef
1 c. cooked brown rice
1 large egg
¼ c. fresh parsley, chopped   1 tsp. honey
1 tsp. sea salt   1 tsp. lemon juice
½ tsp. dried thyme   ½ tsp. Chinese Five Spice
¼ tsp. black pepper
3 c. tomatoes, chopped
½ c. onion, chopped

Place cabbage leaves in large pot with about 2 inches of boiling water. Boil until tender, about 5 minutes. Drain thoroughly and pat leaves dry between paper towels or dish towels. In a large bowl, thoroughly mix ground beef, rice, egg, parsley, thyme, pepper, and ½ of the salt. Place about 1/3 cup of the mixture in each cabbage leaf. Roll up by folding sides over the meat mixture. Then, fold the bottom (small end) of the leaf over the folded sides and roll up the rest of the way. In large skillet or Dutch oven, mix tomatoes, onion, honey, lemon juice, Chinese Five Spice and remaining salt. Place cabbage rolls on top of tomato mixture, seam side down. Spoon some of the tomato mixture over the cabbage rolls. Cover and simmer for 45 minutes. Uncover and continue to simmer for another 15 minutes. Remove cabbage rolls and place on serving platter. Spoon tomato sauce over cabbage rolls and serve.

Stuffed Cabbage Rolls

Amounts per serving		%DV	Amounts per serving		%DV
Calories	278	11%	Vitamin B12	2 mcg	12%
Carbohydrates	16 g	8%	Vitamin C	33 mg	55%
Fiber	3 g	8%	Vitamin D	3 IU	1%
Fat	14 g	19%	Vitamin E	1 mg	5%
Protein	23 g	18%	Calcium	57 mg	6%
Tryptophan	38 mg	*	Iron	3 mg	14%
Tyrosine	99 mg	*	Magnesium	53 mg	13%
Phenylalanine	183 mg	*	Potassium	644 mg	18%
Niacin	6 mg	2%	Zinc	5 mg	34%
Vitamin B6	0.6 mg	5%	Omega-3	103 mg	*
Folate	53 mcg	7%	Omega-6	707 mg	*
Selenium	20 mcg	29%			

*No recommended DV

This is a simple and elegant dish, suitable for company and a treat for the family.

DILLED SALMON

Servings: 4

4 – 4oz portions of wild salmon
1 clove garlic, minced
3 Tbsp. fresh or 3 tsp. dried dill weed, divided
2 tsp. olive oil

Sauce

Juice and zest from ½ organic lemon
1 c. yogurt
dill

Heat olive oil in heavy skillet. Place salmon in skillet, skin side down and sear over medium-high heat for 3 minutes. Sprinkle 2 Tbsp. fresh or 2 tsp. dried dill and garlic on top of salmon. Flip over and cook for another 3-4 minutes. The dill and garlic should be quite brown and crispy. For sauce, mix yogurt, 1 Tbsp. fresh or 1 tsp. dried dill, lemon juice and lemon zest. Serve salmon with sauce.

Dilled Salmon

Amounts per serving		%DV	Amounts per serving		%DV
Calories	196	10%	Vitamin B12	3 mcg	57%
Carbohydrates	1 g	8%	Vitamin C	4 mg	6%
Fiber	0 g	0%	Vitamin D	466 IU	117%
Fat	11 g	16%	Vitamin E	0.4 mg	2%
Protein	24 g	51%	Calcium	88 mg	9%
Tryptophan	260 mg	*	Iron	3 mg	14%
Tyrosine	938 mg	*	Magnesium	37 mg	9%
Phenylalanine	1062 mg	*	Potassium	597 mg	17%
Niacin	8 mg	2%	Zinc	1 mg	9%
Vitamin B6	1 mg	5%	Omega-3	1244mg	*
Folate	30 mcg	7%	Omega-6	356 mg	*
Selenium	41 mcg	59%			

* No recommended DV

Adding ½ cup milk and 1 large egg will make a full meal's worth of protein.

GRANOLA

Servings: 20

4 c. rolled oats (not the quick cooking kind)
2 tsp. vanilla
½ c. coconut oil
¼ c. honey
½ c. maple syrup
½ c. each of:
  walnuts
  pecans
  almonds
  cashews
  brazilnuts
  pumpkin seeds
  raw sunflower seeds
¼ c. sesame seeds
¼ c. chia seeds
1 c. dried unsweetened coconut flakes
2 c. raisins
1 c. dried papaya, chopped
1 c. dates, chopped

Whisk together vanilla, oil, honey, and maple syrup. In a large bowl, combine oats with all of the nuts, seeds, and coconut flakes. Add wet ingredients and mix until all dry ingredients are moistened. Spread out on baking sheets in no deeper than about 1". Bake at 325º for 20 minutes, then stir. Increase heat to 350º and bake for another 10 minutes. Let cool and add raisins, papaya, and dates. Store in airtight container.

Granola

Amounts per serving		%DV	Amounts per serving		%DV
Calories	389	19%	Vitamin B12	0 mcg	0%
Carbohydrates	52 g	17%	Vitamin C	0.6 mg	1%
Fiber	7 g	27%	Vitamin D	0 IU	0%
Fat	19 g	28%	Vitamin E	1.3 mg	6%
Protein	9 g	19%	Calcium	77 mg	8%
Tryptophan	138 mg	*	Iron	3.2 mg	18%
Tyrosine	291 mg	*	Magnesium	126 mg	31%
Phenylalanine	481 mg	*	Potassium	458 mg	13%
Niacin	1 mg	5%	Zinc	2.5 mg	17%
Vitamin B6	0.2 mg	8%	Omega-3	298 mg	*
Folate	30 mcg	7%	Omega-6	4036mg	*
Selenium	66 mcg	94%			

* No recommended DV

MUSHROOM SPINACH OMELETTE

Servings: 1

¼ c. parmesan cheese, grated
2 large eggs
2 medium mushrooms
1 c. raw spinach
1 tsp. olive oil
pinch of fresh or dried thyme
dash sea salt

Beat eggs, salt, and thyme in a small bowl. Heat oil in skillet on low-medium heat. Pour eggs in skillet. Let cook about 1 minute, just until omelette can be lifted with a spatula on one side. Place spinach and mushrooms on one half of the omelette. Lift the other half and fold over the spinach and mushrooms. Turn heat to low and cover skillet with a lid. Cook for about 4-5 minutes more or until eggs are cooked all the way through. Put grated cheese on top of omelette, return cover and cook just until cheese is melted, about 30 seconds. Salt and pepper to taste. This is especially good served with black beans and salsa.

Mushroom Spinach Omelette

Amounts per serving		%DV	Amounts per serving		%DV
Calories	235	12%	Vitamin B12	1.4 mcg	24%
Carbohydrates	3 g	1%	Vitamin C	9 mg	15%
Fiber	0.9 g	4%	Vitamin D	42 IU	11%
Fat	17 g	27%	Vitamin E	2.3 mg	11%
Protein	20 g	40%	Calcium	205 mg	20%
Tryptophan	236 mg	*	Iron	3 mg	16%
Tyrosine	747 mg	*	Magnesium	42 mg	11%
Phenylalanine	936 mg	*	Potassium	384 mg	11%
Niacin	1.1 mg	6%	Zinc	1.7 mg	11%
Vitamin B6	0.2 mg	12%	Omega-3	180 mg	*
Folate	110 mcg	27%	Omega-6	1655 mg	*
Selenium	36.4 mcg	52%			

* No recommended DV

PARMESAN CHICKEN

Servings: 4

4 boneless, skinless chicken breasts
½ c. parmesan cheese, grated
1 c. plain whole milk yogurt
1 tsp. garlic powder
½ tsp. smoked paprika
¼ tsp. oregano
¼ tsp. black pepper
¼ tsp. sea salt

Arrange chicken breasts in a shallow baking pan. Mix together remaining ingredients and spread over chicken. Bake at 375º for 40 minutes.

Parmesan Chicken

Amounts per serving		%DV	Amounts per serving		%DV
Calories	223	11%	Vitamin B12	1 mcg	16%
Carbohydrates	4 g	5%	Vitamin C	1.9 mg	3%
Fiber	0.1 g	8%	Vitamin D	0 IU	0%
Fat	7 g	25%	Vitamin E	0.2 mg	1%
Protein	34 g	11%	Calcium	226 mg	23%
Tryptophan	397 mg	*	Iron	1.0 mg	6%
Tyrosine	1319 mg	*	Magnesium	46 mg	11%
Phenylalanine	1460 mg	*	Potassium	419 mg	12%
Niacin	13 mg	66%	Zinc	1.8 mg	12%
Vitamin B6	0.7 mg	35%	Omega-3	88 mg	*
Folate	10 mcg	3%	Omega-6	361 mg	*
Selenium	25 mcg	35%			

* No recommended DV

This marinade works well for grilling too and can be used for pork chops or ribs.

MARINATED PORK LOIN

Servings: 5

1.5 lb boneless pork loin
¼ c. molasses
3 Tbsp. brown mustard (I like spicy mustard)
3 Tbsp. apple cider vinegar

Whisk together molasses, mustard, and vinegar. Cut pork loin in 5 pieces, about 1" thick. Coat each loin slice with the molasses mixture and place slices in a covered container. Pour any remaining marinade over the top of the meat. Refrigerate overnight. Remove meat from marinade and place on an oiled broiler pan. Broil 4 inches from the heat for 10 minutes on each side brushing with the remaining marinade every 5 minutes.

Marinated Pork Loin

Amounts per serving		%DV	Amounts per serving		%DV
Calories	345	17%	Vitamin B12	0.7 mcg	11%
Carbohydrates	13 g	4%	Vitamin C	0.6 mg	1%
Fiber	0.4 g	1%	Vitamin D	0 IU	0%
Fat	20 g	30%	Vitamin E	0.4 mg	2%
Protein	28 g	55%	Calcium	49 mg	5%
Tryptophan	279 mg	*	Iron	1.9 mg	11%
Tyrosine	941 mg	*	Magnesium	74 mg	18%
Phenylalanine	912 mg	*	Potassium	791 mg	23%
Niacin	6.5 mg	33%	Zinc	2.3 mg	15%
Vitamin B6	0.7 mg	34%	Omega-3	191 mg	*
Folate	9 mcg	2%	Omega-6	1760mg	*
Selenium	50.2 mcg	72%			

* No recommended DV

These meatballs are as easy to make as meatloaf but cook faster and are much more versatile. They are great as a stand-alone with any side dish or on gluten-free pasta sprinkled with grated parmesan cheese, with or without marinara sauce.

MAINSTAY MEATBALLS

Servings: 4

1 lb. grass-fed ground beef
½ c. sun-dried tomatoes, diced
1 c. spinach, cooked and drained
½ tsp. sea salt
¼ tsp. garlic powder
¼ tsp. paprika
½ tsp. black pepper
1/8 tsp. cayenne pepper

Mix spices together. Add to ground beef and mix thoroughly. Add spinach and sun-dried tomatoes to mixture, using hands to mix together well. Roll mixture into 1 ½" balls and place on a baking sheet. Bake at 375º for 15-20 minutes.

Mainstay Meatballs

Amounts per serving		%DV	Amounts per serving		%DV
Calories	244	12%	Vitamin B12	2.2 mcg	37%
Carbohydrates	6 g	2%	Vitamin C	7.2 mg	12%
Fiber	2 g	8%	Vitamin D	0 IU	0%
Fat	15 g	22%	Vitamin E	1.4 g	7%
Protein	24 g	48%	Calcium	84 mg	8%
Tryptophan	25 mg	*	Iron	4.5 mg	25%
Tyrosine	67 mg	*	Magnesium	74 mg	19%
Phenylalanine	86 mg	*	Potassium	772 mg	22%
Niacin	6 mg	31 %	Zinc	5.6 mg	37%
Vitamin B6	0.5 mg	27%	Omega-3	142 mg	*
Folate	77 mcg	19%	Omega-6	57 mg	*
Selenium	17 mcg	22%			

* No recommended DV

These were one of my kids' favorite things to eat when they were growing up and there is ongoing debate about how they got their name. They are still a family favorite for something easy and satisfying. They are very high in potassium and a good source of magnesium and calcium. If you use Greek style yogurt they will be even higher in protein and lower in carbohydrate.

POTATO BOATS

Servings: 2

2 large baked potatoes, cooled
1 c. broccoli, steamed
½ c. plain fat-free yogurt
½ c. lowfat cheddar cheese

Slice potatoes open lengthwise and mash lightly. Salt and pepper to taste. Put half of the yogurt on each potato. Put half of the broccoli on each potato and top with cheese. Bake at 375º degrees for about 20 minutes or until heated through and cheese is melted. To save time, you can put them in the microwave for about 3 minutes or until cheese is melted.

Potato Boats

Amounts per serving		%DV	Amounts per serving		%DV
Calories	379	19%	Vitamin B12	0.5 mcg	9%
Carbohydrates	70 g	23%	Vitamin C	62 mg	104%
Fiber	7 g	26%	Vitamin D	0 IU	0%
Fat	3 g	5%	Vitamin E	0.1 mg	1%
Protein	20 g	40%	Calcium	321 mg	32%
Tryptophan	241 mg	*	Iron	4 mg	21%
Tyrosine	831 mg	*	Magnesium	110 mg	27%
Phenylalanine	943 mg	*	Potassium	1893mg	54%
Niacin	5 mg	23%	Zinc	2 mg	16%
Vitamin B6	1 mg	8%	Omega-3	107 mg	*
Folate	51 mcg	52%	Omega-6	196 mg	*
Selenium	9 mcg	13%			

* No recommended

165

Vegetables

Here you will find some very simple ways to prepare vegetables that are nutritious and easy on the budget. Vegetables contain fiber and other very important nutrients and you should eat a variety of different kinds each day. This doesn't need to be complicated. Simply steaming broccoli or some type of leafy green is really all there needs to be to it. Having a green vegetable and a red, yellow, or orange vegetable with your main course will provide a variety of vitamins, minerals, starch, and fiber. I love plain steamed greens with flax oil drizzled on them when served. I often just fill my steamer basket with whatever vegetables I have on hand. Adding just 1 tsp. of flax oil to the vegetables on your plate adds a wonderful nutty flavor, only 37 calories and over 3000 mgs of omega-3 fat while being very low in omega-6 fats. It's one of the best and easiest ways to counterbalance the omega-6's we consume.

You can use just about any combination of vegetables in this. I often throw in whatever I have in the fridge. You can also experiment with your favorite seasonings too. Sometimes I throw in a little bit of ginger or some red pepper flakes.

RED COOKED VEGETABLES

Servings: 4

½ c. broccoli flowerets
1 c. red cabbage, chopped
½ c. carrots, sliced
½ c. cauliflower flowerets
½ c. celery, chopped
4 cloves garlic, chopped
½ c. mushrooms, sliced
2 Tbsp. olive oil
½ medium onion, sliced
¼ c. green bell pepper, chopped
¼ c. red bell pepper, chopped
½ c. yellow squash, sliced
¼ c. wheat-free soy sauce (tamari)

Heat oil in large skillet. Add all ingredients except tamari and cook over medium heat until vegetables are brown and onions are caramelized, about 7-8 minutes. Add tamari sauce stirring to coat the vegetables thoroughly and cook for one more minute.

Red Cooked Vegetables

Amounts per serving		%DV	Amounts per serving		%DV
Calories	109	5%	Vitamin B12	0 mg	0%
Carbohydrates	10 g	3%	Vitamin C	51 mg	85%
Fiber	3 g	10%	Vitamin D	1.6 IU	0%
Fat	7 g	11%	Vitamin E	1 mg	7%
Protein	4 g	8%	Calcium	44 mg	4%
Tryptophan	46 mg	*	Iron	1 mg	6%
Tyrosine	79 mg	*	Magnesium	25 mg	6%
Phenylalanine	137 mg	*	Potassium	365 mg	10%
Niacin	2 mg	8%	Zinc	0.4 mg	3%
Vitamin B6	0.3 mg	14%	Omega-3	62 mg	*
Folate	41 mcg	10%	Omega-6	740 mg	*
Selenium	2 mcg	3%			

* No recommended DV

There are almost limitless combinations of vegetables that can be used in this recipe. All colors of bell peppers, onions, celery, yellow squash, red cabbage, sugar snap peas, potatoes and even chopped kale are some suggestions. Experiment with your favorites!

ROASTED VEGETABLES

Servings: 4

1 c. broccoli flowerets
½ c. carrots, sliced
1 c. cauliflower flowerets
3 cloves garlic, minced
½ c. mushrooms, sliced
1 medium zucchini, sliced
3 Tbsp. olive oil
salt to taste

Mix all ingredients in a bowl. Use hands to thoroughly coat the vegetables. Bake at 400º for 15 minutes. Gently flip vegetables over to cook other side. Remove when vegetables are browned but not burnt, about 10 more minutes. The tips of the broccoli will tend to get a bit more crispy than the rest but that is OK.

Roasted Vegetables

Amounts per serving		%DV	Amounts per serving		%DV
Calories	120	6%	Vitamin B12	0 mcg	0%
Carbohydrates	7 g	2%	Vitamin C	38 mg	64%
Fiber	2 g	7	Vitamin D	1.6 IU	0%
Fat	10 g	16%	Vitamin E	1.6 mg	8%
Protein	2g	4%	Calcium	31 mg	3%
Tryptophan	21 mg	*	Iron	0.6 mg	3%
Tyrosine	43 mg	*	Magnesium	20 mg	5%
Phenylalanine	65 mg	*	Potassium	350 mg	10%
Niacin	1 mg	5%	Zinc	0.4 mg	3%
Vitamin B6	0.2 mg	12%	Omega-3	133 mg	*
Folate	46 mcg	11%	Omega-6	1047mg	*
Selenium	2 mcg	3%			

* No recommended DV

171

The secret to good winter squash is to make sure it is completely cooked. The outside of the squash (skin) should be brown and very soft to the touch. A fork placed in the flesh of the squash should go all the way in very easily. You want the squash to be really soft to the touch.

STUFFED ACORN SQUASH

Servings: 4

2 acorn squash
2 medium apples
½ c. dried cranberries (cranraisins)
½ c. pecans, chopped
1 Tbsp. maple syrup
2 tsp. coconut oil
2 tsp. butter
1 tsp. cinnamon

Heat oven to 375º. Cut squash in half and scoop out seeds. Brush cut sides with oil. Place with cut sides down on baking pan. Melt butter and pour on pan next to squash. Place pecans in the melted butter and bake alongside the squash for 7-8 minutes or until browned but not burned. Remove pecans from pan and set aside. Continue cooking squash for a total of 30 minutes. While squash is cooking, core, peel, and chop apples. Mix together with dried cranberries, cinnamon, and maple syrup. After 30 minutes, remove squash from oven. Turn right side up and fill each cavity with apple mixture. Return to oven, right side up, for an additional 30 minutes or until squash and apples are soft. Remove from oven and sprinkle roasted pecans on top.

Stuffed Acorn Squash

Amounts per serving		%DV	Amounts per serving		%DV
Calories	310	16%	Vitamin B12	0 mcg	0%
Carbohydrates	49 g	16%	Vitamin C	28 mg	47%
Fiber	9 g	8%	Vitamin D	1.4 IU	0%
Fat	8 g	31%	Vitamin E	0.9 mg	4%
Protein	3 g	7%	Calcium	94 mg	9%
Tryptophan	38 mg	*	Iron	2 mg	12%
Tyrosine	90 mg	*	Magnesium	91 mg	23%
Phenylalanine	132 mg	*	Potassium	910 mg	26%
Niacin	2 mg	9%	Zinc	1 mg	6%
Vitamin B6	0.4 mg	20%	Omega-3	228 mg	*
Folate	43 mcg	11%	Omega-6	3260mg	*
Selenium	1.7 mcg	2%			

* No recommended DV

GINGER SWEET POTATO FRIES

Servings: 4

4 medium sweet potatoes
1 tsp. ginger
2 Tbsp. coconut (you can also use olive oil)
salt to taste

Heat oven to 450º. Peel and cut sweet potatoes lengthwise into fry size pieces and place in a large bowl. Whisk together oil and ginger. Pour over fries and mix well with hands so that each piece is coated. Lay fries on a baking sheet in a single layer with space between each one as much as possible for even browning. Bake for 15-20 minutes and turn over with a spatula. Bake another 15-20 minutes or until fries are brown and crispy. Remove from oven and sprinkle with coarse salt.

Ginger Sweet Potato Fries

Amounts per serving		%DV	Amounts per serving		%DV
Calories	171	9%	Vitamin B12	0 mcg	0%
Carbohydrates	27 g	9%	Vitamin C	3 mg	5%
Fiber	4 g	8%	Vitamin D	0 IU	0%
Fat	7 g	19%	Vitamin E	0.4 mg	2%
Protein	2 g	18%	Calcium	40 mg	4%
Tryptophan	41 mg	*	Iron	0.8 mg	5%
Tyrosine	45 mg	*	Magnesium	33 mg	8%
Phenylalanine	117 mg	*	Potassium	444 mg	13%
Niacin	0.7 mg	4%	Zinc	0.4 mg	3%
Vitamin B6	0.3 mg	14%	Omega-3	3 mg	*
Folate	15 mcg	4%	Omega-6	143 mg	*
Selenium	0.9 mcg	1%			

* No recommended DV

I remove pithy asparagus stems by holding the stem side with one hand and with the other hand, holding the other side, about half way between the tip and the middle. Slowly bend the asparagus spear until it snaps in two. It will snap where the pithy part ends. What is left will be the tender, edible part.

ROASTED BALSAMIC ASPARAGUS

Servings: 4

1 lb. raw asparagus, pithy stems removed
1 Tbsp. olive oil
1 Tbsp. balsamic vinegar
1 dash salt
2 dashes pepper

In a small bowl, mix salt, pepper, oil and vinegar. Place asparagus on a baking sheet or in a shallow baking pan. Coat thoroughly with oil and vinegar mixture. Bake at 400º until lightly browned, about 15- 20 minutes, turning once.

Roasted Balsamic Asparagus

Amounts per serving		%DV	Amounts per serving		%DV
Calories	57	11%	Vitamin B12	0 mcg	0%
Carbohydrates	5 g	2%	Vitamin C	6 mg	9%
Fiber	2 g	8%	Vitamin D	0 IU	0%
Fat	3.5 g	5%	Vitamin E	1.6 mg	8%
Protein	2 g	5%	Calcium	26 mg	3%
Tryptophan	27 mg	*	Iron	2.2 mg	12%
Tyrosine	52 mg	*	Magnesium	15 mg	4%
Phenylalanine	75 mg	*	Potassium	212 mg	6%
Niacin	1 mg	5%	Zinc	0.5 mg	4%
Vitamin B6	0.1 mg	5%	Omega-3	36 mg	*
Folate	52 mcg	13%	Omega-6	36 mg	*
Selenium	2.3 mcg	3%			

* No recommended DV

This recipe works well with most any kind of greens - spinach, swiss chard, mustard greens, collard greens, or kale. The tougher greens like kale and collards need to cook about twice as long. Spinach cooks very fast and will cook down more than the others so you will want to start out with about 50% more.

STIR-FRIED GREENS

Servings: 2

3 c. fresh beet greens, chopped
1 clove garlic, minced
2 tsp. olive oil
½ tsp. red pepper flakes
salt to taste

Heat oil in heavy skillet. Add garlic, beet greens, and red pepper flakes. Cook over medium heat, stirring constantly until greens are tender, about 3-4 minutes. Salt to taste and serve.

Stir-Fried Greens

Amounts per serving		%DV	Amounts per serving		%DV
Calories	56	3%	Vitamin B12	0 mcg	0%
Carbohydrates	3 g	1%	Vitamin C	18 mg	30%
Fiber	2 g	9%	Vitamin D	0 IU	0%
Fat	5 g	7%	Vitamin E	1.6 mg	8%
Protein	1 g	3%	Calcium	70 mg	7%
Tryptophan	21 mg	*	Iron	1.5 mg	9%
Tyrosine	31 mg	*	Magnesium	41 mg	10%
Phenylalanine	36 mg	*	Potassium	449 mg	13%
Niacin	0.3 mg	13%	Zinc	0.2 mg	2%
Vitamin B6	0.1 mg	4%	Omega-3	38 mg	*
Folate	9 mcg	29%	Omega-6	500 mg	*
Selenium	0.8 mcg	1%			

* No recommended DV

Don't be afraid of overcooking the squash. The key to really good winter squash is being well cooked. When it's done, the flesh side should be brown. Cook it to just before the point of burning. That is when it is melt in your mouth good.

CARAMELIZED BUTTERNUT SQUASH

Servings: 4

1 medium butternut squash
2 tsp. olive oil

Cut squash in half lengthwise and scoop out seeds. Rub flesh with oil. Place flesh side down on baking sheet and bake at 350º until skin side is brown and very soft to the touch, about 1 - 1 1/2 hours. Flesh side will be bubbly and starting to smell a little burned.

Caramelized Butternut Squash

Amounts per serving		%DV	Amounts per serving		%DV
Calories	102	5%	Vitamin B12	0 mcg	0%
Carbohydrates	22 g	7%	Vitamin C	31 mg	52%
Fiber	9 g	8%	Vitamin D	0 IU	0%
Fat	2 g	4%	Vitamin E	3 mg	15%
Protein	2 g	4%	Calcium	84 mg	8%
Tryptophan	27 mg	*	Iron	1.2 mg	7%
Tyrosine	62 mg	*	Magnesium	59 mg	15%
Phenylalanine	72 mg	*	Potassium	582 mg	17%
Niacin	2 mg	13%	Zinc	0.3 mg	2%
Vitamin B6	0.3 mg	5%	Omega-3	66 mg	*
Folate	39 mcg	10%	Omega-6	248 mg	*
Selenium	1.0 mcg	1%			

* No recommended DV

This dish is high in potassium and vitamin C and is also very balanced in omega-3's and 6's.

STEAMED KALE AND YELLOW SQUASH

Servings: 2

3 c. raw kale, chopped
1 c. yellow squash, sliced
¼ c. sun-dried tomatoes

Place kale and sun-dried tomatoes in a 2 qt. pot with a steamer basket and 1 inch of water. Bring to a boil, reduce heat and simmer, covered, for 5 minutes. Add squash, replace lid and simmer for 5 more minutes. Remove from pot and toss with seasoning salt before serving.

Steamed Kale and Yellow Squash

Amounts per serving		%DV	Amounts per serving		%DV
Calories	86	11%	Vitamin B12	0 mcg	0%
Carbohydrates	18 g	6%	Vitamin C	128 mg	214%
Fiber	4 g	16%	Vitamin D	0 IU	0%
Fat	1 g	2%	Vitamin E	0.7 mg	1%
Protein	5 g	11%	Calcium	163 mg	16%
Tryptophan	54 mg	*	Iron	2.7 mg	15%
Tyrosine	156 mg	*	Magnesium	61 mg	15%
Phenylalanine	223 mg	*	Potassium	834 mg	24%
Niacin	2 mg	13%	Zinc	0.8 mg	5%
Vitamin B6	0.4 mg	19%	Omega-3	255 mg	*
Folate	52 mcg	13%	Omega-6	257 mg	*
Selenium	1.5 mcg	2%			

* No recommended DV

Lambsquarters is a weed that grows wild all over the US and Europe. It is very nutritious and has a nice mild flavor. I have lots of it popping up in the gardens, lawn, and pasture. It is good to eat from early spring when it first appears to later in the summer when it goes to seed. After they go to seed they get a little bitter. When you see them, just pull them up and pluck the leaves from the stems. They are good raw or cooked.

SAUTEED CAULIFLOWER WITH LAMBSQUARTERS

Servings: 1

½ c. raw cauliflower
1 clove garlic, minced
½ c. lambsquarters leaves
1 tsp. olive oil

Cut cauliflower into pieces ¼ inch thick. Heat oil in skillet over medium heat. Add garlic, cauliflower and lambsquarters. Stir for 3-5 minutes until cauliflower is lightly browned on both sides. Salt to taste.

Sauteed Cauliflower and Lambsquarters

Amounts per serving		%DV	Amounts per serving		%DV
Calories	68	3%	Vitamin B12	0 mcg	0%
Carbohydrates	6 g	2%	Vitamin C	47 mg	78%
Fiber	2 g	10%	Vitamin D	0 IU	0%
Fat	5 g	7%	Vitamin E	0.7 mg	3%
Protein	2 g	5%	Calcium	103 mg	10%
Tryptophan	26 mg	*	Iron	0.6 mg	4%
Tyrosine	73 mg	*	Magnesium	18 mg	4%
Phenylalanine	88 mg	*	Potassium	290 mg	8%
Niacin	0.6 mg	3%	Zinc	0.3 mg	2%
Vitamin B6	0.2 mg	11%	Omega-3	63 mg	*
Folate	37 mcg	9%	Omega-6	539 mg	*
Selenium	1.0 mcg	1%			

* No recommended DV

Salads

Some of the salads here contain 20 grams of protein, qualifying them as Main Courses. Some of them are intended to be served as side dishes. You should find all of them easy to make and tasty. Three of the salad dressings found at the back of this section contain flax oil. Using one of these dressings on a salad every day will help ensure you are consuming the correct ratio of omega-3 fats to omega-6 fats. We are aiming for as close to a 1:1 ratio as possible. You will notice that many foods contain more omega-6 than omega-3. So, we need to be conscious of eating foods whenever possible that contain higher amounts of omega-3 and lower amounts of omega-6. Incorporating flax oil into our diet is an excellent way to counterbalance our omega-6 intake.

This small salad is packed with flavor and has enough protein to serve as a main course. Top with a flax oil dressing to balance the omega fats.

COBB SALAD

Servings: 4

4 cups mixed baby greens
1 large tomato, chopped
4 slices crisp cooked bacon, crumbled
½ medium red onion
2 large eggs, hard-boiled and chopped
1 c. cooked chicken breast, chopped
½ c. blue cheese, crumbled
1 large avocado, sliced

Place 1 cup of raw salad greens on each of 4 salad plates. Arrange tomato, bacon, onion, eggs, chicken, blue cheese, and avocado in sections on top of the greens. Serve with favorite dressing.

Cobb Salad

Amounts per serving		%DV	Amounts per serving		%DV
Calories	308	15%	Vitamin B12	0.7 mcg	12%
Carbohydrates	11 g	4%	Vitamin C	21 mg	35%
Fiber	5 g	20%	Vitamin D	0 IU	0%
Fat	20 g	30%	Vitamin E	2.3 mg	12%
Protein	23 g	46%	Calcium	156 mg	16%
Tryptophan	274 mg	*	Iron	2 mg	12%
Tyrosine	878 mg	*	Magnesium	66 mg	17%
Phenylalanine	1099 mg	*	Potassium	778 mg	22%
Niacin	7 mg	36%	Zinc	2 mg	13%
Vitamin B6	0.6 mg	29%	Omega-3	203 mg	*
Folate	134 mg	33%	Omega-6	1503mg	*
Selenium	26 mcg	36%			

* No recommended DV

189

This is a high protein recipe that can be served as a main course. It is also very high in vitamin C, B vitamins and provides 86% of the daily requirement of selenium.

TUNA SALAD

Servings: 3

2 small (5 oz.) cans tuna packed in water, drained
1 c. snowpeas, chopped
½ c. celery, chopped
½ c. feta cheese
½ medium cucumber, chopped
2 large eggs, hard-boiled and chopped
¼ c. onion, chopped
½ small red bell pepper, chopped

Mix all ingredients. This is very good tossed with Honey Mustard Dressing.

Tuna Salad

Amounts per serving		%DV	Amounts per serving		%DV
Calories	211	11%	Vitamin B12	2.5 mcg	42%
Carbohydrates	8 g	3%	Vitamin C	38 mg	63%
Fiber	1.8 g	7%	Vitamin D	11.7 IU	3%
Fat	9 g	14%	Vitamin E	0.9 mg	5%
Protein	24 g	48%	Calcium	179 mg	18%
Tryptophan	283 mg	*	Iron	2.6 mg	14%
Tyrosine	863 mg	*	Magnesium	43 mg	11%
Phenylalanine	1011 mg	*	Potassium	417 mg	12%
Niacin	8.2 mg	41%	Zinc	1.8 mg	12%
Vitamin B6	0.5 mg	24%	Omega-3	260 mg	*
Folate	57 mcg	29%	Omega-6	528 mg	*
Selenium	60 mcg	86%			

* No recommended DV

MOLASSES PINTO BEAN SALAD

Servings: 6

3 c. cooked pinto beans (or 2-15 o.z cans drained)
1 clove garlic, minced
½ c. molasses
2 tsp. olive oil
1 small onion, chopped
1 large green bell pepper
1 Tbsp. mustard seed
½ tsp. red pepper flakes
½ c. sun-dried tomatoes
2 ½ Tbsp. apple cider vinegar

Cover dried tomatoes in water and simmer for 10 minutes. Remove from water and let cool. Put tomatoes, garlic, molasses, olive oil, mustard seed, pepper flakes, and vinegar in a blender. Blend until smooth. Combine beans, onion, and bell pepper in a bowl. Pour the liquid from the blender into the beans and stir. Salt and pepper to taste. Cover and refrigerate for 2 hours or overnight.

Molasses Pinto Bean Salad

Amounts per serving		%DV	Amounts per serving		%DV
Calories	229	11%	Vitamin B12	0 mcg	0%
Carbohydrates	45 g	15%	Vitamin C	26 mg	43%
Fiber	7 g	28%	Vitamin D	0 IU	0%
Fat	3 g	5%	Vitamin E	1.1 mg	5%
Protein	7 g	15%	Calcium	130 mg	13%
Tryptophan	89 mg	*	Iron	3.8 mg	21%
Tyrosine	192 mg	*	Magnesium	118 mg	30%
Phenylalanine	378 mg	*	Potassium	938 mg	27%
Niacin	1.3 mg	13%	Zinc	1.2 mg	8%
Vitamin B6	0.4 mg	19%	Omega-3	263 mg	*
Folate	81 mcg	29%	Omega-6	430 mg	*
Selenium	16.4 mcg	23%			

* No recommended DV

This is my friend, Katharine's, recipe that she created specially for this book. It is very high in vitamin C, vitamin B12, vitamin D, selenium, and calcium. She emphasizes that good quality sardines make all the difference and she recommends Trader Joe's brand. This salad has enough protein to serve as a main course.

KATHARINE'S GREEK GOD SALAD

Servings: 4

1 c. feta cheese, crumbled
1 medium cucumber, chopped
2 - 4 oz. cans sardines, packed in olive oil
2 Tbsp. lemon juice
1 c. black olives, pitted and halved
1 medium red onion, chopped
1 small red bell pepper, chopped
1 small yellow bell pepper, chopped
3 large tomatoes, chopped
4 Tbsp. red wine vinegar
1 tsp. dried oregano
salt and pepper to taste

Drain oil from sardine cans and whisk together with lemon juice, vinegar, and oregano. Set sardines aside. In a bowl, combine all other ingredients except sardines. Add oil and vinegar mix and toss. Divide onto 4 salad plates and top with sardines.

Katharine's Greek God Salad

Amounts per serving		%DV	Amounts per serving		%DV
Calories	415	21%	Vitamin B12	5 mcg	80%
Carbohydrates	19 g	6%	Vitamin C	134 mg	224%
Fiber	4 g	18%	Vitamin D	124 IU	31%
Fat	30 g	46%	Vitamin E	4.6 mg	23%
Protein	20 g	39%	Calcium	434 mg	43%
Tryptophan	226 mg	*	Iron	3.8 mg	21%
Tyrosine	681 mg	*	Magnesium	65 mg	16%
Phenylalanine	839 mg	*	Potassium	847 mg	24%
Niacin	4 mg	22%	Zinc	2.3 mg	16%
Vitamin B6	0.6 mg	28%	Omega-3	944 mg	*
Folate	72 mcg	18%	Omega-6	3432mg	*
Selenium	31 mcg	44%			

* No recommended DV

This is one of my very favorite salads and I eat it a lot, especially around Thanksgiving and Christmas when there is a lot of leftover turkey around. I eat it as a main course because it is high in protein.

TURKEY WALNUT SALAD

Servings: 1

2 cups romaine and mixed baby greens
3 oz. roasted turkey breast, chopped
2 Tbsp. walnuts, chopped
1 Tbsp. blue cheese
1 Tbsp. dried cranberries (cranraisins)

Arrange turkey, walnuts, blue cheese, and cranberries on top of lettuce. Serve with Raspberry Vinaigrette.

Katharine's Greek God Salad

Amounts per serving		%DV	Amounts per serving		%DV
Calories	350	17%	Vitamin B12	0.5 mg	9%
Carbohydrates	12 g	4%	Vitamin C	23 mg	38%
Fiber	4 g	15%	Vitamin D	0 IU	0%
Fat	20 g	30%	Vitamin E	0.5 mg	2%
Protein	33 g	67%	Calcium	152 mg	15%
Tryptophan	386 mg	*	Iron	3 mg	16%
Tyrosine	1328 mg	*	Magnesium	75 mg	19%
Phenylalanine	1399 mg	*	Potassium	617 mg	18%
Niacin	7 mg	35%	Zinc	2.8 mg	19%
Vitamin B6	0.7 mg	34%	Omega-3	2094mg	*
Folate	160 mcg	40%	Omega-6	8359 mg	*
Selenium	31 mcg	44%			

* No recommended DV

This salad has enough protein to be served as a main course. As a light lunch it could be served with gluten-free crackers. For a fuller meal, serve with soup and gluten-free bread.

HAWAIIAN CHICKEN SALAD

Servings: 4

2 c. chicken breast, cooked and chopped
½ c. celery, chopped
2 small cantaloupe
¼ c. onion, chopped
1 small red bell pepper, chopped
1 c. pineapple chunks
½ c. yogurt
dash salt and pepper

Cut cantaloupes in half and remove seeds. Cut a small amount off the bottoms to make them more stable. Mix remaining ingredients. Spoon ¼ of the mixture into each cantaloupe half.

Hawaiian Chicken Salad

Amounts per serving		%DV	Amounts per serving		%DV
Calories	213	11%	Vitamin B12	0 mcg	0%
Carbohydrates	16 g	5%	Vitamin C	32 mg	52%
Fiber	9 g	8%	Vitamin D	0 IU	0%
Fat	16 g	25%	Vitamin E	1.7 mg	9%
Protein	5 g	11%	Calcium	60 mg	6%
Tryptophan	74 mg	*	Iron	1.8 mg	10%
Tyrosine	878 mg	*	Magnesium	82 mg	20%
Phenylalanine	345 mg	*	Potassium	591 mg	17%
Niacin	2 mg	13%	Zinc	1.2 mg	8%
Vitamin B6	0.3 mg	5%	Omega-3	134 mg	*
Folate	115 mcg	29%	Omega-6	2678mg	*
Selenium	22 mcg	31%			

* No recommended DV

CABBAGE SALAD

Servings: 6

3 c. cabbage, chopped
1 c. carrots, grated
½ c. raisins
½ c. plain yogurt
1 Tbsp. honey
1 Tbsp. lemon juice
2 tsp. prepared yellow mustard
½ tsp. salt

Mix together yogurt, lemon juice, mustard, honey, and salt.
Combine with cabbage, carrots, and raisins and toss.

Cabbage Salad

Amounts per serving		%DV	Amounts per serving		%DV
Calories	84	11%	Vitamin B12	0.1 mg	2%
Carbohydrates	20 g	7%	Vitamin C	20 mg	33%
Fiber	2 g	9%	Vitamin D	0 IU	0%
Fat	0.3 g	0%	Vitamin E	0.2 mg	1%
Protein	2 g	5%	Calcium	73 mg	7%
Tryptophan	19 mg	*	Iron	0.6 mg	3%
Tyrosine	72 mg	*	Magnesium	17 mg	4%
Phenylalanine	101 mg	*	Potassium	299 mg	9%
Niacin	0.4 mg	2%	Zinc	0.4 mg	2%
Vitamin B6	0.1 mg	6%	Omega-3	8 mg	*
Folate	27 mcg	7%	Omega-6	41 mg	*
Selenium	1.6 mg	2%			

* No recommended DV

This tasty salad does not require any additional dressing and is a good source of vitamin C and provides 40% of folate.

BEET SALAD

Servings: 4

4 c. mixed baby greens
6 medium beets, cooked
½ c. feta cheese
½ c. walnuts, chopped
¼ c. olive oil
2 Tbsp. red wine vinegar
dash salt and pepper

Cut beets into 1" squares and place in a shallow container. Shake together oil, vinegar, salt and pepper. Pour over beets and marinate in refrigerator while preparing the rest of the salad. Toast walnuts at 350º for about 8 minutes, stirring once. Remove from oven. Place 1 cup of mixed greens on each of 4 salad plates. Divide beets equally, placing on top of greens. Top with walnuts and feta cheese.

Beet Salad

Amounts per serving		%DV	Amounts per serving		%DV
Calories	237	11%	Vitamin B12	0.3 mcg	5%
Carbohydrates	15 g	5%	Vitamin C	18 mg	30%
Fiber	5 g	21%	Vitamin D	0 IU	0%
Fat	18 g	25%	Vitamin E	2.6 mg	13%
Protein	6 g	11%	Calcium	159 mg	16%
Tryptophan	77 mg	*	Iron	2.3 mg	13%
Tyrosine	197 mg	*	Magnesium	62 mg	15%
Phenylalanine	211 mg	*	Potassium	746 mg	21%
Niacin	0.8 mg	4%	Zinc	1.2 mg	8%
Vitamin B6	0.3 mg	5%	Omega-3	161 mg	*
Folate	160 mcg	40%	Omega-6	1470mg	*
Selenium	4.1 mcg	6%			

* No recommended DV

SPINACH SALAD

Servings: 4

4 c. raw baby spinach
1 medium avocado, sliced
1 medium pink grapefruit
½ c. unsalted mixed nuts

Peel grapefruit and separate the sections. Remove the membrane from each section by laying the section on its side and cutting off the inside edge. Peel away the membrane and remove seeds. Arrange avocado and grapefruit sections on top of spinach. Sprinkle with nuts. Serve with your favorite vinaigrette dressing.

Spinach Salad

Amounts per serving		%DV	Amounts per serving		%DV
Calories	213	11%	Vitamin B12	0 mcg	0%
Carbohydrates	16 g	5%	Vitamin C	32 mg	52%
Fiber	9 g	8%	Vitamin D	0 IU	0%
Fat	16 g	25%	Vitamin E	1.7 mg	9%
Protein	5 g	11%	Calcium	60 mg	6%
Tryptophan	74 mg	*	Iron	1.8 mg	10%
Tyrosine	177 mg	*	Magnesium	82 mg	20%
Phenylalanine	345 mg	*	Potassium	591 mg	17%
Niacin	2 mg	13%	Zinc	1.2 mg	8%
Vitamin B6	0.3 mg	5%	Omega-3	134 mg	*
Folate	115 mcg	29%	Omega-6	2678mg	*
Selenium	0.6 mcg	1%			

* No recommended DV

This little salad is packed with tangy-sweet flavor as well as crunch!

GREEN AND ORANGE SALAD

Servings: 2

2 c. watercress, chopped
2 medium seedless tangerines (mandarin oranges)
½ c. raw snowpeas

Place watercress on a salad plate. Peel tangerines and separate the sections. Arrange tangerine sections and snowpeas on top of watercress. Serve with your favorite dressing.

Green and Orange Salad

Amounts per serving		%DV	Amounts per serving		%DV
Calories	61	3%	Vitamin B12	0 mcg	0%
Carbohydrates	14 g	5%	Vitamin C	0.2 mg	0%
Fiber	2.4 g	10%	Vitamin D	--	--
Fat	0 g	0%	Vitamin E	0.5 mg	3%
Protein	2 g	4%	Calcium	84 mg	8%
Tryptophan	19 mg	*	Iron	1 mg	5%
Tyrosine	59 mg	*	Magnesium	24 mg	6%
Phenylalanine	78 mg	*	Potassium	307 mg	9%
Niacin	0.5 mg	3%	Zinc	0.2 mg	1%
Vitamin B6	0.2 mg	8%	Omega-3	27 mg	*
Folate	27 mcg	7%	Omega-6	65 mg	*
Selenium	0.6 mcg	1%			

*No recommended DV

BASIC VINAIGRETTE

Servings: 4

¼ c. flax oil
2 Tbsp. lemon juice
2 Tbsp. apple cider vinegar

Shake all ingredients in a jar until well blended. Serve. Store any remaining in the refrigerator.

*Note that this dressing has a very high omega-3 to omega-6 ratio. Using this dressing on a salad will go a long way towards balancing omega fat intake.

Basic Vinaigrette

Amounts per serving		%DV	Amounts per serving		%DV
Calories	123	6%	Vitamin B12	0 mcg	0%
Carbohydrates	0.7 g	0%	Vitamin C	3.2 mg	5%
Fiber	0 g	0%	Vitamin D	0 IU	0%
Fat	14 g	21%	Vitamin E	1.9 mg	10%
Protein	0 g	0%	Calcium	11 mg	0%
Tryptophan	0 mg	*	Iron	0.1 mg	1%
Tyrosine	0 mg	*	Magnesium	0.8 mg	0%
Phenylalanine	0 mg	*	Potassium	14mg	0%
Niacin	0 mg	0%	Zinc	0 mg	0%
Vitamin B6	0 mg	0%	Omega-3	6200 mg	*
Folate	0.9 mcg	0%	Omega-6	1810mg	*
Selenium	0 mcg	0%			

* No recommended DV

RASPBERRY VINAIGRETTE

Servings: 4

1 Tbsp. raw honey
¼ c. flax oil
juice of 1 orange
½ c. fresh raspberries, washed and stemmed
2 Tbsp. red wine vinegar

Mash raspberries in a bowl. Whisk together with remaining ingredients. Store any remaining in a jar in the refrigerator and shake well before serving.

*Note that this dressing has a very high omega-3 to omega-6 ratio. Using this dressing on a salad will go a long way towards balancing omega fat intake.

Raspberry Vinaigrette

Amounts per serving		%DV	Amounts per serving		%DV
Calories	162	8%	Vitamin B12	0 mcg	0%
Carbohydrates	11 g	4%	Vitamin C	25 mg	41%
Fiber	2 g	8%	Vitamin D	0 IU	0%
Fat	14 g	21%	Vitamin E	2.1 mg	11%
Protein	0.5 g	1%	Calcium	20 mg	2%
Tryptophan	3 mg	*	Iron	0.3 mg	2%
Tyrosine	5 mg	*	Magnesium	8 mg	2%
Phenylalanine	19 mg	*	Potassium	87 mg	2%
Niacin	0.2 mg	1%	Zinc	0.1 mg	1%
Vitamin B6	0.0 mg	0%	Omega-3	6200mg	*
Folate	15 mcg	4%	Omega-6	1810 mg	*
Selenium	0.1 mcg	0%			

* No recommended DV

HONEY MUSTARD DRESSING

Servings: 2

1 Tbsp. raw honey
1 Tbsp. sweet and spicy mustard
1 Tbsp. flax oil
1 ½ Tbsp. red wine vinegar

Whisk all ingredients together or shake in a jar.

*Note that this dressing has a very high omega-3 to omega-6 ratio. Using this dressing on a salad will go a long way towards balancing omega fat intake.

Honey Mustard Dressing

Amounts per serving		%DV	Amounts per serving		%DV
Calories	98	5%	Vitamin B12	0 mcg	0%
Carbohydrates	9 g	3%	Vitamin C	0.2 mg	0%
Fiber	0.3 g	1%	Vitamin D	0 IU	0%
Fat	7 g	1%	Vitamin E	1 mg	5%
Protein	0.3 g	11%	Calcium	5.4 mg	1%
Tryptophan	1 mg	*	Iron	0.2 mg	1%
Tyrosine	11 mg	*	Magnesium	4.1 mg	1%
Phenylalanine	13 mg	*	Potassium	20 mg	1%
Niacin	0 mg	0%	Zinc	0.1 mg	0%
Vitamin B6	0 mg	0%	Omega-3	3100mg	*
Folate	0.7 mcg	0%	Omega-6	905 mg	*
Selenium	2.4 mcg	3%			

* No recommended DV

CREAMY FAT-FREE DRESSING

Servings: 4

½ c. plain fat-free yogurt
1 Tbsp. honey
2 Tbsp. lemon juice
1 clove garlic, minced and mashed
1 Tbsp. fresh parsley
½ tsp. dried dill weed

Whisk all ingredients together in a small bowl or shake in a jar until well blended. Store any remaining in the refrigerator.

Creamy Fat-Free Dressing

Amounts per serving		%DV	Amounts per serving		%DV
Calories	36	2%	Vitamin B12	0.2 mcg	3%
Carbohydrates	8 g	3%	Vitamin C	5.1 mg	8%
Fiber	0.1 g	0%	Vitamin D	0 IU	0%
Fat	0.1 g	0%	Vitamin E	0 mg	0%
Protein	2 g	4%	Calcium	67 mg	7%
Tryptophan	11 mg	*	Iron	0.2 mg	1%
Tyrosine	90 mg	*	Magnesium	8 mg	2%
Phenylalanine	99 mg	*	Potassium	102 mg	3%
Niacin	0.1 mg	0%	Zinc	0.3 mg	2%
Vitamin B6	0 mg	0%	Omega-3	0.5 mg	*
Folate	6.1 mcg	2%	Omega-6	4.0 mg	*
Selenium	1.3 mcg	2%			

* No recommended DV

Desserts and Snacks

What we are looking for in desserts and snacks is nutritive value. When we eat something, no matter what it is, it should be providing us with a good health benefit. The desserts and snacks here demonstrate that healthy food doesn't have to be restricted to mealtimes. None of them are made with refined sugar and all of them are meant to be complimentary to the food you have eaten throughout the rest of the day. I hope that some of these will serve as an inspiration to experiment, find and create recipes that are free of sugar and other processed food.

This is a rich, nutritious, and super fast way to satisfy a sudden chocolate craving!

FLOURLESS CHOCOLATE MUG CAKE

Servings: 1

1 tsp. coconut oil
1 large egg
1 Tbsp. half-and-half
1 Tbsp. maple syrup
½ tsp. vanilla
5 drops liquid stevia
2 Tbsp. raw cacao powder (or cocoa)

Pour coconut oil in the bottom of a coffee mug. Swirl the oil around to cover the bottom of the mug and up to about 1 ½" of the sides. Add remaining ingredients to the mug and beat with a fork until completely moistened. The timing is crucial for this so you will need to check it between 40 and 45 seconds. In my 1000 watt microwave, 45-50 seconds is usually just perfect although sometimes it needs an additional 5 seconds. It is done as soon as the sides start pulling away from the cup. It will still look quite gooey on the top. Unmold it onto a dessert plate immediately. This is almost a cross between cake and pudding with the cake being very moist with it's own chocolaty sauce.

Flourless Chocolate Mug Cake

Amounts per serving		%DV	Amounts per serving		%DV
Calories	223	11%	Vitamin B12	0.7 mcg	12%
Carbohydrates	25 g	8%	Vitamin C	0.2 mg	0%
Fiber	9 g	8%	Vitamin D	18 IU	4%
Fat	13 g	19%	Vitamin E	0.5 mg	3%
Protein	9 g	18%	Calcium	57 mg	6%
Tryptophan	121 mg	*	Iron	3 mg	14%
Tyrosine	350 mg	*	Magnesium	99 mg	25%
Phenylalanine	463 mg	*	Potassium	260 mg	7%
Niacin	0.3 mg	2%	Zinc	1 mg	9%
Vitamin B6	0.1 mg	5%	Omega-3	62 mg	*
Folate	28 mcg	7%	Omega-6	740 mg	*
Selenium	18 mcg	25%			

* No recommended DV

This version of deviled eggs is a wonderful combination of tangy, creamy and crunchy.

DEVILED EGGS

Servings: 6

1 avocado, peeled and pitted
1 cucumber, peeled and diced
6 large eggs, hard-boiled and peeled
1 tsp. prepared horseradish
2 tsp. lime juice
2 Tbsp. pimento, chopped
½ tsp. smoked paprika
¼ tsp. salt

Cut hard-boiled eggs in half lengthwise. Scoop out yolks and put in a medium sized bowl. Add avocado and mash together with lime juice, horseradish, and salt and pepper to taste. Fold in chopped pimentos and cucumber until well mixed. Spoon mixture back into the cavity of the egg halves. Sprinkle with paprika.

Deviled Eggs

Amounts per serving		%DV	Amounts per serving		%DV
Calories	134	11%	Vitamin B12	0.6 mcg	9%
Carbohydrates	4 g	1%	Vitamin C	8.5 mg	14%
Fiber	2 g	10%	Vitamin D	0 IU	0%
Fat	10 g	16%	Vitamin E	1.2 mg	6%
Protein	7 g	14%	Calcium	31 mg	3%
Tryptophan	86 mg	*	Iron	0.9 mg	5%
Tyrosine	274 mg	*	Magnesium	16.2 mg	4%
Phenylalanine	415 mg	*	Potassium	246 mg	7%
Niacin	0.7 mg	3%	Zinc	1 mg	9%
Vitamin B6	0.2 mg	8%	Omega-3	78 mg	*
Folate	51 mcg	13%	Omega-6	1170mg	*
Selenium	16 mcg	22%			

* No recommended DV

This works as a dessert or as breakfast if you add some additional protein. 2 large eggs or a 10 oz. glass of 2% milk would provide the additional needed protein.

GRAINLESS PANCAKES

Servings: 2

1 medium banana
½ c. strawberries
1 large egg
¼ coconut flour
½ c. plain yogurt
1 tsp. vanilla
2 tsp. maple syrup
¼ tsp. baking soda
pinch of salt

Mix all ingredients except banana and strawberries. Heat a small amount of coconut oil or butter in a skillet. Drop 3 inch rounds into heated oil. Cook over low-medium heat until browned on one side, about 3 minutes. Flip and cook about 3 minutes on second side. Serve with banana and strawberries sliced on top. You can add other toppings like fruit syrup and whipped cream.

Grainless Pancakes

Amounts per serving		%DV	Amounts per serving		%DV
Calories	337	17%	Vitamin B12	0.7 mcg	12%
Carbohydrates	36 g	12%	Vitamin C	27 mg	45%
Fiber	6 g	25%	Vitamin D	8.8 IU	2%
Fat	19 g	29%	Vitamin E	0.5 mg	3%
Protein	9 g	19%	Calcium	151 mg	15%
Tryptophan	90 mg	*	Iron	1.7 mg	9%
Tyrosine	324	*	Magnesium	58 mg	15%
Phenylalanine	486 mg	*	Potassium	600 mg	17%
Niacin	0.8 mg	4%	Zinc	1.5 mg	10%
Vitamin B6	0.4 mg	19%	Omega-3	58.5 mg	*
Folate	42 mcg	10%	Omega-6	526 mg	*
Selenium	15.6 mcg	22%			

* No recommended DV

223

KALE CHIPS

Servings: 4

1 bunch raw kale (about 3 cups chopped)
1 Tbsp. olive oil
seasoning of choice
coarse salt to taste (optional)

Wash the kale and pat dry. Make sure the kale is thoroughly dry. This is really important so it doesn't turn out limp. Cut or tear the leaves away from the stem. Discard the stems. Tear the leaves into 2", chip size, pieces. You can drizzle the oil over the leaves and use your hands to cover each leaf lightly with oil. This works best with an oil spritzer. It will coat the leaves more evenly and go faster. You can sprinkle them lightly at this point with your favorite seasoning – I like The Spice Hunter's Fajita Seasoning – but it isn't necessary. Bake at 375º for about 15 minutes until the "chips" are crispy and brown but not burnt. Sprinkle with coarse salt if desired.

Kale Chips

Amounts per serving		%DV	Amounts per serving		%DV
Calories	110	5%	Vitamin B12	0 mcg	0%
Carbohydrates	10 g	3%	Vitamin C	121 mg	201%
Fiber	2 g	8%	Vitamin D	0 IU	0%
Fat	8 g	11%	Vitamin E	1 mg	5%
Protein	3 g	7%	Calcium	136 mg	14%
Tryptophan	40 mg	*	Iron	1.7 mg	10%
Tyrosine	118 mg	*	Magnesium	34 mg	9%
Phenylalanine	170 mg	*	Potassium	449 mg	13%
Niacin	1 mg	5%	Zinc	0.4 mg	3%
Vitamin B6	0.3 mg	14%	Omega-3	232 mg	*
Folate	29 mcg	7%	Omega-6	798 mg	*
Selenium	0.9 mcg	1%			

* No recommended DV

These make a nice snack, side dish, or a fun take-along finger food.

PIZZA BUTTONS

Servings: 8

8 large mushrooms
½ c. mozzarella cheese, shredded
¼ c. pepperoni, minced
½ c. marinara sauce
4 cloves garlic
1 Tbsp. olive oil
½ tsp. oregano

Remove mushroom stems. Place upside down on baking sheet. Brush with olive oil. Sprinkle ½ clove garlic (1/2 tsp.) in each mushroom cap. Bake at 350º for 5 minutes. Remove from oven. Place 1 Tbsp. of marinara in each cap, about 2 tsp. of pepperoni, 1 Tbsp. cheese, and a small pinch of oregano on top. Return to oven and bake for an additional 6-8 minutes until cheese is melted and starting to brown.

Pizza Buttons

Amounts per serving		%DV	Amounts per serving		%DV
Calories	103	5%	Vitamin B12	0.2 mcg	4%
Carbohydrates	4 g	1%	Vitamin C	1.4 mg	2%
Fiber	0.7 g	3%	Vitamin D	5.1 IU	4%
Fat	7 g	3%	Vitamin E	0.7 mg	3%
Protein	6 g	12%	Calcium	107 mg	11%
Tryptophan	68 mg	*	Iron	0.4 mg	2%
Tyrosine	234 mg	*	Magnesium	11 mg	3%
Phenylalanine	237 mg	*	Potassium	167 mg	5%
Niacin	2 mg	9%	Zinc	0.8 mg	5%
Vitamin B6	0.1 mg	5%	Omega-3	51 mg	*
Folate	8 mcg	2%	Omega-6	634 mg	*
Selenium	7 mcg	10%			

* No recommended DV

This dessert tastes like a major indulgence and is an excellent source of fiber, B vitamins, vitamin C, potassium, and magnesium. You will want to use medjool dates because they are bigger and softer than other types and will blend smoother without leaving little bits in the mousse.

MOCHA MOUSSE

Servings: 2

1 ripe avocado
1 ripe banana (fresh or frozen)
2 Tbsp. raw cacao (or cocoa)
¼ c. espresso or strong brewed coffee
4 medjool dates
1 tsp. vanilla extract
1 Tbsp. maple syrup

Peel and pit avocado. Put avocado and all other ingredients in blender and blend until smooth and creamy. Spoon into 2 dessert glasses and refrigerate until cold – about 30 minutes.

Mocha Mouse

Amounts per serving		%DV	Amounts per serving		%DV
Calories	365	18%	Vitamin B12	0 mcg	0%
Carbohydrates	61 g	20%	Vitamin C	15 mg	25%
Fiber	13 g	53%	Vitamin D	0 IU	0%
Fat	16 g	24%	Vitamin E	2.1 mg	11%
Protein	5 g	9%	Calcium	53 mg	5%
Tryptophan	49 mg	*	Iron	2 mg	11%
Tyrosine	101 mg	*	Magnesium	183 mg	47%
Phenylalanine	335 mg	*	Potassium	1150 mg	33%
Niacin	4.6 mg	23%	Zinc	1.3 mg	9%
Vitamin B6	0.6 mg	30%	Omega-3	126 mg	*
Folate	102 mcg	26%	Omega-6	1776mg	*
Selenium	1.7 mcg	2%			

* No recommended DV

You want to be sure to use canned coconut milk for this - not the kind that comes in the carton. The canned coconut milk is much richer. Shake the can really well before opening and measuring it. Also, you can greatly increase the nutritional content, including protein, B vitamins, calcium, and magnesium, by substituting whole dairy milk for the coconut milk.

DAIRY-FREE PUMPKIN CUSTARD

Servings: 8

2 c. cooked pumpkin
1 c. canned coconut milk
2 large eggs
½ c. maple syrup
1 tsp. cinnamon
½ tsp. ground ginger
¼ tsp. ground cloves
½ tsp. salt

Beat eggs in a large bowl. Add remaining ingredients and mix until smooth. You can make this into a pie by pouring the mixture into an unbaked pie shell or to bake as a custard, pour the mixture into an oiled pie pan. Bake at 425º for 15 minutes. Leave custard in the oven and reduce heat to 350º. Bake another 35-45 minutes until slightly brown on top and around the edges.

Dairy-Free Pumpkin Custard

Amounts per serving		%DV	Amounts per serving		%DV
Calories	146	7%	Vitamin B12	0.2 mcg	3%
Carbohydrates	20 g	7%	Vitamin C	3 mg	5%
Fiber	1 g	4%	Vitamin D	0 IU	0%
Fat	7 g	11%	Vitamin E	0.6 mg	3%
Protein	3 g	5%	Calcium	32 mg	3%
Tryptophan	34 mg	*	Iron	1.7 mg	10%
Tyrosine	100 mg	*	Magnesium	22 mg	6%
Phenylalanine	130 mg	*	Potassium	249 mg	7%
Niacin	0.5 mg	2%	Zinc	0.9 mg	6%
Vitamin B6	0.1 mg	3%	Omega-3	14 mg	*
Folate	16 mcg	4%	Omega-6	223 mg	*
Selenium	4.3 mcg	6%			

* No recommended DV

TRAIL MIX

Servings: 15

1 c. dried bananas
1 c. cacao nibs (or crush a cacao candy bar)
1 c. raw almonds
1 c. raw cashews
1 c. dried unsweetened coconut flakes
1 c. raisins
1 c. pumpkin seeds
1 c. walnuts
coarse salt to taste

Roast nuts and pumpkin seeds at 350º for about 10 minutes. Stir, sprinkle with coarse salt and add coconut. Roast about 7 more minutes until coconut begins to brown. Let cool completely then add dried bananas, cacao nibs and raisins. Store in airtight container.

Trail Mix

Amounts per serving		%DV	Amounts per serving		%DV
Calories	300	15%	Vitamin B12	0 mcg	0%
Carbohydrates	26 g	9%	Vitamin C	1 mg	2%
Fiber	5 g	19%	Vitamin D	0 IU	0%
Fat	21 g	32%	Vitamin E	2.7 mg	13%
Protein	9 g	18%	Calcium	46 mg	5%
Tryptophan	100 mg	*	Iron	4 mg	21%
Tyrosine	211 mg	*	Magnesium	136 mg	34%
Phenylalanine	366 mg	*	Potassium	474 mg	14%
Niacin	1 mg	5%	Zinc	2 mg	13%
Vitamin B6	0.1 mg	7%	Omega-3	34 mg	*
Folate	15 mcg	4%	Omega-6	3979mg	*
Selenium	4.8 mcg	7%			

* No recommended DV

This is a very easy and tasty snack and it would be easy to eat too many of them. They are high in calories at 100 each and also high in omega-6's compared to omega-3's so you don't want to make a habit of these. But, each one has 129% of your daily requirement of selenium! So, I like to make up a few, keep them in the fridge and indulge in one every once in a while for a delicious way to help make sure I'm getting enough selenium.

BRAZILIAN DATES

Servings: 6

6 large medjool dates
6 large brazilnuts
1 Tbsp. dried unsweetened coconut, finely ground

Slice dates open enough to remove the pit. Place a brazilnut in the date folding the date around the nut. Roll in dried coconut.

Brazilian Dates

Amounts per serving		%DV	Amounts per serving		%DV
Calories	100	5%	Vitamin B12	0 mcg	0%
Carbohydrates	19 g	6%	Vitamin C	0 mg	0%
Fiber	2 g	8%	Vitamin D	0 IU	0%
Fat	4 g	5%	Vitamin E	0.3 mg	2%
Protein	1 g	2%	Calcium	23 mg	2%
Tryptophan	9 mg	*	Iron	0.3 mg	2%
Tyrosine	25 mg	*	Magnesium	31 mg	8%
Phenylalanine	43 mg	*	Potassium	201 mg	6%
Niacin	0.4 mg	2%	Zinc	0.3 mg	2%
Vitamin B6	0.1 mg	3%	Omega-3	0.8 mg	*
Folate	5 mcg	1%	Omega-6	972 mg	*
Selenium	90 mcg	129%			

* No recommended DV

This is a favorite for kids and adults alike. Each of them has nearly half of the daily requirement of vitamin C and only 88 calories.

STRAWBERRY DREAMSICLES

Servings: 6

2 c. plain whole milk yogurt
2 c. strawberries, fresh or frozen
1 tsp. vanilla
2 Tbsp. honey

Place all ingredients in a blender and blend until smooth. Pour into popsicle molds or paper cups with wooden popsicle sticks inserted in the middle. Freeze.

Strawberry Dreamsicles

Amounts per serving		%DV	Amounts per serving		%DV
Calories	88	4%	Vitamin B12	0.3 mcg	5%
Carbohydrates	13 g	4%	Vitamin C	29 mg	48%
Fiber	1 g	4%	Vitamin D	0 IU	0%
Fat	3 g	4%	Vitamin E	0.2 mg	1%
Protein	3 g	6%	Calcium	107 mg	11%
Tryptophan	21 mg	*	Iron	0.3 mg	1%
Tyrosine	154 mg	*	Magnesium	16 mg	4%
Phenylalanine	164 mg	*	Potassium	205 mg	6%
Niacin	0.3 mg	1%	Zinc	0.6 mg	4%
Vitamin B6	0.1 mg	3%	Omega-3	53 mg	*
Folate	17.4 mcg	4%	Omega-6	96 mg	*
Selenium	2 mcg	3%			

* No recommended DV

References

Agnoli A, Andreoli V, Casacchia M, Cerbo R. (1976). Effect of s-adenosyl-l-methionine (SAMe) upon depressive symptoms. *Journal of Psychiatric Research, 13,* 43–54.

Akbaraly T., & Brunner E. (2009). Dietary pattern and depressive symptoms in middle age. *British Journal of Psychiatry, 195,* 408–413.

Ambrogini P., Ciuffoli S., Lattanzi D., Minelli A., Bucherelli C., Baldi E., Betti M., Cuppini R. (2011, October 24). Maternal dietary loads of α-tocopherol differentially influence fear conditioning and spatial learning in adult offspring. *Physiology & Behavior,* *104*(5), 809-15. doi: 10.1016/j.physbeh.2011.07.026.

Amminger PG., Berger GE., Schäfer MR., Klier C., Friedrich MH., Feucht M. (2007, February 15). Omega-3 fatty acids supplementation in children with autism: a double-blind randomized, placebo-controlled pilot study. *Biological Psychiatry, 61(*4), 551-3.

Amr M., El-Mogy A., Shams T., Vieira K., Lakhan SE. (2013, March 9). Efficacy of vitamin C as an adjunct to fluoxetine therapy in pediatric major depressive disorder: a randomized, double-blind, placebo-controlled pilot study. *Nutrition Journal,12,* 31. doi:10.1186/1475-2891-12-31.

Anglin RE., Samaan Z., Walter SD., McDonald SD. (2013, February). Vitamin D deficiency and depression in adults: systematic review and meta-analysis. *British Journal of Psychiatry, 202,* 100-7. doi: 10.1192/bjp.bp.111.106666.

Armstrong D., et al. (2007).Vitamin D deficiency is associated with anxiety and depression in fibromyalgia. *Clinical Rheumatology, 2,* 551-4.

Bae YJ., & Kim SK. (2012, December). Low dietary calcium is associated with self-rated depression in middle-aged Korean women. *Nutrition Research and Practice, 6*(6), 527-33. doi: 10.4162/nrp.2012.6.6.527.

Bakhtiyari M., Ehrampoush E., Enayati N., Joodi G., Sadr S., et al. (2013, April). Anxiety as a consequence of modern dietary pattern in adults in Tehran-Iran. *Eating Behaviors, 14*(2), 107-12. doi: 10.1016/j.eatbeh.2012.12.007.

Benton D., & Cook R. (1991, June 1).The impact of selenium supplementation on mood. *BiologicalPsychiatry, 29*(11), 10928.

Bertone-Johnson ER., Powers SI., Spangler L., Larson J., Michael YL., et al. (2012, July 1). Vitamin D supplementation and depression in the women's health initiative calcium and vitamin D trial. *American Journal of Epidemiology, 176*(1), 1-13. doi: 10.1093/aje/kwr482. Epub 2012 May 9.

Bloch M., Qawasmi A. (2011, October). Omega-3 fatty acid supplementation for the treatment of children with attention-deficit/hyperactivity disorder symptomatology: systematic review and meta-analysis. *Journal of the American Academy of Child and Adolescent Psychiatry, 50*(10), 991-1000.

Brocardo PS., Assini F., Franco JL., Pandolfo P., Müller YM., et al. (2007, May). Zinc attenuates malathion-induced depressant-like behavior and confers neuroprotection in the rat brain. *Toxicological Sciences, 97*(1), 140-8. Epub 2007 Feb 27.

Brody S. (2002, August 15). High-dose ascorbic acid increases intercourse frequency and improves mood: a randomized controlled clinical trial. *Biological Psychiatry, 52*(4), 371-4.

Broersen LM., Kuipers AA., Balvers M., van Wijk N., Savelkoul PJ., et al. (2013). A specific multi-nutrient diet reduces Alzheimer-like pathology in young adult AβPPswe/PS1dE9 mice. *Journal of Alzheimers Disease, 33*(1), 177-90. doi: 10.3233/JAD-2012-112039.

Canadian Mental Health Association - Moose Jaw: Women and Depression n/d

Christensen O., & Christensen E. (1988). Fat consumption and schizophrenia. Acta Psychiatrica Scandinavica, *78*(5), 587-591.

Clayton EH., Hanstock TL., Hirneth SJ., Kable CJ., Garg ML., Hazell PL. (2009, August). Reduced mania and depression in juvenile bipolar disorder associated with long-chain omega-3 polyunsaturated fatty acid supplementation. *European Journal of Clinical Nutrition, 63*(8), 1037-40.

Coleman, R. Psychiatric Disorders Caused by Vitamin Deficiencies. (Livestrong. November 22, 2010, http://www.livestrong.com/article/314558-psychiatric-disorders-caused-by-vitamin-deficiencies/#ixzz1iKm2wCNO).

Cope EC., & Levenson CW. (2010, November). Role of zinc in the development and treatment of mood disorders. *Current Opinion in Clinical Nutrition & Metabolic Care, 13*(6), 685-9. doi: 10.1097/MCO.0b013e32833df61a.

Cope EC., Morris DR., Levenson CW. (2012, July). Improving treatments and outcomes: an emerging role for zinc in traumatic brain injury. *Nutrition Reviews, 70*(7), 410-3. doi: 10.1111/j.1753-4887.2012.00486.x.

Davison KM., & Kaplan BJ. (2012, February). Nutrient intakes are correlated with overall psychiatric functioning in adults with mood disorders. *Canadian Journal of Psychiatry, 57*(2), 85-92.

Davison KM. & Kaplan BJ. (2011, December). Vitamin and mineral intakes in adults with mood disorders: comparisons to nutrition standards and associations with sociodemographic and clinical variables. *Journal of the American College of Nutrition, 30*(6), 547-58.

Demyttenaere K, Bruffaerts R, Posada-Villa J, Gasquet I, Kovess V, et al., WHO World Mental Health Survey Consortium. (2004). Prevalence, severity, and unmet need for treatment of mental disorders in the World Health Organization World Mental Health Surveys. *JAMA*, 291(21), 2581-2590.

Derbeneva SA., Bogdanov AR., Pogozheva AV., Gladyshev OA., Vasilevskaia LS., Zorin SN., Mazo VK. (2012). Effect of diet enriched with selenium on the psycho-emotional and adaptive capacity of patients with cardiovascular diseases and obesity. *Vopr Pitan, 81*(4), 35-41.

Devore EE., Grodstein .F, van Rooij FJ., Hofman A., Stampfer MJ., Witteman JC., Breteler MM. (2010, July). Dietary antioxidants and long-term risk of dementia. *Archives of Neurology, 67*(7), 819-25. doi: 10.1001/archneurol.2010.144.

DiGirolamo AM., Ramirez-Zea M., Wang M., Flores-Ayala R., Martorell R., et al. (2010, November). Randomized trial of the effect of zinc supplementation on the mental health of school-age children in Guatemala. *American Journal of Clinical Nutrition, 92*(5), 1241-50. doi: 10.3945/ajcn.2010.29686.

Eby GA., Eby KL. (2006). Rapid recovery from major depression using magnesium treatment. *Medical Hypotheses, 67*(2), 362-70. Epub 2006 Mar 20.

Ellsworth-Bowers ER., & Corwin EJ. (2012, June). Nutrition and the psychoneuroimmunology of postpartum depression.

Nutrition Research Reviews, 25(1), 180-92. doi: 10.1017/S0954422412000091.

Eschenauer G., Sweet BV.(2006). Pharmacology and Therapeutic Uses of Theanine. *American Journal of Health-System Pharmacy, 63*, 26-30.

Fava M., Alpert J., Nierenberg AA., Mischoulon D., Otto MW., Zajecka J., Murck H., Rosenbaum JF. (2005). A double-blind, randomized trial of St. John's wort, fluoxetine, and placebo in major depressive disorder. *Journal of Clinical Psychopharmacology, 25*(5), 441-447.

Gautam M., Agrawal M., ,Gautam M., Sharma P., Gautam AS., Gautam S. (2012, July). Role of antioxidants in generalised anxiety disorder and depression. *Indian Journal of Psychiatry, 54*(3), 244-7. doi: 10.4103/0019-5545.102424.

German L., Kahana C., Rosenfeld V., Zabrowsky I., Wiezer Z., Fraser D., Shahar DR. (2011, January). Depressive symptoms are associated with food insufficiency and nutritional deficiencies in poor community-dwelling elderly people. *Journal of Nutrition Health and Aging. 15*(1), 3-8.

Gosney MA., Hammond MF., Shenkin A., Allsup S. (2008). Effect of micronutrient supplementation on mood in nursing home residents. *Gerontology, 54*(5), 292-9. doi: 10.1159/000131886.

Harvard Mental Health Publications, Harvard Mental Health Letter, September, 2004.

Heurteaux C., Lucas G., Guy N., El Yacoubi M., et al. (2006). Deletion of the background potassium channel TREK-1 results in a depression-resistant phenotype. *Nature Neuroscience* 9, 1134-1141 Published online: 13 August 2006. doi:10.1038/nn1749.

Hiremath SB., Anand S., Srinivas LD., Rashed MR. (2010, December). Effect of calcium on anxiolytic activity of diazepam and verapamil in rats. *Indian Journal of Pharmacology, 42*(6), 406-8. doi: 10.4103/0253-7613.71889.

Hughes RN., Lowther CL., van Nobelen M. (2011, January). Prolonged treatment with vitamins C and E separately and together decreases anxiety-related open-field behavior and acoustic startle in hooded rats. *Pharmacology Biochemistry and Behavior, 97*(3), 494-9. doi: 10.1016/j.pbb.2010.10.010. Epub 2010 Oct 28.

Jacka FN., Kremer PJ., Leslie ER., Berk M., Patton GC., et al. (2010, May). Associations between diet quality and depressed mood in adolescents: results from the Australian Healthy Neighbourhoods Study. *Australian and New Zealand Journal of Psychiatry, 44*(5), 435-42. doi: 10.3109/00048670903571598.

Jacka FN., Mykletun A., Berk M., Bjelland I., Tell GS. (2011, July-August). The association between habitual diet quality and the common mental disorders in community-dwelling adults: the Hordaland Health study. *Psychosomatic Medicine,73*(6), 483-90. doi: 10.1097/PSY.0b013e318222831a.

Jacka FN., Overland S., Stewart R., Tell GS., Bjelland I., Mykletun A. (209, January). Association between magnesium intake and depression and anxiety in community-dwelling adults: the Hordaland Health Study. *Australian and New Zealand Journal of Psychiatry, 43*(1), 45-52. doi: 10.1080/00048670802534408.

Jazayeri S., Tehrani-Doost M., Keshavarz S., et al. (2008, March). Comparison of therapeutic effects of omega-3 fatty acid eicosapentaenoic acid and fluoxetine, separately and in combination, in major depressive disorder. *Australian and New Zealand Journal of Psychiatry, 42*(3), 192-8.

Jia F., Yue M., Chandra D., Keramidas A., Goldstein PA., Homanics GE., Harrison NL. (2008, January 2). Taurine is a potent activator of extrasynaptic GABA(A) receptors in the thalamus. Journal of Neuroscience, 28(1), 106-15.

Joshi M., Akhtar M., Najmi AK., Khuroo AH., Goswami D. (2012, December). Effect of zinc in animal models of anxiety, depression and psychosis. *Human and Experimental Toxicologyl,* *31*(12), 1237-43. doi: 10.1177/0960327112444938.

Kalueff A., et al. (2006). Behavioral anomalies in mice evoked by Tokyo disruption of the vitamin D receptor gene. *NeuroscientificResearch, 54,* 254-60.

Kalueff A., et al. (2004). Increased anxiety in mice lacking vitamin D receptor gene. *Neuroreport, 15,* 1271-74.

Kalueff AV., Lou YR., Laaksi I., Tuohimaa P. (2004, June 7).Increased anxiety in mice lacking vitamin D receptor gene. *Neuroreport, 15*(8), 1271-4.

Keenan E., Finnie M., Jones P., Rogers P., Priestley C. (2011, March 15). How much theanine in a cup of tea? Effects of tea type and method of preparation. *Food Chemistry, 125*(2), 588-594. Khoraminya N., Tehrani-Doost M., Jazayeri S., Hosseini A., Djazayery A. (2013, March). Therapeutic effects of vitamin D as adjunctive therapy to fluoxetine in patients with major depressive disorder. *Australian and New Zealand Journal of Psychiatry, 47*(3), 271-5. doi: 10.1177/0004867412465022. Epub 2012 Oct 23.

Kiecolt-Glaser JK., Belury MA., Andridge R., Malarkey WB., Glaser R. (2011, November). Omega-3 supplementation lowers inflammation and anxiety in medical students: a randomized controlled trial. *Brain Behavior and Immunity, 25*(8), 1725-34. doi:10.1016/j.bbi.2011.07.229.

Kimura K., Ozeki M., Juneja LR., Ohira H. (2007, January). L-Theanine reduces psychological and physiological stress responses. *Biological Psychology, 74*(1), 39-45.

Kryscio RJ., Abner EL., Schmitt FA., Goodman PJ., Mendiondo M., Caban-Holt A., Dennis BC., Mathews M., Klein EA., Crowley JJ.; SELECT Investigators (2013, January). A randomized controlled Alzheimer's disease prevention trial's evolution into an exposure trial: the PREADViSE Trial. *Journal of Nutritional Health and Aging, 17*(1), 72-5. doi: 10.1007/s12603-012-0083-3.

Lakhan S., & Vieira K. (2008, January). Nutritional Therapies for Mental Health Disorders. *Nutrition Journal, 7,* 2. doi:10.1186/1475-2891-7-2

Leung BM., & Kaplan BJ. (2009, September). Perinatal depression: prevalence, risks, and the nutrition link--a review of the literature. *Journal of the American Dietetic Association, 109*(9), 1566-75. doi: 10.1016/j.jada.2009.06.368.

Leung BM., Kaplan BJ., Field CJ., Tough S., Eliasziw M., Gomez MF., McCargar LJ., Gagnon L.; APrON Study Team. (2013, January 16). Prenatal micronutrient supplementation and postpartum depressive symptoms in a pregnancy cohort. *BMC Pregnancy Childbirth, 13,* 2. doi: 10.1186/1471-2393-13-2.

Levine J., Barak Y., Gonzalves M., Szor H., Elizur A., Kofman O., Belmaker RH. (1995). "Double-blind, controlled trial of inositol treatment of depression". *American Journal of Psychiatry* 152 (5): 792–794. PMID 7726322.

Li Y., Zhang J., McKeown RE. (2009, January 30). Cross-sectional assessment of diet quality in individuals with a lifetime history of attempted suicide. *Psychiatry Research,165*(1-2), 111-9. doi: 10.1016/j.psychres.2007.09.004.

Lin H., Mao S., Gean P. (2009, October). Block of γ-Aminobutyric Acid-A Receptor Insertion in the Amygdala Impairs Extinction of Conditioned Fear. *Biological Psychiatry, 66*(7).

Liu C., & Xie B. (2007). Perceived stress, depression and food consumption frequency in the college students of China Seven Cities. *Physiology & Behavior, 92,* 748–754.

Lobato KR., Cardoso CC., Binfaré RW., Budni J., Wagner CL., et al. (2010, June 19). alpha-Tocopherol administration produces an antidepressant-like effect in predictive animal models of depression. *Behavioural Brain Research, 209*(2), 249-59. doi: 10.1016/j.bbr.2010.02.002.

Maddock J., Berry DJ., Geoffroy MC., Power C., Hyppönen E. (2013, January 21). Vitamin D and common mental disorders in mid-life: Cross-sectional and prospective findings. *Clinical Nutrition.* pii: S0261-5614(13)00030-7. doi: 10.1016/j.clnu.2013.01.006. [Epub ahead of print].

Maes M., De Vos N., Pioli R., Demedts P., Wauters A., et al. (2000, June). Lower serum vitamin E concentrations in major depression. Another marker of lowered antioxidant defenses in that illness. *Journal of Affective Disorders, 58*(3), 241-6.

McAfee AJ., McSorley EM., Cuskelly GJ., et al. (2011, January). Red meat from animals offered a grass diet increases plasma and platelet n-3 PUFA in healthy consumers. *British Journal of Nutrition, 105*(1), 80-9. doi: 10.1017/S0007114510003090.

McCleane GJ., & Watters CH. (2007). Pre-operative anxiety and serum potassium. *Anaesthesia, 45(7).* Article first published online: 22 Feb 2007 doi: 10.1111/j.1365-2044.1990.tb14837.x.

McClung J., Karl JP., Sonya J Cable SJ., Williams KW., Nindl B., Young AJ., Lieberman HR. (2009). Randomized, double-blind, placebo-controlled trial of iron supplementation in female soldiers during military training: effects on iron status, physical performance, and mood. *American Journal of Clinical Nutrition, 90*(1), 124-131. First published May 27, 2009, doi: 10.3945/ ajcn.2009.27774.

Medhavi Gautam, Mukta Agrawal, Manaswi Gautam, Praveen Sharma, Anita Sharma Gautam, Shiv Gautam (2012). Role of antioxidants in generalised anxiety disorder and depression. *Indian J Psychiatry, 54*(3):244-7.

Milaneschi Y., Hoogendijk W., Lips P., Heijboer AC., Schoevers R., et al. (2013, April 9). The association between low vitamin D and depressive disorders. *Molecular Psychiatry.* doi: 10.1038/mp.2013.36. [Epub ahead of print].

Mokhber N., Namjoo M., Tara F., Boskabadi H., Rayman MP., et al. (2011, January). Effect of supplementation with selenium on postpartum depression: a randomized double-blind placebo-controlled trial. J *Journal of Maternal-Fetal and Neonatal Medicine, 24*(1), 104-8. doi: 10.3109/14767058.2010.482598. Epub 2010 Jun 8.

Moretti M., Colla A., de Oliveira Balen G., dos Santos DB., Budni J., et al. (2012, March). Ascorbic acid treatment, similarly to fluoxetine, reverses depressive-like behavior and brain oxidative damage induced by chronic unpredictable stress. *Journal of Psychiatric Research, 46*(3), 331-40. doi:10.1016/j.jpsychires.2011.11.009. Epub 2011 Dec 9.

Morris MS., Picciano MF., Jacques PF., Selhub J. (2008, May). Trends of Vitamin B6 Status in US Population Sample. *American Journal of Clinical Nutrition, 87,* 1446-54.

Mozaffari-Khosravi H., Nabizade L., Yassini-Ardakani SM., Hadinedoushan H., Barzegar K. (2013, April 19). The Effect of 2 Different Single Injections of High Dose of Vitamin D on Improving the Depression in Depressed Patients With Vitamin D Deficiency: A Randomized Clinical Trial. *Journal of Clinical Psychopharmacology.* 2013 Apr 19. [Epub ahead of print].

Murck H. (2002, December).Magnesium and affective disorders. *Nutritional Neuroscience, 5*(6), 375-89.

Nagwa M., Hazem A., Amr G., Rehab K., (2008, September). Role of polyunsaturated fatty acids in the management of Egyptian children with autism. *Clinical Biochemistry, 41*(13), 1044-8.

Nathan P., Lu, K., Gray, M.; Oliver, C. (2006). The Neuropharmacology of L-Theanine(N-Ethyl-L-Glutamine). *Journal of Herbal Pharmacotherapy 6* (2), 21–30. doi:10.1300/J157v06n02_02. PMID 17182482.

National Institute of Mental Health. The Numbers Count: Mental Disorders in America. www.nimh.nih.gov/health/publications/the-numbers-count-mental-disorders-in-america/index.shtml.

Naylor GJ., & Smith AH. (1981). Vanadium: a possible aetiological factor in manic depressive illness. *Psychology and Medicine, 11,* 249-256.

Nogovitsina OR., & Levitina EV. (2006, January-February). Effect of MAGNE-B6 on the clinical and biochemical manifestations of the syndrome of attention deficit and hyperactivity in children. *Eksp Klin Farmakol, 69*(1), 74-7.

Okura Y., Tawara .S, Kikusui T., Takenaka A. (2009, May-June). Dietary vitamin E deficiency increases anxiety-related behavior in rats under stress of social isolation. *Biofactors, 35*(3), 273-8. doi: 10.1002/biof.33.

Osher Y.,& Belmaker RH. (2009). Omega-3 fatty acids in depression: a review of three studies. *CNS Neuroscience and Therapeutics, 15*(2), 128-33.

Owen AJ., Batterham MJ., Probst YC., Grenyer BF., Tapsell LC. (2005, February). Low plasma vitamin E levels in major depression: diet or disease? *European Journal of Clinical Nutrition, 59*(2), 304-6.

Palatnik A., Frolov K., Fux M., Benjamin J. (2001). "Double-blind, controlled, crossover trial of inositol versus fluvoxamine for the treatment of panic disorder". *Journal of Clinical Psychopharmacology* **21** (3): 335–339. doi:10.1097/00004714-200106000-00014. PMID 11386498.

Parker G., & Gibson NA. (2006) Omega-3 Fatty Acids and Mood Disorder. *The American Journal of Psychiatry, 163.*

Partyka A., Jastrzębska-Więsek M., Szewczyk B., Stachowicz K., Sławińska A., et al. (2011). Anxiolytic-like activity of zinc in rodent tests. *Pharmacological Reports, 63*(4),1050-5.

Pasco JA., Jacka FN., Williams LJ., Evans-Cleverdon M., Brennan SL, et al. (2012 June). Dietary selenium and major depression: a nested case-control study. *Complementary Therapies in Medicine, 20*(3), 119-23. doi: 10.1016/j.ctim.2011.12.008.

Payne ME., Steck SE., George RR., Steffens DC. (2012, December). Fruit, vegetable, and antioxidant intakes are lower in older adults with depression. Journal of the Academy of Nutrition and Dietetics *112*(12), 2022-7. doi: 10.1016/j.jand.2012.08.026.

Poleszak E, Szewczyk B, Kedzierska E, Wlaź P, Pilc A, Nowak G. (2004, May). Antidepressant and anxiolytic-like activity of magnesium in mice. *Pharmacology Biochemistry and Behavior, 78(1), 7-12.*

Popa TA., & Ladea M. (2012, December 15). Nutrition and depression at the forefront of progress. *Journal of Medicine and Life, 5*(4), 414–419.

Premkumar M., Sable .T, Dhanwal D., Dewan R. (2013, December). Vitamin D homeostasis, bone mineral metabolism, and seasonal affective disorder during 1 year of Antarctic residence. *Archives of Osteoporosis, 8*(1-2), 129. doi: 10.1007/s11657-013-0129-0. Epub 2013 Mar 9.

Reis LC., & Hibbeln JR. (2006). Cultural symbolism of fish and the psychotropic properties of omega-3 fatty acids. *Prostaglandins, Leukotrienes and Essential Fatty Acids, 75*, 227–236.

Sánchez-Villegas A., Delgado-Rodríguez M., Alonso A., Schlatter J., Lahortiga F., Serra Majem L., Martínez-González MA. (2009, October). Association of the Mediterranean dietary pattern with the incidence of depression: the Seguimiento Universidad de Navarra/University of Navarra follow-up (SUN) cohort. *Archive of General Psychiatry, 66*(10), 1090-8.

Sánchez-Villegas A., & Toledo E. (2012, March). Fast-food and commercial baked goods consumption and the risk of depression. *Public Health Nutrition, 15*(3), 424-432 DOI: http://dx.doi.org/10.1017/S1368980011001856, Published online: 11 August 2011.

Sánchez-Villegas A., Toledo E., de Irala J., Ruiz-Canela M., Pla-Vidal J., Martínez-González M. (2012). Fast-food and commercial baked goods consumption and the risk of depression. *Public Health Nutrition, 15,* 424-432. doi:10.1017/S1368980011001856.

Sánchez-Villegas A., Verberne L. (2011). Dietary Fat Intake and the Risk of Depression: The SUN Project. *PLoS ONE, 6*.

Sánchez-Villegas A, Verberne L, De Irala J, Ruíz-Canela M, Toledo E, et al. (2011). Dietary Fat Intake and the Risk of Depression: The SUN Project. *PLoS ONE 6*(1): e16268. doi:10.1371/journal.pone.0016268.

Sarris J., Mischoulon D., Schweitzer I. (2011, August, 9). Omega-3 for bipolar disorder: meta-analyses of use in mania and bipolar depression. *Journal of Clinical Psychiatry.* Epub 2011 August 9. PMID: 21903025.

Sartori SB., Whittle N., Hetzenauer A., Singewald N. (2012 January). Magnesium deficiency induces anxiety and HPA axis dysregulation: modulation by therapeutic drug treatment. *Neuropharmacology,* 62(1), 304-12. doi: 10.1016/j.neuropharm.2011.07.027.

Shor-Posner G., Lecusay R., Miguez MJ., Moreno-Black G., Zhang G., et al. (2003). Psychological burden in the era of HAART: impact of selenium therapy. *International Journal of Psychiatry and Medicine, 33*(1), 55-69.

Smith BA., Cogswell A., Garcia G. (2013, March 6). Vitamin D and Depressive Symptoms in Children with Cystic Fibrosis. *Psychosomatics.* pii: S0033-3182(13)00013-3. doi: 10.1016/j.psym.2013.01.012. [Epub ahead of print].

Spasov AA., Lezhitsa IN., Kharitonova MV., Kravchenko MS. (2008, July-August). Depression-like and anxiety-related behaviour of rats fed with magnesium-deficient diet. *Zh Vyssh Nerv Deiat Im I P Pavlova, 58*(4), 476-85.

Stewart R., & Hirani V. (2012 February-March). Relationship between depressive symptoms, anemia, and iron status in older residents from a national survey population. *Psychosomatic Medicine,* 74(2), 208-13.doi:10.1097/PSY.0b013e3182414f7d. Epub 2012 Jan 27.

Tassabehji NM, Corniola RS, Alshingiti A, Levenson CW. (2008, October 20). Zinc deficiency induces depression-like symptoms in adult rats. *Physiology and Behavior, 95*(3), 365-9. doi: 10.1016/j.physbeh.2008.06.017.

Terada Y., Okura Y., Kikusui T., Takenaka A. (2011).Dietary vitamin E deficiency increases anxiety-like behavior in juvenile and adult rats. *Bioscience, Biotechnology, Biochemistry, 75*(10), 1894-9.

Torres S., Nowson C., Worsley, A. (2011). Dietary electrolytes are related to mood. *British Journal of Nutrition : an international journal of nutritional science*, 100(5), 1038-1045.

Toyoda A., & Iio W. (2013). Antidepressant-like effect of chronic taurine administration and its hippocampal signal transduction in rats. *Advances in Experimental Medicine and Biology, 775,* 29-43. doi: 10.1007/978-1-4614-6130-2_3.

Tsimihodimos V., Kakaidi V., Elisaf M. (2009, June). Cola-induced hypokalaemia: pathophysiological mechanisms and clinical implications. *International Journal of Clinical Practice, 63*(6), 900-2. doi: 10.1111/j.1742-1241.2009.02051.x.

UNICEF Office of Research (2013). 'Child Well-being in Rich Countries: A comparative overview', Innocenti Report Card 11, UNICEF Office of Research, Florence.

Verhoeven V., Vanpuyenbroeck K., Lopez-Hartmann M., Wens J., Remmen R. (2012, April). Walk on the sunny side of life--epidemiology of hypovitaminosis D and mental health in elderly nursing home residents. *Journal of Nutritional Health and Aging, 16*(4), 417-20.

Walker SP., Wachs TD., Grantham-McGregor S., Black MM, Nelson CA., et al. (2011, October 8). Inequality in early childhood: risk and protective factors for early child development. *Lancet, 378*(9799),1325-38. doi: 10.1016/S0140-6736(11)60555-2.

Ward MS., Lamb J., May JM., Harrison FE. (2013, February). Behavioral and monoamine changes following severe vitamin C deficiency. *Journal of Neurochemistry,_124*(3), 363-75. doi: 10.1111/jnc.12069. Epub 2012 Nov 30.

Weng TT., Hao JH., Qian QW., Cao H., Fu JL., et al. (2012, April). Is there any relationship between dietary patterns and depression and anxiety in Chinese adolescents? *Public Health Nutrition,15*(4), 673-82. doi: 10.1017/S1368980011003077.

Westover A, & Marangell L. (2002). A cross-national relationship between sugar consumption and major depression? . *Depression and Anxiety, 16*, 118–120.

Whittle N., Lubec G., Singewald N. (2009, January). Zinc deficiency induces enhanced depression-like behaviour and altered limbic activation reversed by antidepressant treatment in mice. *Amino Acids, 36*(1), 147-58. doi: 10.1007/s00726-008-0195-6.

Yassaei S., Vahidi A., Farahat F. (2012, September-October). Comparison of the efficacy of calcium versus acetaminophen on reduction of orthodontic pain. *Indian Journal of Dental Research,_23*(5), 608-12. doi: 10.4103/0970-9290.107349.

Yi S., Nanri A., Poudel-Tandukar K., Nonaka D., Matsushita Y., Hori A., Mizoue T. (2011, October 30). Association between serum ferritin concentrations and depressive symptoms in Japanese municipal employees. *Psychiatry Research, 189*(3), 368-72. doi: 10.1016/j.psychres.2011.03.009.

Yin C, Gou L, Liu Y, Yin X, Zhang L, Jia G, Zhuang X. (2011, November). Antidepressant-like effects of L-theanine in the forced swim and tail suspension tests in mice. *Phytotherapy Research, 25*(11), 1636-9. doi: 10.1002/ptr.3456.

Zeratsky, K. Junk Food Blues: Are Depression and Diet Related? (Mayo Clinic August 11, 2011, http://mayoclinic.com/health/depression-and-diet/AN02057).

Zhang L., Kleiman-Weiner M., Luo R., Shi Y., Martorell R., Medina A., Rozelle S. (2013, May). Multiple Micronutrient Supplementation Reduces Anemia and Anxiety in Rural China's

Elementary School Children. *Journal of Nutrition, 143*(5), 640-7. doi: 10.3945/jn.112.171959.

27741396R00149

Made in the USA
Middletown, DE
21 December 2015